Avoid Mosquitoes

— and Other Impossibilities

Nancy Sellin

iUniverse, Inc.
New York   Bloomington

Avoid Mosquitoes—and Other Impossibilities

iUniverse books may be ordered through booksellers or by contacting:

iUniverse
1663 Liberty Drive
Bloomington, IN 47403
www.iuniverse.com
1-800-Authors (1-800-288-4677)

ISBN: 978-0-595-52646-8 (pbk)
ISBN: 978-0-595-51897-5 (dj)
ISBN: 978-0-595-62699-1 (ebk)

Printed in the United States of America

iUniverse rev. date: 1/08/09

DEDICATION

This book is dedicated to Dale Sellin, without whom I never would have joined the Peace Corps and gone to Liberia, or moved to New York City to pursue an acting career—two decisions that forever changed my life.

CONTENTS

Acknowledgments ix

Chapter 1.   The Journey Begins 1

Chapter 2.   Wedding Night 7

Chapter 3.   The Training 10

Chapter 4.   Terrence 15

Chapter 5.   Steve 25

Chapter 6.   Wisdom Teeth 27

Chapter 7.   New York City, Polyester, and the Money Bus 28

Chapter 8.   The Hostel, Club Beer, and Jif 34

Chapter 9.   Fisebu 41

Chapter 10. Elephant Tusk Band 52

Chapter 11. Liberian Suntan 55

Chapter 12. The Flight to Greenville 63

Chapter 13. Student Teaching in America 70

Chapter 14. Religious Instruction 73

Chapter 15. Arrival in Greenville 76

Chapter 16. The Carpenters 81

Chapter 17. Turkish Coffee 91

Chapter 18. Letters From Home and Moving In 95

Chapter 19. Charlies, Curtains, and Dresses...................101

Chapter 20. David and Ralph...104

Chapter 21. The First Day of School 107

Chapter 22. The Bananas...113

Chapter 23. The First Day of School—Again 116

Chapter 24. R & R...125

Chapter 25. Mac Cat...132

Chapter 26. Puppy Crisis..138

Chapter 27. Husking Rice 140

Chapter 28. Chicken and Chop.................................144

Chapter 29. Country Wife 155

Chapter 30. Bush Hike..159

Chapter 31. Big Boy..171

Chapter 32. The Coming of the Rain 172

Chapter 33. The Electrical Storm.............................176

Chapter 34. CARE Food 180

Chapter 35. VD 184

Chapter 36. U.S. Army Privates...............................187

Chapter 37. Tropical Itch 191

Chapter 38. Staff Meeting 193

Chapter 39. Christmas 195

Chapter 40. East Africa and Amos Midamba.....................200

Chapter 41. A Party..209

Chapter 42. Soldier Ants 213

Chapter 43. The Decision to Relocate 215

Chapter 44. The Baby...219

Chapter 45. Buchanan...223

Chapter 46. Penelope 227

Chapter 47. Back Home..232

Chapter 48. Through My Eyes..................................234

ACKNOWLEDGMENTS

A memoir is, by its very nature, subjective. What I remember about events and people carries my own bias and emotional content.

I hope that all who read this very personal memoir will appreciate it as a colorful tapestry of experiences and compassionate portraits and realize that the subjects of those portraits, by virtue of their very presence, have had an indelible influence on the pattern and texture of my life, even today.

On occasion, I have combined several events into one story. Out of respect for the perceived sensibilities of known people, I have changed some of the names.

I want to thank the following people for their honesty, help, encouragement, and support:

To my son, Sean Loginovs, for indulging me when I interrupted whatever he was doing to read him the first draft of the book as it was pouring out of me.

To my mother, Virginia Trombley-Anderson, for her generosity and unfailing belief in me.

To my sisters, Ginger Horner and Pamela Stephens, for laughing and crying in all the right places and for understanding everything others didn't.

To Carole Belle, David Drake, Laura Fitzpatrick-Nagel, Jane Hayden, Jeff Heisler, Maureen McElheron, Carol Silverstein, Shari Upbin, Sal Yamusa, and especially Dale Sellin, for reading various stages of drafts and giving me honest, useful feedback. In addition, I want to thank Kim (Carpenter) Abrams for corroborating the accuracy of certain facts, people, and events.

Finally, I want to thank my editor Paul Hawley, for his clarity of vision, for his attention to detail, and for making sure I said precisely what I meant to say.

CHAPTER 1

The Journey Begins

Nancy and Dale in 1965

I joined the Peace Corps to save the world. My husband, Dale, had been talking about Kennedy's Peace Corps since its inception in 1961. He liked being in on the ground floor of practically anything. He was the first person to register at our brand-new college in Anchorage, Alaska; he received the Dean's one-year scholarship at least twice, earned free tuition for three out of his four years, and was the first person to get 100 percent on a calculus test given by the toughest professor at the university. I guess it should not have surprised me that he wanted to be among the first from Alaska to enlist in the Peace Corps. We enlisted at the beginning of my senior year and left for Africa after my graduation in 1965.

My Instamatic camera was loaded and ready to go. I had my army regulation ammunition box with silica gel packets to keep the moisture at bay. I was going to capture on film my first impressions of Africa so that I could revisit and re-experience the place for the rest of my life. I would share the profound new experiences of a foreign culture with fascinated family and friends, and I would be shrouded in a veil of mystique and sought after to reveal the living secrets of the darkest and most colorful continent in the world. I knew that experience is by far the most powerful teacher, and choosing how you experience an event is the true revealer of who you are.

From the end of my junior year in high school through my graduation from college, I lived in Anchorage, Alaska. Having lived my entire life, up to that point, in the moderate, rainy climate of Tacoma and Puyallup, Washington, I was not prepared for the freezing, almost desert-dry condition of Alaska's largest city. This was well before the days of Thinsulate, and my family could not afford goose down, so I braved those freezing winter temperatures in JCPenney's finest low-budget ski coats—layers of bulk, but no warmth. I was cold all the time—even in the summer's hottest 78-degree temperatures, when I would sunbathe on the only lakefront in town, trying to produce some hint of color on my Alaskan pallor. At least in the winter my cheeks would sport a rosy glow from the cold and from the mildly chapped condition that even Corn Husker's lotion couldn't alleviate.

By the time I had lived in Alaska five years, my blood had thickened. I had adjusted enough so that I could even walk to school in below-freezing temperatures with only earmuffs on my head so as not to muss my fashionable bouffant hairdo. Years later I would laugh as I related the stories of cold, brittle hairspray and frozen nose hairs. Alaska was probably the place least likely to prepare me for what I was to experience in the humid, tropical climate of West Africa.

Our group, Group VII, had to go through eight weeks of intensive training. The first day, the trainers told us we would spend the first four weeks at San Francisco State College, and then they would send us to the Virgin Islands for a month so we could adjust to a climate and people more similar to what we would find in Liberia.

The training we received at San Francisco State College was rather academic, except for the living conditions. They drove us in yellow school buses to a secluded army barracks somewhere in the hills of San Francisco where we had to assemble our living quarters from the mattresses, cot springs, army blankets, and odds and ends stacked in one corner of the barracks. I quickly learned that even "altruistic" people could be rude and greedy, grabbing and hoarding provisions even though others hadn't gotten their share.

Steve Wilson was the preppy from Connecticut, who arrived sporting a tennis racket, Bermuda shorts, appropriate Lacoste shirt, and a mouthful of large, white teeth, which flashed impressively as he laughed arrogantly and monologued about his accomplishments back home. "I was valedictorian of my class and captain of the tennis team," he boasted. I disliked him instantly.

Steve took it upon himself to round up a number of "teammates" and appoint himself the captain. Then they set about gathering up as many of the provisions as they could pile into one corner of the barracks. He managed to direct the traffic of his team like a drill sergeant, telling his people where to set up their bunks and where to put their belongings. The amazing part of it all was the uncanny speed with which his teammates followed his lead—as if their very survival depended on it. After everyone had taken all the provisions, it was obvious that some had taken more than their share.

It naturally fell upon Steve to become the magnanimous distributor of his team's abundant wealth, as he took "this" from that team member and "that" from another team member to bestow on the grateful less fortunate. I was *not* one of the grateful less fortunate. Life has a way of providing opportunities for growth, and if you don't take advantage of them, life will present you with the same wolf in different sheep's clothing until you do. Therefore, it was not surprising that Steve Wilson was to become my opportunity and my nemesis. In a few hours, the buses came back and picked us up to go to the campus for a college cafeteria dinner.

Our days of training consisted of lectures about Liberia—history and what to expect, strength and endurance-building classes, and the living conditions themselves, which tested our adaptability to lack of privacy and modern conveniences. There was a special class on how to stay healthy. The same men who conducted the training also administered the Peace Corps program in-country—men who lived in the capital city of Monrovia in air-conditioned houses and got paid a healthy salary to live in the American style to which they were accustomed, men who had plenty of money left over to accumulate a wealth of precious African artifacts that filled their spacious tropical homes to the walls. We, of course, were not aware of any of this until we arrived overseas.

Part of the trainers' job was to de-romanticize the Peace Corps experience so we would be aware of what we were getting in for. It was made clear that, should we choose to leave the Peace Corps before our two-year stint was up, our two-dollar-a-day salary, which was put into a bank in America to be given to us upon our return to the States for readjustment purposes, would be used to pay for our airfare home. Even if it was a return for a medical emergency, it would be a "that's the breaks" situation. Not in my wildest twenty-one-year-old dreams did I imagine I would be one of those who would leave the country shy of the required two years.

The training was a process of self-deselection. If you were *at* the training, you were *in* the Peace Corps, unless they found something unusual that called for them to deselect you. They discovered one girl had a tendency for epilepsy, something she knew nothing about, and they sent her home. Other than the unusual, the only way you'd be out was if you deselected yourself.

As I heard the talk about the hardships and inconveniences we would face, I thought how lucky I was to have been a Girl Scout. The Girl Scout motto was "be prepared," and it suited me to a tee. My mother's compulsive nature had been passed on to me and I accepted it as my sworn duty, not realizing that, in a country where ease and flow was a way of life, my overdeveloped sense of responsibility and tendency to perfectionism would eventually lead me into anxiety and depression. Not to mention the staunch denial of the sad truth that my marriage was a mistake.

Dale and I had married at the beginning of my senior year in college. We both had extremely conservative parents who raised us to be virgins until marriage. This was the sixties, and, although it was unusual for newlyweds to be virgins, it wasn't impossible. (After all, I had prided myself on being "sweet sixteen and never been kissed" and fiercely defended any of my friends who were the brunt of rumors that intimated they were "unclean." Oh, the shock, in tenth grade, when Cindy turned up pregnant! Well, she was obviously the exception, poor girl.) Ignorance is bliss, but it's also food for depression.

Although Dale talked constantly about joining the Peace Corps, I was reluctant. I dutifully acted enthusiastic, while secretly harboring the belief that he would certainly change his mind by the time of my graduation three years later. After Kennedy's death, however, Dale's resolve became even stronger, and by the time 1965 rolled around, Vietnam was in full swing. It was clear that Dale had a choice: he could go into the service or join the Peace Corps. My fear of Dale going to war was greater than my fear of going into the Peace Corps. They wouldn't accept a married man into the Peace Corps without his spouse, so I made up my mind rather quickly. Then I spent the second half of my senior year convincing myself that going into the Peace Corps was my lifelong dream—that I was going to help the less fortunate and teach them the profound success secrets of the American way of life.

I was the epitome of the "hubris of the young." I spouted Kennedyisms and basked in the awe of others' admiration as they told me how brave I was, how courageous. As they voiced their fears and concerns about the hardships, dangers, and the sicknesses that surely awaited me, their words stung the truth of my own fears just below the surface, which I willfully pushed further down by convincing myself what an adventure I was going to have. If I had openly admitted my fear, I might never have gone to Liberia—and I would have missed the most profoundly affecting experience of my life. No doubt I would have stayed snugly settled into a confined, unfulfilled suburban life, which probably would have led me into anxiety and depression anyway.

Back then, therapy was a thing "crazy people" did, so I had no one to help me see the truth I learned much later—that fear and excitement can be best buddies, that it was okay to admit being afraid and still pursue risky adventures. Back then, you didn't admit being afraid, and if you did, it was a sign of weakness. Our family creed was either "There's nothing to be afraid of" or "Don't do that, it's dangerous." I didn't realize that being afraid and doing it anyway was the way most successful people live their lives.

We got our letter of acceptance in the spring of 1965. We were to report to San Francisco State College on November 3 to begin the first phase of the two-month training. Dale called them immediately, to have them issue our plane tickets from Anchorage to Seattle, then on to San Francisco. Our plan was to cash in the tickets from Anchorage to Seattle and use the money to drive down the Alcan Highway, touristing our way through rugged, unpaved, and dusty terrain. We would spend some time with his parents in Tacoma, then fly to San Francisco for the training.

CHAPTER 2

Wedding Night

We had been married a scant year when we loaded our blue, economy, no-frills Valiant to travel down the Alcan. The trip had two purposes. It was a chance to really see Alaska and to have a belated honeymoon. The prospect of traveling through Alaska's hinterland and hobnobbing with Aleuts, Tlingits, and Eskimos thrilled me, but the prospect of a belated honeymoon did not.

During the short time we had been married, our sex life had dwindled from three times a week to once a month, and that only because I felt obliged to do my duty. A few weeks before we got married, the elderly Lutheran minister who married us said it was his responsibility to give us a written questionnaire on sex and then counsel us afterwards. The purpose of the questionnaire was to ascertain how much knowledge we had so he could inform us of our marital responsibilities in that regard.

After we had filled it out, he called us into his office and went over the points with us. He began the consultation by saying that Dale had slightly more knowledge of sex than I had, and this was desirable because he was the man, and men should know more about sex than women. He reassured me that Dale could teach me all about it.

My mother's response to my questions about sex at age sixteen was "You don't need to know anything, it will all come naturally," so the minister's comment seemed to fit right in line with hers. The only thing that terrified me was when the minister said that a happily married couple should be having sex three or four times a week. I couldn't even *imagine* the sex act, let alone three or four times a week!

In those days, weddings in my corner of the world didn't seem to be as elaborate a social event as they are today. Dinner was not part of a reception. Generally, the wedding took place in a church, sparsely decorated, and the reception was held downstairs in the church hall.

The oral fare was wedding cake, coffee, tea, punch (absolutely no alcohol), mixed nuts, and mints. The guests received a small, wrapped piece of groom's cake (fruitcake) so they could put it under their pillows to inspire good dreams. A reception was exactly what the word implied: the bride and groom and their parents stood in a reception line at the door, welcomed the guests into the room, then disappeared upstairs to get pictures taken while the guests enjoyed their punch and salted mixed nuts.

After cutting the wedding cake, we were supposed to leave the reception quickly, in anticipation of consummating our unbridled desires in the bedroom.

My fear became more intense as we raced toward our brand-new Plymouth Valiant amid rice and well-wishers. My parents told me the next day that, after we left, they invited many of the guests (my teetotaling in-laws were not invited) over to the house for the real party and we were assured we had really missed a good one. Though I was a teetotaler myself, how I would have loved to attend, delaying the inevitable for a few more hours.

While driving to the hotel, I suddenly got hungry and asked my new husband if he wanted to get something to eat. I was relieved when he said yes. Since McDonald's was the most recent novelty in our rustic town, we both agreed it would be fun to eat there. However, since we felt self-conscious in our dressy wedding getaway suits, we went through the drive-in window and ate our mushy hamburgers and greasy french fries in the car. Once we consumed our meal, there was nothing else to do but drive to the hotel—the Captain Cook—the newest and most beautiful hotel in Anchorage.

At my wedding shower my mother-in-law had given me a full-length negligee set, made from layers of sheer nylon, with a fleshy colored lace bodice. I'm sure she must have sent to Seattle for it because she never would have found anything so beautiful in Anchorage's most fashionable department store—JCPenney.

My mother's sage advice kept ringing in my ears—"It will all come naturally." Dale was very ready to let nature take its course, but I was not. My expectation was to experience a magical, sexual union such as the world had never known—letting nature take its course—guiding us into the miracle of transformation.

What followed was a fumbling attempt to mingle the self-conscious bodies of two virgins into some semblance of a sex act. Once it was over, Dale must have perceived the look on my face as pleasure, because he had tears of joy in his eyes. *My* tears were from the devastating revelation that I had just married someone with whom I might never be able to enjoy sex.

Over time, the pain of intercourse gradually decreased, and there was desire and pleasure, but once Dale was satisfied, we were both at a loss about what to do next. In an effort to make me feel better, Dale once said, "That's okay. Lots of women are frigid."

As we lay on the wedding bed after the consummation of our marriage, Dale glanced down and noticed he was no longer wearing the rubber. Assuming it was somewhere among the bedclothes, he proceeded to look for it. When he couldn't find it, we both looked— everywhere. We finally decided to let the mystery be, until the next day when I began to feel an uncomfortable fullness and frequent urges to urinate.

My first trip to a gynecologist, later that day, resulted in the embarrassment of the doctor pulling the condom from my vagina. Dangling the condom in front of my face and wrinkling up his nose, he reprimanded, "You really shouldn't use rubbers—it's not good for a man's pleasure." Thinking of it now, some forty-five years later, I feel a combination of pity for the doctor and sadness at my inability to stand up for myself. That day, however, I felt only shame.

CHAPTER 3

The Training

John and Virginia Lyon and us

Back at the army barracks, Steve had successfully established himself as alpha dog while we settled into our eight-week training. There were four married couples in our group of seventy-five Peace Corps Volunteers (PCVs), and we became hanging buddies with one couple—John and Virginia Lyon, a down-to-earth, ordinary-looking pair who had been married five years and still enjoyed sex. The singles in the group hung out together and pretty much ignored the married couples. I found myself feeling left out a good deal of the time, but too shy—or too bound by convention—to take the initiative of breaking the married/single barrier. We played a lot of gin rummy with John and Virginia and learned how to drink warm Johnny Walker Red from paper Dixie cups.

One of the most important parts of the training was the study of prescription medicine and self-diagnosis. Liberia was a third-world country with few medical facilities or doctors outside of the capital of Monrovia.

There was the occasional country hospital, such as the one I visited in a small up-country village, but one quick look would tell even the most undiscerning eye that this was not a place you'd want to set foot in if you were ill. The halls and rooms were stark and bare of any medical equipment except beds without sheets or pillowcases and families of giant cockroaches skittering across the floor. The resident doctor wore a brand-new, clean white jacket over a pair of unwashed Bermuda shorts and dingy country cloth shirt. Neither his age nor his manner inspired my confidence. He must have been all of twenty-two, spoke very little English, and said he had studied medicine from an American nurse who lived in Monrovia. One look at the huge room with twenty beds in it and the two patients (one woman and one man) sleeping on bare mattresses, and I had more trust in the juju witch doctor—at least he had experience with all the local ailments and a vast knowledge of herbal and tribal medicine. It was obvious we would have to rely heavily on those two weeks of intensive medical training we got in San Francisco.

A three-inch thick medical manual was sitting at each desk as we entered the classroom. The trainers instructed us to open our manuals to the first page. There, in big, bold, capital letters, were the first two words: **AVOID MOSQUITOES.** When you're living in a tropical country four degrees north of the equator, where most people live in mud and stick huts with dirt floors and no indoor or outdoor plumbing, and where the only water source is a slow-moving stream in which all bathing and laundry and drinking is done, and malaria is as prevalent as the common cold, it is *impossible* to **AVOID MOSQUITOES.** But none of us got the joke until our first day in Liberia. A joke with a belated punch line is always the best laugh, and that one sustained us for months!

After we were properly terrified by grim tales of mosquitoes and malaria, and drilled about the importance of taking our weekly dose of malaria pills, we moved on to the tsetse fly and sleeping sickness, which they assured us was not so common. Most flies do not carry the encephalitis germ—just do not let a tsetse fly bite you. Suddenly I imagined myself sitting behind a mahogany desk interviewing flies: "Are you a tsetse fly or a housefly? Do you sustain yourself by biting people or by feeding off dead things? Are you a carrier of the encephalitis germ?" There was no cure or preventive medication for sleeping sickness, so we would just have to take our chances.

Amebic dysentery covered nearly two hours. "**Don't** drink unboiled water. **Don't** brush your teeth with unboiled water. **Don't** drink tap water anywhere in the country. **Don't** drink water or use ice cubes from restaurants—even at the Dukor Intercontinental, the swankiest European hotel in Monrovia. Bathe only in rain water or water pumped from the ground and under no circumstances utilize water from lakes, pools, ponds, rivers, or streams."

The symptoms of dysentery are not pretty: severe abdominal cramps accompanied by frequent and massive diarrhea, black or red stool (caused from blood oozing from raw intestinal walls), fever, weakness, and life-threatening dehydration. At the first sign of any loose stool (they called it "runny tummy" in Liberia), we were supposed to take Polymagma (two huge pink horse pills) after each episode for three weeks, and drink plenty of boiled, filtered water. Dysentery comes on fast and strong, so unless you were stationed in Monrovia, you had to self-diagnose and self-medicate. Our medical kit contained enough Polymagma for a dozen occasions. If we needed more, we could get some from one of the recently graduated doctors working in Monrovia for the U.S. Public Health Service. Anyway, if you needed more than a dozen treatments, you should seriously look at what you were putting in your mouth.

Under no circumstances should you walk barefoot. Aside from fatal snakebite, you could get schistosomiasis, which is caused by a bug that likes to live in stagnant water. I won't even elaborate on the description of the schisto bug boring its way through your pores, undetected by you until the illness manifests its grotesque symptoms.

For two weeks we continued to study about diseases too exotic to remember, their accompanying symptoms, and treatments. Then we were given the medical manual and a rather large medical kit crammed full of every imaginable prescription and nonprescription drug. The married couples received one kit to share between them. I guess they figured that married people only get half as many illnesses as single people. Actually, in our case, it turned out to be true.

At the end of the first week, we began receiving our first series of inoculations. So what's a shot or two? Over the course of the next weeks, we received twenty-one shots, most of which we reacted to with the appropriate headache, nausea, soreness, and fever. We all complained a lot, but no one would dream of taking a sick day for fear everyone would think we "couldn't take it." Dale, however, had a reaction I never would have suspected. We were standing in line waiting for our first series of five shots, joking with other PCVs, and sharing inoculation stories. I got my shots just ahead of Dale. On my third shot, I heard a loud thump behind me, and when I turned around, I found all six foot five inches of Dale passed out cold on the floor. I had no idea he suffered from fear!

Dr. Rubin Aka, the diminutive Peace Corps doctor from India, counseled the women on birth control. "Any woman," he said delicately, "who is having sex or might have sex within the next two years should be on the pill." If you were married, you had to see Dr. Aka in a private session to talk about it. He was a gregarious man who enjoyed his job. After he gave me a pelvic exam, he examined my breasts. I was quite skinny, which made my ribs show and my breastbone prominent. He looked at me with a serious expression and asked me if I'd ever had rickets. Even though I didn't exactly know what rickets was, I knew it had something to do with lower classes and poverty, and I was appropriately insulted.

Then he talked to me about the pill. Even though he admitted the FDA had only recently approved the pill, and nobody was sure of its long-term effects, the pill was the only viable option for women in the Peace Corps. First, you didn't want to get pregnant. Second, you didn't want to get pregnant. And third, you didn't want to get pregnant. Liberia was a backward country. There was no way the Peace Corps could support a woman who got pregnant—they would send you home. And God forbid you should be raped. Well, you see the problem. The pill was 99 percent effective against pregnancy.

Dr. Aka gave me a brief rundown of possible symptoms. The pill simulated the condition of pregnancy. Some women experienced morning sickness (nausea and vomiting) until the body became accustomed to the high influx of hormones, though the symptoms were not likely to show up until a few weeks after beginning the pill. Weight gain of up to twenty pounds was common, blood clots and water retention possible. That's it! Surely I was brave enough to endure these mild symptoms for the convenience and protection offered by the pill. He was a doctor, a man, a protector. I succumbed.

VD (venereal disease, now referred to as STDs or sexually transmitted diseases) was not a major issue at that time. We were advised to watch for the symptoms of gonorrhea and syphilis, which could be easily cured by penicillin. All of us were warned about the dangers of sleeping with the natives for fear of VD. I left his office armed with two years' supply of Ortho-Novum, the only oral contraceptive on the market and, by today's standards, an incredibly strong dose.

We were given a long list of items that were in short supply or not available at all in Liberia. The list included foodstuffs such as milk, butter, beef, fresh vegetables, pork, cheese, and nonfood items such as Excedrin, hairspray, and Kotex. Since I was not yet comfortable with using Tampax, I brought a two-year supply of Kotex. I was certainly going to be prepared in that department! What I wasn't prepared for was how easily things mildew in Liberia, so after a couple of months in the country, I had to dump my entire supply and rely on the occasional small-plane shopping trip to Monrovia to obtain sanitary napkins imported from Germany and Denmark. Europe's version of Kotex was no better than ours was—they were equally nonabsorbent so that much of the menstrual blood accumulated on top and, when it dried, would make the pad stick to your pubic hair, which pulled when you walked. Because I had begun taking the pill by that time, we didn't have to worry about moldy rubbers.

CHAPTER 4

Terrence

San Francisco had a large black community. Since Liberians are black, our trainers thought it would be a good experience to become familiar with the ways of black people. This, of course, sounds prejudiced and arrogant today, but in 1965 I had no familiarity with anyone of any color, except the occasional Eskimo and Alaskan Indian, so it seemed reasonable and sensible. I wonder, now, how it must have sounded to the black Peace Corps Volunteers, though they appeared not to notice. I don't see how they could have been unaware of the not-so-subtle implications of prejudice with which we are so familiar today.

We were given a list of ghetto schools to contact to arrange a visit, first to observe the teaching in the classroom, then to volunteer to tutor a needy student at their home. Dale was to go to a high school, and I was to go to an elementary school. It was suggested that we not stay in the ghetto late at night, and if we went in after dark, two of us should go together whenever possible.

I was raised to be wary of anything different, and I had enough bigots in my family to make me a little nervous about the whole business. Nevertheless, deep inside me lurked an adventuresome spirit that longed to break free of the narrow-mindedness of my upbringing. And my parents weren't here to mirror my fear. I knew I didn't want to live in apprehension my entire life, and the only way to grow was to reach beyond my comfort zone.

My parents always said I was the risk taker in the family—always wanting to try something different or looking at things from a "strange" (I prefer "unique") point of view; and it is true that I often felt like a round peg in a square hole, craving my own niche. My parents, in their belief that the world is a dangerous place, and knowing that I was sensitive and impressionable, sought to control me through fear of the unknown. They were successful in holding the reins too tight. This tightness, which I ultimately internalized, conflicts with my creative desires even to this day; and resolving this conflict continues to be one of my life's challenges.

I located a school in the heart of the ghetto. The principal, Mrs. Douglas, had had other PCVs visit the school and tutor youngsters, so she was pleased to invite me to follow suit. She said I would have to use a firm hand with the children, and she would show me how to do it. I should come to the school the following day to observe, and she would make her schedule free to come into the classroom in the afternoon to speak to the children while I was there.

All classes were self-contained except for lunchtime. Mrs. Douglas had a particular child in mind who came from a large family and desperately needed some kind of tutoring in every subject, and I could follow his schedule all day. She said the child was in fourth grade, and his name was Terrence Jackson. He was a small child, although he was a year older than the other children in his class because he had flunked the last year and really should have flunked third grade, too.

His younger sister was in the same class. She was the smart one—getting all A's except in math. Terrence was just lazy and refused to learn. Maybe the principal would reconsider giving him the special privilege of having a tutor after all—he really didn't deserve it. But she felt sorry for his mother, who had five other children, so she guessed she would give Terrence one more try even though she'd about reached the end of her rope with him. She told me this was his last chance, and I shouldn't expect too much—I'd know what she meant as soon as I saw him in the classroom, and she was definitely going to warn Terrence of his precarious standing.

I gulped, thinking that Terrence's last chance rested with me, but decided not to say anything just yet. She told me to get to the school by 7:30 a.m. What I saw the following day shocked me so much I still get a blood rush when I think about it.

I felt exhilarated riding the bus early in the morning through the ghetto. Nobody bothered me, and when I asked directions to the school, a woman kindly told me—and even walked a block with me to make sure I found my way. She pointed out a large, four-story, red brick building with a twelve-foot-high fence around it and bars on the windows. On one side of the building was a large concrete yard with a giant bullhorn attached high on one corner of the fence.

I arrived at 7:15 and stood outside a locked gate until a policeman came to let me in. When I had spoken with the principal the previous day, I had thought it rather unusual that the principal was a woman; where I came from, principals were men, and secretaries were women. Women were supposed to be the weaker sex, the gentler, sensitive sex, the nurturing ones. I wondered how effective a woman could be, running a tough ghetto school. I soon found out.

Mrs. Douglas was a stocky, intimidating woman with a husky voice. She was loud and opinionated, strict and systematic. Everyone had to do things her way, and woe to those who strayed. She had devised the whole management system, and she was a hands-on dictator. Nobody escaped her careful scrutiny or her swift, sharp tongue. It was a maximum-security prison, and she was the warden.

She met me at the gate and ushered me upstairs to her office on the top floor. It was a room big enough for her desk, three student desks, and a couple of extra chairs. One wall was all glass. It had a sliding door opening onto a small balcony that overlooked the concrete yard. I was intrigued. I imagined her standing behind her glass wall surveying her courtyard domain. But I wondered what she would see. There was not a single piece of playground equipment in the yard—not a swing, a slide, or a jungle gym. Not a seesaw, a merry-go-round, or a basketball hoop. There was nothing that indicated, even remotely, that children played there.

After a few minutes, the children began to arrive and filter into the yard. As the principal talked about her four-year reign and the rise of reading and math scores of her subjects, I gazed out of the window and watched the children stroll into the yard. What was most curious was the distinct lack of playfulness in their demeanor. I was used to seeing elementary-aged children running and hopping, chasing and teasing, tagging each other and shouting loudly. These children talked quietly, rarely smiled or touched each other. They walked into the courtyard and hardly moved from their spots—hundreds of children from first to sixth grades, milling around quietly, without apparent supervision. I couldn't make any sense out of it.

At 7:45, a loud bell rang, and thirty-five teachers appeared from out of nowhere and marched quickly into the yard. The principal opened the glass door and stepped onto the balcony. "All right! Shut up! You heard the bell! Line up!" she bellowed through a microphone. She was a black Hitler, standing behind a podium in front of the masses, shouting her stern message in a language that transported me to my own childhood.

The more than occasional spats that took place in my home when I was growing up were treated in only one way. My mother reacted to my older sister and me with the warning words, "You'd better stop that fighting or you're going to get it!" If that didn't work, she'd raise her voice to the next decibel level: "All right! If you two don't stop it right now, I'm coming in there!" Then came "That's it! You just wait till your father gets home—then you're really going to get it!"

That generally did the trick. Dad's wrath was something to reckon with. His favorite way to stop chaos was to get red-angry and shout, "Shut up! Stop crying, or I'll give you something to cry about!" The next action was the spanking—followed by my inevitable hysteria. I vowed that when I grew up, I would never, ever say *shut up* to anyone. In Dad's twilight years, he often expressed remorse at having to play the tyrant whose children were sometimes afraid to see him walk through the door.

The children scurried to get in line. Mrs. Douglas missed nothing. One of the children apparently wasn't moving fast enough to suit her, and she yelled his name loudly through the microphone. If people in the neighborhood had been asleep, they were awake now. Within moments, little soldier lines formed in front of each of the thirty-five teachers. "Miss Washington, watch your line!" she shouted to one of the teachers. Whenever someone did something she didn't like, she repeatedly demonstrated her gift of farsightedness by singling them out and yelling their names through the loudspeaker for the entire world to hear.

Had this woman never heard of treating people with dignity? Had she never taken a course in education or management where the first cardinal rule was never to embarrass or single out a person's misbehavior in front of others? Had she never heard that the way to improve self-esteem is through praise, not criticism and ridicule? I knew this day was going to be one for the books.

After roll call, the children were allowed to follow their teachers to their classrooms. I stood out like a sore thumb: I was the only white person in the entire multitude.

Terrence was a sweet-faced youngster with very dark skin and bright, coal-black eyes. As we walked along to the class, we sized each other up. I was wondering if what the principal had said about him was true. Was he lazy, resistant to learning, just a do-nothing kid who was an embarrassment to his family? And what would happen to him if his "last chance" failed? What would be his fate? What had they told him about me? Was I the miracle worker come to save him, and was I his only hope of redemption, or was I just a young white girl who needed a black person to practice on? How had the principal set me up?

The classroom was arranged in the traditional way—student desks in rows facing the teacher desk and blackboard up front. I was not surprised that the class was teacher-directed, teacher-oriented, and teacher-centered. There was lecture, copying from the board, and assignments in books. The only way the students participated was by answering questions when the teacher called on them or by reading aloud, one at a time, from the textbook. There were no learning centers, no cooperative learning in groups, no hands-on teaching or learning. All the children were expected to understand the lesson by listening to the teacher talk and doing the writing assignment from their books. They were expected to sit quietly and to complete all the work in the time allotted.

The teacher strolled up and down the rows with a ruler in her hand, tapping a desk here and there to bring a child back to attention or using it as a pointer for errors. From the looks of it, Terrence was at sea. He was staring at the book, but his eyes weren't taking it in. He had his pencil in his hand, but he wasn't writing. When the teacher approached his desk, she shook her head, sighed in judgment, gestured, and glanced disapprovingly in my direction. Terrence turned his head slightly to look at me. I hoped my face remained neutral.

The morning went pretty much like that. At lunch, I was allowed to sit with the children. Terrence was directed to escort me. I didn't want to put him in an embarrassing situation, so after I got my lunch, I released him from his obligation so he could have some time to go out and play with his friends.

There were a few rubber balls and a couple of jump ropes in the yard, but most of the children played self-invented games without benefit of props. Terrence stood by himself in one corner of the yard, occasionally trying to participate, but always falling away to be alone again. I pretended that I wasn't watching him. After about ten minutes I could see him, out of the corner of my eye, working his way toward me. When he was near enough, I acknowledged him. I asked him if he was assigned to be with me and would get in trouble if he played instead. He said no, that he wanted to stand here. He said I was his tutor, and he wanted people to know that. So what I had thought might be an embarrassment was actually a status symbol, and if anyone needed a status symbol, Terrence did.

Now that I knew what my role was, I played my part to the hilt. Wherever Terrence went, I went. I asked him to show me around the yard. I asked him to introduce me to his classmates. He changed before my eyes. He seemed to actually grow in stature and acquire a sort of lilt to his step. "This is my tutor," he would say as he strutted around the yard, with me following close behind. He was becoming an instant celebrity. He was, in some strange way, safe while he was with me. It was as if he had some kind of immunity from teasing or ridicule.

He was a delightful child. He was bright and alert, his quick eye catching every nuance of my conversation. He was open and had a familiar sensitivity I could relate to. I guessed he was a middle child and had become slightly lost in the shuffle of daily living. He said his mother worked two jobs—she was a cleaning woman by day and took in laundry by night. The two older children picked up and delivered the laundry after school.

Terrence's younger sister was self-sufficient, self-motivated, and self-assured. Terrence said she wanted to be a doctor when she grew up, and if her performance in the class was any prediction of success, she would accomplish whatever she set her mind to. The two younger boys—twins—kept pretty much to each other and, in that way, were a self-sustaining pair. Dad was out of the picture entirely. Only Terrence didn't seem to fit. He was asked to be a self-starter, find his own niche, occupy his own free time, and go it alone. The mother was used to, and fortunate enough to have, five other children who managed pretty well without her constant intervention. They had found a way to use each other for support and leave Mom to bring home the bacon. Terrence floundered. He wasn't a troublemaker—he just didn't know how to manage.

In the afternoon the principal was true to her promise and made her scheduled visit to the classroom. As soon as she walked in, the children straightened in their seats. Books were flipped closed, papers and pencils put away, and hands folded neatly atop the empty desks. She took the floor and said she was going to speak about the progress of each student. She called the first row of children to stand in front of the class. One by one she went down the row, like a general's inspection, singling out each student by name and announcing their accomplishments and failures. Apparently, this was a regular occurrence, because the children knew exactly what to do.

Standing at attention and showing no facial emotion, they listened to the definitive statements of who they were. The principal encapsulated each child into a neat little package. Then she took her leather switch and executed the punishment (based on her singular judgment) to each child's backside. Those who had the most failures received the most swats. It was painful to watch and even more painful to hear. No one came out a winner. The children whose accomplishments were praised were aware of the cost. Getting a good review was by no means the pleasure it should have been. The manner in which the praise was bestowed was a demand for continued perfection and an expectation of even greater production.

Every one of those kids must have lived in fear that they could be next. The children who were given less worthy reports took it as stone faced as they could. Terrence couldn't have been stonier. The principal tore him apart, belittling him unmercifully in front of the entire class. I was humiliated. I was back in second grade.

Miss Lahey was a strict, old-maid schoolmarm, who was about seventy-five years old when I was in her class. She had a tendency to shake when she wrote on the blackboard so that her letters had a wavy quality to them. She had a strict rule about chewing pencils. The school supplied those thick primary pencils for us until we got into third grade and began writing in script. I remember Miss Lahey admonishing, smartly, anyone who chewed their pencil. As second graders, we often ended up

Nancy Sellin

with the pencils in our mouths from time to time. Once or twice my own pencil found its way into mine, but not enough to attract Miss Lahey's attention. Until one day.

We were taking a spelling test that, uncharacteristically, I had forgotten to study for. We were supposed to know words with two vowels together, specifically "ea" and "ee" words. I became flummoxed and couldn't remember whether *feet* was spelled with two *e*'s or an *ea*, or whether or not *neat* was spelled *neet*. My confusion turned into panic and before I knew it, I was chewing my pencil. Just after I had finished making it look like corn-on-the-cob, Miss Lahey descended on me, grabbed me by the back of the neck, and shoved me to the front of the room. She held up my mottled pencil and ridiculed me in front of the class.

At this moment, looking at Terrence, I knew what he was feeling. But he was a boy, and his boy code didn't permit his lower lip to tremble or his eyes to fill with tears. It didn't allow him to ask to be excused because his bladder suddenly felt the urge to let go. He knew he'd never have been excused and would have been humiliated further as his plea was refused.

Then something happened I didn't expect. Tears began to trickle from my eyes. I tried desperately to hold them back, but it was no use. No one noticed until I raised my hand to wipe away the tears with the back of my sleeve. First, one student turned to look at me. Then another, until a ripple passed through the room. I was unprepared for the flow of tears, which continued to fall down onto the front of my sweater, and I prayed for them to stop. I was making a spectacle of myself in front of all these strangers, and I had absolutely no control over it.

As the principal continued her diatribe at Terrence, curious glances flew my way. Then, without warning, Terrence abruptly left the front of the room, walked right past the principal and over to me. The principal stopped in midsentence. Her jaw dropped open as all heads turned toward us standing together at the back of the room. After a moment, as if by agreement, all heads turned in unison to look back at the principal. Even she knew that when a mystery is too overpowering, you just have to let it be. She closed her mouth, looked at the teacher, and said, "That will be all for today."

My tears stopped as abruptly as they had begun. Terrence took my hand and led me to his desk, where I spent the rest of the afternoon helping him do his lessons. I was grateful that no one mentioned the incident. No one asked me if I was all right. No one asked me what had happened or why I had been crying. The tears came from nowhere and disappeared into nowhere. I hadn't even made the sound of a sniffle. I couldn't remember feeling much of anything—except the wetness rolling down my face.

After school I walked home with him and met his mother and the rest of the children. Then we sat at the kitchen table and ate peanut butter on Wonder bread, washed down with ice-cold milk. I was famished, and it was delicious! I tried to talk but the peanut butter kept sticking to the roof of my mouth, so I could only slur my words and laugh.

We spent the rest of the "tutoring" afternoon looking at comic books, Terrence describing all of his superheroes and their various adventures. He was animated and expressive, a very different child than I had witnessed in the classroom, where expression was not encouraged— not even allowed. No scholastics took place that afternoon, or in the next two tutoring sessions either, but at the fourth session, his mother told me Terrence's teacher had said he was doing a little better and had even passed a math test.

We developed an unspoken routine. I would spend the day in the Peace Corps training at San Francisco State College. Then, at six o'clock, I would take the bus to the ghetto. Although I never asked him to, Terrence always met me at the bus stop and walked with me the seven blocks to his house. In that seven blocks, we lingered and talked to everyone we met. Terrence was pleased to be able to take me around and show me off; he said he was making sure I would be safe in the neighborhood.

After we got to his house, we would spend the first half of our tutoring session playing and talking and eating our peanut butter sandwiches, and the second half going over his upcoming lessons. Then around eight o'clock, he would walk me back to the bus and wave me on my way. This is how Terrence and I passed our four weeks together.

I spent a lovely Thanksgiving dinner with the family, and that was the last time I ever saw or heard from them.

I wondered what this San Francisco ghetto experience had to do with Liberians except for the color of their skin. And I couldn't begin to imagine the impact of slavery in shaping the present-day lives of those ghetto children or the Liberians, but more often than not, insight comes with hindsight, and this experience proved to be no exception.

CHAPTER 5

Steve

Toward the end of the fourth week of the training, I'd about had it with Steve. He had taken to having late-night card parties in the open space outside our bedroom. There were only four rooms with doors; probably these were offices when the barracks were a boot-camp training facility. The other three married couples had quickly secured the most secluded ones, and Dale and I, always hesitant and eager to please, had taken the least private one just outside the community space. There was no insulation in the building and certainly no soundproofing. Dale had wanted to make love a few times, but the walls were thin. On top of that, my self-consciousness took priority over my marital duty, and he knew better than to push it. Once or twice, I heard the squeaky springs in John and Virginia's bedroom late at night, which made me feel guilty, but my desire to please Dale was not sufficient to overcome either my self-consciousness or my guilt.

Steve's raspy donkey laugh penetrated the thin barracks walls at two and three in the morning, shaking me awake and making me furious. Dale tried to pacify me by telling me to simply ignore it. That made me angry with him for not taking seriously his role of protector and telling Steve where to get off. I don't know which made me angrier—Steve's inconsiderate behavior or Dale's pacifist attitude.

Once or twice, against Dale's urging me to "Be nice, now, be nice," I timidly asked Steve if he would be a little quieter, to which he always waved me off with a "Sure, sure, sorry," as he laughed again, baring those huge equine teeth. It would be quieter for a few minutes and then begin to escalate again. His stifled laugh was almost more annoying than the full bray. I'm a person who has always needed my sleep, so the mornings after these nights were hard for me. I pumped myself full of coffee to try to stay alert, but more often than not, all the coffee did was make me edgy. Oh well, it was only a few more days—I guessed I could stand it.

On the last day, the trainers told us that thirty-five of us were not going to be sent to the Virgin Islands after all, for the second phase of our training. We would be going directly to Liberia for special in-country training. We would be sent home for the month of December to gather supplies, go to the dentist, celebrate Christmas, and say our good-byes. Dale and I decided to spend the entire month in Washington State at my in-laws, rather than split the time between Anchorage and Tacoma.

CHAPTER 6

Wisdom Teeth

We were advised to have our wisdom teeth extracted to avoid dealing with any complications that might arise while in the country. Dental surgeons were nonexistent in Liberia, and sending us anywhere else outside the country would be very expensive. Most of us were at the age when wisdom teeth were just emerging or had newly emerged, and it was not uncommon to experience impacted or abscessed wisdom teeth. I made an appointment with a dental surgeon in Tacoma, had eight shots of Novocain, and had all four wisdom teeth extracted at once.

One of the extractions took an especially long time. Finally, the dentist admitted that I actually had only three wisdom teeth—he had not taken X-rays and had been probing deep into my jaw for no reason! He probably even charged me for it.

At that time, it didn't even occur to me to complain. I was a good little girl, respected authority, and did what I was told. Fortunately, I only had to take one dose of pain medication, which I probably didn't even need, and was good as new. On the other hand, Dale's jaws swelled up like two balloons, and he spent the next three days in bed doped up on pain medicine. We took our passport photos that week, so Dale has a permanent visual reminder of the experience.

CHAPTER 7

New York City, Polyester, and the Money Bus

Kids looking inside a money bus

On January 3, 1966, our group was to meet at Kennedy airport for our flight to Liberia. Dale and I decided to arrive a day early to take in some of the sights of New York City. Our plan was to take a midnight nonstop flight, sleep on the plane, drop our duffel bags off in our hotel room, and then tour the city for the rest of the day.

Los Angeles was the largest city either of us had ever been to, except that Dale had once accompanied his father to Tokyo. Our friends and relatives, none of whom had ever been to New York or knew anything about it, warned us severely about walking the streets after dark.

The horror stories of New York were fresh in our minds—rude, unhelpful people, muggings, and prostitutes hanging out in every doorway. We knew nothing at all about the diversified areas of New

York City—East side, West side, downtown, uptown, Greenwich Village, Harlem. We did, however, know that hotel chains have similar accommodations anywhere in the country. We called ahead to book a room at the New York Hilton.

Our flight arrived on time. We collected our bags and headed outside only to find that New York City was smack in the middle of a transit strike. Cabs were in high demand, so we stood in line and waited our turn. During the two-hour wait, we had many opportunities to observe how native New Yorkers haggled over the price of rides. We decided if we didn't want to spend all our money on a single cab ride (we also had to get back to the airport the following day), we would have to stand firm.

When our turn came, the cabbie took one look at us and recognized us as the patsies we were. He was sweet as sugar, spouting comforting words: "Don't worry, I'll get you where you want to go—no problem, get in, I'll take good care of you."

We naturally assumed we had, with beginner's luck, gotten the only altruistic cabbie in New York City. Relieved, we smiled and hopped in. Once he had us in his cab, we were trapped. He spent the entire next hour regaling us about the hardships of driving a cab in this strike, the meanness of people, his inability to pay his rent, and how he was doing us this huge favor because he could see we were nice people. He felt terrible that he was forced to charge us triple the fare, but he knew we'd understand his predicament.

By the time we reached our destination, we knew that if we ever wanted to leave his cab, we'd better pay up. We emptied our pockets and came up with exact fare (we knew nothing about the custom of tipping). He counted the money as we were leaving the cab, but the string of angry obscenities that followed us out threw us for a loop. We were pretty shaken when we stumbled into the lobby of the Hilton.

Composing ourselves, we approached the desk clerk to inquire about our reservation. After scouring his reservation list, he informed us he had no reservation in our name and that the hotel was completely booked. We must have turned white as ghosts because he quickly engaged us in conversation. "When did you make the reservation? Where are you from? How long are you staying?" He looked at our duffel bags. "Where are you going from here? How was it getting from the airport in this strike?" At that moment he seemed like the nicest person we'd ever met.

We poured out our entire life history in five minutes, ending with our tale of woe about the cab ride. I can see now why Americans so easily tell strangers their life histories. It has nothing to do with our friendliness. We are clearly a nation of emotionally needy people who will reveal anything to anybody who will listen.

The desk clerk listened with a sympathetic ear, recognizing us as the fearful innocents we were. He handed us the keys to the bridal suite, told us he'd give it to us for the price of a regular room, and encouraged us to enjoy our stay. This certainly contradicted everything we'd heard about New Yorkers, and we felt much better. Only then did our eyes begin to take in the beauty and elegance of our surroundings, and we quickly realized this was like no other Hilton we'd ever seen. We put the duffels in the room and suddenly felt famished.

We managed to find a reasonable place to eat outside the hotel and got last-minute tickets to see Henry Fonda in *Generation* on Broadway. I'd been involved in school drama programs since sixth grade, had majored in drama in high school, and had starred in numerous community theatre productions, so seeing a Broadway show was a dream come true. The evening was magical, and I knew in the deepest recesses of my heart that I would be back to stay—that my turn would come.

The flight to Liberia the following day was six hours late for departure. We neglected to call to see if the flight was on time, so we were the first of our PCV group to arrive and had plenty of time to really see the airport. Of course, in 1966, the occasional magazine stand was the only attraction, so we spent a good deal of the time browsing through trashy novels. It was exciting to mingle with the various nationalities always present at international airports. The Africans in their tribal dresses and colorful robes especially intrigued us, and, although we couldn't really understand a word they said, we tried to have a conversation which consisted, on both sides, of nodding our heads a lot and saying "yes" enthusiastically.

Within three hours, other members of our group began to arrive. It was great to see the familiar faces of people with whom we had gone through the training. We knew we would be spending the next two years of our lives with some of them. When Steve Wilson arrived, shaking everyone's hand like a politician in an election year, I looked the other way. The New York–based PCVs were the last to arrive, just in time to board the plane. The five of them dragged in looking like they had been to an all-nighter, which turned out to be true. They were the most blasé of all the PCVs, both during the training and in the country itself. They seemed always to be easy going and unflustered, and I assumed it was because, living in New York City, they had been everywhere and done everything. I longed to have some of their style and vowed that someday I would.

The party atmosphere in our section of the plane settled down after a couple of hours and people began to doze off. Dozing, waking up, and cruising the aisles to chat or play cards became pretty much the pattern for the next fourteen hours. I looked down as we flew over the city of Dakar and passed into the denser, tropical rain forest of the Liberian countryside, with no idea what would await me outside the cool, temperature-controlled cabin of the jet.

Stopping to refuel in Dakar was the only chance we had to deplane. My eyes burned from the cigarette smoke drifting in from the smoking section of the plane, so I eagerly took advantage of the forty-five-minute stopover outside the plane. It was a rustic one-room terminal with no air conditioning and only one bathroom. I was glad for the bag of nuts and gum we had bought at Kennedy airport. Flying was still relatively rare for most civilians, so takeoffs, landings, and the occasional turbulence were white-knuckle experiences for me. I had never been on such a long flight before, and, although my knees were not yet stiff, as they would be later from years of theatre acting and gymnastic workouts, my body ached to stretch out and move freely in unfiltered air. I was not prepared, however, for what that air would be like.

Polyester fabric was the latest craze in the States. The advantage of polyester was that it didn't wrinkle no matter what you did to it. You could squeeze it into a tight ball and put three hundred pounds of weight on top of it, and it still wouldn't show a crease. It washed easily and dried quickly. It was the perfect choice for a humid country like

Liberia, where we'd have to wash everything by hand and dry our clothes in the open air. During the month we were home, I made every piece of clothing I brought with me (except underwear) out of this miracle fabric. I thanked my mother every day for putting up with the frustration of teaching me how to sew when I was in high school. I felt dually smug as I noticed the wrinkled 100 percent cotton blouses of the New York–based PCVs.

The *dis*advantage of early polyester is that it doesn't breathe and doesn't conform to your body—it definitely has a life of its own. It clings to your body when you sweat, feels like rubber, and holds the odor of perspiration. It turned out to be a terrible choice for a humid, tropical country like Liberia, especially at a time when there was no such thing as unscented antiperspirant. To this day, my stomach turns over at the smell of Secret deodorant mixed with perspiration.

Within minutes of deboarding the plane, my blouse was sticking to me like glue. I looked around at the confident New York PCVs, chatting with each other, their wrinkled all-cotton shirts easily gracing their sweaty bodies. "Pride cometh before a fall," I chuckled at my own arrogance. Some of us choose to learn the hard way. Every time I pulled my blouse away from my body, it immediately found its way back, like a magnet to its perfect mate.

I thought of all those beautiful polyester blouses and tent dresses rolled neatly in my duffel. I was grateful to reboard the plane. Even the smoke didn't seem to bother me so much. I made up my mind, right there at the airport, that I would much rather freeze to death than burn to death. However, on reflection, both seem rather gruesome. It took a few months in the country before my Alaskan blood had thinned enough so I didn't perspire quite so much, and there were even those times, in the rainy season, I would get cold and have to don a sweater. Those times were the best! I loved getting cold—a welcome break from the relentless, humid heat.

Excitement mounted as we started our descent toward Monrovia's Roberts International Airport. This was it! A new experience. Our home for the next two years. A new life. I never dreamed to what extent the experience of living in Liberia would affect the rest of my life—my perceptions, my choices, and my priorities, my values.

I stepped out of the plane, and a solid wall of heat came up and hit me in the face. I swooned and nearly lost my balance. After I caught my breath, I grabbed my Instamatic camera and began taking pictures. I didn't want to miss a moment of those first impressions. I had never seen such vibrant colors. It seemed like all of my senses were vibrating. If I could have taken a picture of the humidity, I would have. At the edge of the airport, women dressed in brightly colored fabrics lined the path, seated on the red ground selling their wares—intricately patterned African cloth spread with bananas, pineapples, rice, hot peppers, palm nuts, coconuts.

The men in their Bermuda shorts and country shirts were selling baskets, cloth, jewelry, wood, and ivory carvings. It was almost too exciting to bear, and I took pictures of everything. My excitement must have been contagious because the Liberians posed willingly, laughed, and begged me to show them the pictures. I tried to explain that pictures have to be developed, but it was useless.

After picking up our duffels, we were loaded, fifteen at a time, into money buses and driven to Monrovia. A money bus is an open-sided van that seats eight people comfortably. It cost a dime anywhere you wanted to go inside the city, and twenty-five cents to and from the airport. The trip to the Peace Corps hostel took forty-five minutes and would have taken longer, except that the drivers had no concept of speed limit or safety. Our duffel bags were loaded onto a top rack and strapped in. We took our chances inside. I would have taken pictures, but I was holding on for dear life.

Blowing in the breeze, we drove at breathtaking speed along a red laterite dirt road; by the time we arrived in Monrovia, we were covered from head to toe in a layer of red dust. After blowing my nose, I realized why Liberians cover nose and mouth with a cloth when they ride the money bus. It might also be, as I discovered later, that when the money bus is loaded with passengers carrying chickens, goats, and fish, the odor is potent—a male goat especially. But I don't think the Liberians were as bothered as I was by human body odor or animal smells. The natural, undeodorized, human musk was not only acceptable, it was desirable. Deodorant was difficult to come by, and its use was simply not a custom, particularly for the majority of people with little or no money to speak of. We would just have to get used to it.

33

CHAPTER 8

The Hostel, Club Beer, and Jif

I was relieved to arrive at the Peace Corps hostel. It was a large whitewashed building with many rooms. Giant ceiling fans hovered over us like swooping eagles. Each room held four bunk beds. The men and women were separated. There was a large kitchen area with several water filter kegs and a kerosene refrigerator. Though the kitchen had a stove, there were really no facilities for thirty-five of us to cook or eat in, so it was suggested we reserve the use of the kitchen for our return visits to Monrovia over the next two years. We could go to the market and bring back fruit, but the main meals would have to be eaten at a restaurant one-half mile away. *Just walk along the main dirt road. You can't miss it.*

We put dibs on our bunks and decided to explore the neighborhood. I put on one of my clean polyester blouses and skirt and grabbed my camera and purse. We decided not to take the money bus to town. Walking the five miles to the center of town, I snapped pictures of the dirt road, the money buses, and Liberians sauntering along, their heads piled high with all manner of goods. A tall, handsome Liberian dressed in a three-piece pinstriped business suit, complete with tie, carried a briefcase on his head, leaving his hands free to wave at us. A small child with a large tummy and protruding belly button, balancing a pail of water on his head, shouted, "Peace Corps!" and asked us for "fah cen." We had been told not to give away money because it encouraged begging, but it was evident the custom of begging from PCVs was already in full swing in the capital city of Monrovia.

Everyone along the road shared a friendly greeting. Even people in the open money buses shouted hello as they passed. My eyes weren't wide enough to capture the depth of my impressions. I was so glad I had brought plenty of film. I would relive these moments repeatedly in pictures. If I had had any trepidation about the friendliness of these beautiful people, it vanished in a matter of minutes. I took a deep breath, looked at my husband, and said, "I love it here."

We spent the rest of the day exploring. Monrovia was a study in contrasts. On a street with cars whizzing by, a woman squatted beside an iron pot frying fritters, the odor of sewage mixing with hot palm oil. I lifted my eyes to the white tropical homes dotting the green hills, most of them probably occupied by European businessmen and their families and, as I learned later, our Peace Corps leaders. If you stood in just the right place, you could see the presidential mansion—modeled after our own White House. I vowed to visit the mansion soon and maybe even meet President Tubman.

Another street revealed a row of boxy one-room abodes with tin roofs, most of which were in dire need of repair, not a square corner among the lot. An elegant air-conditioned bar and restaurant graced an adjacent street while, just around the corner, a group of women haggled over the price of fish resting on a cardboard box in the noonday sun. I think the flies already had the best of the fish. We went into the restaurant for a cold drink and ran into John and Virginia Lyon, so we joined them. One of the PCVs from New York joined us too.

Being the enthusiastic newcomers that we were, we decided to order the local beer. We were mindful that our Peace Corps training had warned us to drink only bottled beverages in restaurants. Neither Dale nor I were beer connoisseurs—one beer was pretty much like another—but even we noticed that Club Beer was no ordinary beer. The first clue was that it came in a burnt umber–colored, unlabeled bottle, so you couldn't really see the beer color inside. The second clue was that the metal cap was rusty, and when the waiter opened the bottle, its rim was caked with rust and something else. Dale and I threw a quick glance at each other. We noticed John and Virginia had a similar reaction, and the four of us shared a chuckle. Without missing a beat, cool Stan, from New York, grabbed his napkin, wiped the rim clean, and took a swig. We followed suit. John and Virginia asked the waiter for glasses. Holding the beer in my mouth, I couldn't help noticing it was on the warm side. I swallowed quickly.

Stan was the epitome of cool, chatting about the latest book he had read and enjoying his beer. John and Virginia, in unison, poured their beer into the clear glasses. We were entranced as we watched enormous globs of sediment plop into the glasses and swirl around for some moments before settling to the bottom. It was too much. Almost on cue, the four of us burst out laughing. We tried to control ourselves (after all, we didn't want to offend the waiter), but every time we tried to stifle the laugh, it would erupt. Stan didn't seem to have the faintest idea what we were laughing at, which made us laugh even harder. If the truth be known, we actually grew to like the smooth taste of the beer, though we never cared for it warm or drank the sediment; and to the Europeans in our town who wouldn't think of drinking anything but Heineken, we would never admit that we liked it.

I was like a kid in a candy store. That afternoon, we tried to hit every store in Monrovia. I couldn't absorb it fast enough. There were all kinds of shops run by either Lebanese merchants or Liberian merchants. The Lebanese shops were stocked with imported goods from various countries: pharmaceuticals, clothes, canned goods, and stacks of African fabrics from which most of the natives made their clothes. The Liberian stores sold rice and other local foods like peppers, flour, green peanuts (groundnuts), farina, plantains, country cloth, and baskets.

After we'd been in the country a few weeks, we learned you could get dibs on a hunk of beef (from a country cow), which you had to rub generously with gobs of mashed papaya and soak for at least eight hours to make it tender. If you didn't do that, you couldn't even bite into it. Even so, you had to put up with loose stool for a couple of days after you ate it. It was worth it just to have a nice piece of tough steak occasionally. Fresh eggs were a rare treat and were usually gone by the time you got there, but you could get powdered eggs that tasted like glue. The advantage of living in a place, though, is that your neighbors give you the scoop about where you could occasionally find beef or eggs, who had them, and when the Fante fishermen were due to come in with their fresh catch on the beach. The fresh fish weren't fresh anymore by the time they reached the market at 6:30 a.m.

If there was a single item that drew my attention that first day in Monrovia, it was the gorgeous 100 percent cotton African cloth. It hadn't occurred to me, until that day, that the cloth would have to have been made in other countries and imported to Africa. I wondered which European white men designed the cloth that had become so "indigenous" to the African people. I came away with an armload of it. As soon as I could get hold of a sewing machine, my polyester clothes would be history. Fortunately, as I was to discover a month later, you could get many things in Liberia by simply passing the word. Within a few days of reaching our final destination in Greenville, I was in possession of a small hand-treadle machine. Brand name: Singer.

When we arrived back at the Peace Corps hostel after dinner in town, Steve Wilson and two friends were in the small kitchen cooking up a whale of a dinner. Rice, fish, collard greens, fried plantains, and fresh baked bread. He had been cooking and baking all afternoon. If anyone else wanted to use the kitchen, he would smile and say, "Sorry, it's in use." I chuckled as I heard several of our group voice their complaints.

I was tired so I fell into bed quickly and slept heavily. I was awakened abruptly at 2:00 a.m. by loud laughter in a nearby room. I recognized Dale's voice and realized he and a few others were playing cards far into the night. I drifted back to sleep. When I awoke again, it was 5:30 a.m. and quiet. I felt a little queasy, so I got up for a drink of water and wondered what I had eaten the day before that could have made me sick. I met the Peace Corps group director in the hall, and he told me that Dale, two other PCVs, and a Liberian driver had driven to Fisebu, a small village about five hours upcountry from Monrovia. Over the next few days, our group would be dispersed and sent to towns and villages all over Liberia for the second month of our training. The Peace Corps wanted to send Dale and me to Fisebu, and they had gone to check out the accommodations for our arrival three days later. Dale didn't want to wake me, and anyway he'd be back sometime the next day. He had left me twenty dollars. It was plenty.

I would have the day to myself, and I wasn't about to spend it sick in bed. Anyway, the wave of nausea had passed, and I was hungry. I went to the kitchen, got some water, and looked in the fridge. There were the leftovers from Steve's feast the night before. I took a few large spoonfuls. It wasn't bad. I thanked him under my breath.

Suddenly there was activity in the hostel, as everyone seemed to jump out of bed at the same time. I dressed quickly and joined three of my group to walk to breakfast. We shared stories of yesterday's explorations, and I filed away the exciting things I would do today.

Alice had found a lady who did a thing called tie-dye, using only dyes from local plants. I couldn't wait to visit her and learn her secrets. Then some PCVs were going to the Mansion, and I could go along. After that, I would explore the waterfront where the Fante fishermen lived in their shacks beside rows of fish hung on lines to dry in the sun. They dried the fish for three days and then took them to the market to sell. Since I would never think of competing with the flies for their fish, I would pass up that delicacy and leave it to the locals whose stomachs were stronger than mine. All these discoveries, however, would have to wait until another day.

I had a big breakfast of French toast with syrup. Hot coffee was okay to drink because it was made with boiled water. Liberia had the greatest coffee in the world. It was fresh, strong, and delicious—and it was a smell like home.

After breakfast, we decided to walk into town. The early morning air was unladen by the weight of later-day humidity, and I felt such a surge of excitement being in this incredible place I didn't want to move through it too fast. I was in heaven and I wanted to savor every moment! I had already taken four rolls of film, but I had brought twenty rolls with me and could purchase more in town. It was one of the few times in my life I wished I was an artist. I knew in an instant why they call Africa the most colorful continent in the world. But it was only the beginning.

On the walk to town, I began to feel queasy again. I pretended I was fine, praying it would pass. By the time we got to town, I was really sick. I told the group I was going to have to go back to the hostel, but I knew walking was out of the question. Though nobody offered to escort me back, one of them hailed me a taxi and told the driver where to take me. The road was bumpy, and he drove like most Liberians— fast and reckless. As he pulled into the driveway of the hostel, I lost my breakfast all over his backseat. He was furious! I tried to apologize, but I was too weak and couldn't compete with his string of demands to clean up his taxi and pay him some exorbitant amount of money. I paid him whatever he wanted and left him still screaming as I dragged myself into the hostel to find something with which to clean vomit from the interior of his taxi. The hostel was empty except for the Liberian hostel workers. One of them took pity on me and told me he would take care of the cab. I never forgot his kindness and brought him a gift next time I visited the hostel.

After I rinsed out my clothes, I went to bed and slept for two hours. I was so embarrassed I told no one. When I awoke, I felt great—as if I'd never been sick a day in my life. I was famished, so I dressed, took a money bus to town, and had a big lunch. I ran into my friends and joined them for the rest of the afternoon. It was as if the entire experience that morning had been a dream.

I arrived back at the hostel in the early evening, and one of the PCVs told me that the director had been looking for me. It sounded urgent. Now what? The director sat me down and told me everything was okay.

I said, "What's okay?"

He said the car Dale was in had been speeding and had not seen an approaching money bus, had swerved to avoid hitting it, and had flipped over on its top. Nobody was hurt—except Dale probably had a slight concussion, and he might be a little disoriented for a while. He was on his way home in another car. I would have to make sure he didn't go to sleep for the next eight hours.

He assured me we were very lucky because head injuries were the main cause of traffic deaths in the country. No local hospital was equipped to deal with that kind of thing, and by the time the injured could be transported to another country, it was often too late. I thought of thanking him for the words of reassurance, but I didn't. The word spread quickly. When the car showed up three hours later, Dale received a hero's welcome. I was just relieved he knew my name.

The next morning I awoke again at five-thirty with the same feeling of nausea, only this time it didn't go away and I had to make a beeline for the bathroom. Again, reviewing what I had eaten yesterday, it finally dawned on me that I had morning sickness—the birth control pills had finally kicked in. I wondered how I was ever going to juggle this one, and for how long I would need to. But within a problem there is always a gift, and this was the beginning of my love affair with European saltines and Danish butter. A quick trip to the Peace Corps doctor in Monrovia let me in on the secret of eating saltines before I got out of bed in the morning. Sometimes it didn't work, and the nausea got to me before the saltines. Those were the tough mornings because, once the nausea came on, it had its full run for about three hours. But most of the time the saltines beat the nausea to the punch. I started setting the alarm for 3:30 a.m., eating two or three plain saltines, setting the alarm again for 4:30, and going back to sleep. Then I'd wake up an hour later, eat some more saltines, set the alarm, and go back to sleep. This continued for the next two months, until my body got used to the high levels of estrogen released by the pill. I carried saltines with me everywhere.

One day I was complaining about how dry they were, and Steve Wilson flashed a wry smile my way, "Ohhh ... you haven't discovered Danish butter!" My mouth watered as he described its creamy texture and buttery fragrance. Later that day, I found he had left a tin of it on my bunk. It just goes to show you, there's good in everyone. I went to the kitchen and found a can opener. The whoosh of fragrance that came out was a mixture of fresh cream and rich sweet butter. I spread a good dollop on a crispy saltine and took a bite. Adding a bit of Jif peanut butter made it even better. Dale tried it too. We were hooked. When we got to our final post a month later, we discovered we couldn't get Jif peanut butter, so we had it shipped in by the case from Monrovia.

And thus began my addiction to saltines, Danish butter, and Jif. I justified my addiction by maintaining it was a good source of protein. Even today, I can recall the taste and how it melted on my tongue. I'm sure that my weight gain over the next few months had more to do with the Danish butter than the birth control pills. (P.S.: Dale never gained an ounce!)

CHAPTER 9

Fisebu

My neighbors in Fisebu

Fisebu was the true stereotype of an upcountry West African village. The natives lived in mud and stick huts with thatch roofs and dirt floors. The PCVs lived in mud and stick houses with dirt floors and tin roofs. One of the requirements for getting a PCV to work in your village was that they had to live in a house with a tin roof. There were four PCVs in the village: Carol and Rick, a small, wholesome-looking married couple who were the only Peace Corps teachers in the village, and two single guys who were building a sewage system for the town.

The trainers had sent Dale and me there to learn about teaching. Dale had already completed one year of teaching in a junior high school in Anchorage, Alaska (a horrendous experience from which he was sure he'd never recover), and I had completed only one semester of student teaching in a fourth grade class.

Carol was the elementary school teacher in the village, and her husband was in the secondary school. They invited us to stay at their house while we were in training, and we happily took them up on their offer. They were into their second year in the country and had set up the village's first school, and people seemed to like them. I was impressed with how fluidly they moved through their daily lives. They had met as two singles in Fisebu, had fallen in love, and were practically living together at a time when it was frowned upon. Six months earlier they had decided to be married in Fisebu by a visiting Baptist missionary. Both sets of parents flew in from the United States.

Having the two of us as houseguests for a month didn't seem to faze them in the least. My goodness, how I wished I could be that easygoing! (I'm still wishing it.) I wondered how a person could live in a house with a dirt floor and not have a layer of dirt on everything. But I learned that a dirt floor gets packed down hard so eventually there's very little loose dirt even when it's swept. The mud and stick walls were painted white, and there were homemade African cloth curtains on the shuttered windows. A large table in the kitchen could seat eight people. There was no electricity, but a kerosene refrigerator kept food cool. In that month, I saw how it was to live as a PCV in Liberia. Of course, living in someone else's house and living on your own are two different things.

Carol was a facile teacher. Although she was soft-spoken and not much taller than the children she taught, she was clearly at ease with them and the material. I'd been trained to use a lot of hands-on techniques—arts and crafts, visual and auditory aids, acting games, and physical involvement. The Liberian school system still practiced mostly rote memorization and recitation. Carol had a nice blend of the two. She had a gift for taking the familiar and incorporating the new. She had decorated her classroom with travel posters, and she had an abundance of books and supplies neatly organized for easy access by the children. Each child had his own desk.

It was clear that, when the children walked into the classroom, they knew there was an established routine to be followed. The kids ranged in age from seven to twelve. I watched Carol smile and move in a relaxed way from child to child, helping them at their own levels. I could see she was a seasoned professional, and I suddenly wished I could have come to Liberia with a little more teaching experience. But she made it look so easy that it made me feel confident in my own ability to create the same wonderful learning environment for my future students.

Carol was not one to complain, so I would never know what struggles she had gone through to make it look that easy. Also, she was not interested in giving formal instruction to prospective teachers, so when I queried her about the difficulties she had initially encountered, she shrugged it off. I didn't see the layers beneath the surface—I saw only the polished result. And of course, the Peace Corps showed us only the most well-oiled machines. My two-dimensional vision turned out to be a protective device. Had I foreseen the difficult challenges that lay ahead of me, I might have given up in despair.

We got up at dawn. Liberians got up with the sunrise and pretty much went to bed when it got dark. Very few people had electricity, so it was simply more convenient to go to bed when it got dark, unless someone was having a celebration around a campfire somewhere. The market opened at 6:30 a.m. Carol and I arrived at ten after six to witness the efficient setup. An influx of women and children arrived, all at once, precisely at six fifteen. Children helped carry goods to the market before school opened at eight o'clock. The loads they carried were heavy, so they needed to help each other lift the goods off their heads. It seemed like the entire village had something to sell, trade, or buy. I thought what a sensible custom it was, this carrying things on your head. I recalled that, in my high school home economics class, we practiced good posture by walking around with books on our heads. It was kind of a lark, but most of us never got the hang of it. All Liberian men, women, and children learn to carry things on their heads. And I never once saw a Liberian with poor posture.

On this market day, as on every other market day, nobody came empty-headed. They took a length of African cloth and twisted it into a sort of soft, thick rope. Then they made it into a circle, which fit perfectly on the top of their heads, to form a cushion. With this arrangement, round-bottom bowls could just as easily be toted as flat baskets, or square containers. They even carried heavy logs bound together this way.

Outside the city of Monrovia, there were no cabs or money buses and very few cars, which most of the time were broken down from wrestling with the humidity. Scarcity of parts was another reason you might see so many cars sitting unused. So there was nothing for it but to walk and carry your goods the best way you knew how.

The PCVs from the civilized country of America carried their goods in their arms, under hunched shoulders, huffing and puffing, having to set down their load frequently to catch their breath, while the primitive Liberians popped their loads atop their heads and glided along smoothly, looking for all the world like proud, elegant fashion models on a runway. This was only one of the countless times I asked myself, "What's wrong with this picture, and why are Americans so smug?" One of the most endearing sights I saw was a two-year-old boy carrying a cup of water nestled in the cloth rag on his head. The tin cup was full to the brim, but he didn't spill a drop. His sister, who might have been a year older and not much bigger, had graduated to carrying a bucket.

A woman carried at least a fifty-pound bag of rice that hung around her ears like an enormous Renaissance hat. Folds of African cloth, cut in two-yard lengths and piled four feet high, rode atop another head. Most of the cloth was sold in these two-yard lengths, not in bolts or rolls like in America. Two-yard lengths were the customary measure for cut cloth because it was the perfect length to wrap around the lower half of the body and tie at the waist, creating an instant wraparound skirt. Another two-yard length was the right amount to make a sleeveless top with a fitted bodice and flared and pleated at the waist to the middle of the hip line. To complete the ensemble, you took another two-yard length and wrapped it in any creative way around your head. The fashion was called a lappa suit and was as standard as jeans and T-shirts are in America today.

The cloth pattern could be very basic (still gorgeous) or quite elaborate—perhaps with gold thread woven through it—for a more formal occasion.

Each person had her own market spot. Everywhere I looked, I saw market vendors whipping out pieces of the colorful cloth, shaking them into the air, and watching them float to the ground like giant butterflies spreading their wings. One cloth was laid with grapefruit. Another was laid with green oranges. It was then that I learned that oranges in their natural state are green on the outside and orange on the inside. Only the well-bred hybrids have the orange peels I was used to seeing. Pineapples adorned another cloth.

I had never bought a fresh pineapple before. Dole in the can was my gourmet fare back home, so I had no idea how to tell if one was ripe. I assumed it was ripe if it was golden yellow on the outside, but after seeing green oranges, I wasn't so sure.

One of my neighbors soon instructed me on the foolproof method of picking the perfect pineapple. First, if the skin was yellow, it was too ripe—most likely the fruit would be mushy and bruised in the center. If it was mostly green with just a hint of yellow, then you went to the next level—you squeezed it. When you pushed your thumbs into it—if it gave too much—too ripe. When you got the perfect squeeze down, you smelled it. If it smelled sweet and strong of pineapple—too ripe. Only a hint of the pineapple perfume was allowed. If it passed the sight, touch, and smell tests, then came the final exam. You held the pineapple under your arm and gently pulled out one of the top leaves. If it didn't come out with a strong pull—too green. If it came out too easily—too ripe. If it came out with moderate resistance, then, like Baby Bear's porridge, it was just right.

This method of selecting pineapple turned out to be the definitive test for pineapples in America, too. I guess nobody could figure out how to hybridize pineapples yellow on the outside. When I returned Stateside, I would go to the pineapples in the produce section of the supermarket and notice, without exception, women testing pineapples for ripeness by using only the sight and smell method. I sometimes shared my secret with them. Some were intrigued and asked me how I knew this, so I eagerly told them a tidbit or two about living in Liberia. But most people just looked at me like I should mind my own business. Consequently, most of my Liberian experiences became my own private treasures until they finally found their way into this book some forty-five years later.

There was no organized farming system in Liberia, so everyone grew what they wanted to grow and brought whatever they couldn't use to the market. Most people tried to grow a little in excess of what they needed in order to exchange with others who grew something else. Rice was the staple of Liberia, but very little of it was grown in the country. Most of it had to be imported, although there always seemed to be plenty of it. You could buy it still in its husk for five cents a can (fifteen-ounce tin cans were the standard measure) or ten cents already husked.

The early birds bought it crude first thing in the morning for five cents. Then they would husk and sift it right there in the market and sell it for ten cents. The process of husking went something like this: First, they put a few cups of rice in a large knee-high mortar. Then, using a giant wooden pole as a pestle, they pounded the rice until it separated from the husk. Then they put it all in a large, flat basket and with expert deftness, tossed the rice high in the air, letting the breeze blow the husks to the four winds. They executed this process repeatedly until only the white rice remained. I figured I could save a lot of money if I learned how to do that myself. I vowed that's just what I would do once I was settled in my own house.

Papaya was another great discovery. Ripeness was easy to see, smell, and feel: golden skins, soft to the touch, and a smell as sweet as fruity perfume. I wondered why they never made "essence of papaya" perfume from the papaya fragrance. It makes your mouth water. Aside from papaya's famed properties for tenderizing meat (just look at the label on any meat tenderizer, and you're likely to find papaya listed as one of the ingredients, unless they've discovered a cheap chemical to replace it), it is delicious in fresh fruit salad or sliced and served with fresh-squeezed lime juice over it. The only warning is, since it is an excellent natural meat tenderizer, it also tenderizes the bulk in your colon, so ingesting too much of it may have you running to the bathroom more often than you'd like. But it's not such a bad thing to have around for the opposite affliction.

Grapefruit was the sweetest thing to come off the tree. Like oranges, the skins were more green than yellow. The Liberians showed us the most efficient way to eat both grapefruits and oranges. First, you peel enough skin off one end to make a small circular hole. Then you put your mouth over the hole and squeeze the fruit, sucking all the juice out. After your fruit is squeezed flat, you break it open, peel it, and eat the pulp.

Everyone had peppers to sell—hot peppers in all sizes and shades of red. They couldn't have been treated with more reverence if they had been diamonds. Some were displayed, with obvious care, in rows ranging from the smallest to the largest. Others were piled high in hand-woven baskets. The purchaser sifted through the displays picking out just the right peppers in just the right color.

The pepper was the most essential ingredient in Liberian cooking, with the exception of rice. I had never had the occasion to include peppers in my limited culinary experience back home. I had never used anything more than a few sprinkles of ground chili pepper (which I got from the supermarket shelf) to liven up some canned chili. I would not enjoy the full impact of the use of the pepper until I got to Greenville and learned how to cook Liberian food properly. And, although I learned to fully appreciate their value, I could never tolerate more than a little for myself, so the joy of picking the perfect pepper never really became a priority for me.

I come from a family of three daughters, and we were raised in the fifties, so shopping was a significant pastime in my family. At first it was just window shopping, but the more money my father made, the easier it was to get into the swing of the acquisition mentality. By the time I entered the Peace Corps, I was an expert. Naturally, I couldn't leave Fisebu without acquiring some artifacts. I wasn't looking for anything imported from Europe or Lebanon. Liberia didn't have any tourist attractions or gift shops, but this was just fine with me, because I wanted the *real* thing—preferably used.

My eyes were constantly searching for items people used in their day-to-day living. Every time I was invited to someone's hut, I would scan the room for something I might want. Each hut became its own gift shop. Everything in Fisebu was fresh and new to me and I thoroughly enjoyed giving in to my coveting urge while it lasted. It was the same kind of urge that led me to shoot thirteen rolls of film the first three days in the country—I just couldn't seem to get enough.

I was strolling through the village, as I often did, sometime close to sunset, greeting everyone and stopping to chat with a few people along the way. A man was sitting outside his hut weaving baskets. They were the traditional straw-colored baskets in all shapes and sizes that were the primary containers used for everything in Liberia except liquids. He asked me if I wanted to buy some baskets, and I asked him how much. He confidently pointed to each basket naming off prices ranging from one to two and a half dollars. I thought the prices were incredibly reasonable, and I picked out one of the one-dollar baskets.

I reached into my bag to give him the dollar and his expression suddenly changed. He looked at me with a surprised, toothless grin and said, "Oh, no, no, mother, not one dollar, too muh, too muh!" I didn't understand what he was trying to say so I offered him the dollar again. He threw up his hands, took the dollar, and gave me seventy-five cents. I stood there dumbfounded as he explained to me that I must never pay the first price for anything! He laughed loudly at my ignorance. His wife came outside to see what was so funny, and when he told her what had happened, she laughed, too.

He gave me the basket, and they invited me inside like an old friend. When the man got up, I noticed he had been sitting on a wooden stool about six inches high. It was rectangular, with a curved seat and four squat legs. It had been crudely carved out of a solid piece of wood, and the seat had a simple geometric design on it. I asked him if I could see it. He handed it to me, and I noticed that the design had a name carved into it. He said it was his country stool, and his name was Kokuloson. He was the son of Kokulo, and that was his name carved on the stool. I asked him timidly if he might be willing to sell me the stool. He told me I didn't want that old stool and that he would carve me a brand-new one—much better. I reiterated that I would much rather have the old one. Then his manner changed. He stood up tall, looked at me straight in the eye, and said firmly, "Ten dollar!"

I looked at him right back and said just as firmly, "One dollar!"

He paused for a second, then said, "Three dollar!"

I said, "Okay!" and handed him the three dollars. He slapped the dollars into his hand and ushered me into the hut, laughing all the while. I knew, without a doubt, he would have taken one dollar. I also knew, without a doubt, I would have paid ten.

We usually spent our evenings playing cards around the kitchen table. The two large kerosene lanterns hung above the table, gently purring like two sleeping kittens. Carol and Rick were eager to teach us how to play bridge, and Dale and I caught on quickly. Bridge is a game played in partners and requires intense concentration and memory, and we became hooked on the challenge. We easily learned the rules but never became competitive players.

PCVs, European merchants, Dale on the right, Greenville

Bridge suited our Peace Corps life to a tee because evenings left plenty of time to practice. Over the next two years, we were always getting together with other PCVs and the Europeans in our town. Once you became a bridge player, you realized, rather quickly, that there are two distinct categories of players: the game players and the players who have to win. We fit into the first category. We played seriously, but if we made a mistake or didn't play too well one night, it was no big deal—we'd do better next time.

The "win" players couldn't tolerate any alternative but winning. God forbid if you were partnered with one of them—they treated you like an idiot if you made a mistake in bidding or playing out a hand. I dreaded those occasions when several of us would get together and play round-robin because I knew I'd eventually end up partnered with one of the "win" mentality. They would get just as angry with themselves if they made a mistake, but that didn't make me feel any better. I would inevitably start each game with a disclaimer: "Gee, I'm only learning the game, and I don't know how to play too well, but I'll do my best—please be patient with me if I make an error in judgment."

They pretended to understand for a few minutes but something in them couldn't resist being critical. Dale usually laughed loudly when one of them told him how stupid he was, but I could tell his laughter was a cover for his feelings of inadequacy because he had a habit of chewing the inside of his cheek when he felt insecure or nervous. If someone insulted me, I couldn't have laughed if I'd tried—my tears were too close to the surface. Thank goodness, the times of extreme tension were rare. There were those occasions when we were partnered against two "win" players, and we'd beat them. I was secretly pleased, but it was a hollow victory because the losers would be seething.

Carol and Rick were relaxed players, and we had a highly enjoyable month learning and playing bridge. We would finish our dinner around five thirty, read a book for a while, and then Carol and I would get the green plantains out. That was the signal for the guys to light the lanterns and get the bridge table set.

Plantains look exactly like green bananas, only much larger. The first time I bought them in the market in Monrovia, they were greenish yellow. I remarked to Dale how large and beautiful the bananas were. When the skins never seemed to ripen to that traditional sunny yellow color, I began to wonder what kind of bananas they were so I decided to peel one. They didn't peel, so I took a knife and cut one in half. The inside looked exactly like a banana except that it was a pale apricot color. I just assumed they weren't ripe so I would wait until they were. A couple of days later, the skin was a sort of rotten-looking black with yellow spots. Again, I had no luck peeling them, and cutting them open, I noticed they were mushy and looked like overripe bananas. The taste was bitter and starchy. I figured I had gotten a rotten batch and threw them out.

When Carol and I went to market the first day in Fisebu and purchased green plantains, she chuckled when I told her my story. She promised me I would be in for a real treat.

While the guys cleared the table for bridge, Carol and I put a quart of palm oil in an iron pot on the stove. Then we took the sharpest knives we had and began cutting the skin off the green plantains. Handling the raw fruit left a powdery residue on our hands. Once they were peeled, we painstakingly sliced them into paper-thin disks as fast as we could because the fruit turns brown very quickly after its exposure to the air. Once we had a nice sized pile, we popped the fruit—one slice at a time—into the sizzling hot palm oil. As we turned the slices frequently, being careful not to let them stick to each other, they reached a crisp golden brown in about two minutes. With lightning speed, we removed each slice, laid them on a plate, and sprinkled them with salt. Voilà! Liberian "french fries"—and deliciously addictive.

The ripe fried plantains were also tasty, but not as compelling as the green ones. You wait until the skin turns black all over. Then you cut the skin off carefully, revealing a soft banana-colored fruit. You slice the fruit in strips and place them in the hot oil, turning frequently until golden brown, and serve plain. It tastes like sweet fried bananas with a little more texture. After I moved to New York City, I was thrilled to find plantains in the Hispanic markets and thoroughly enjoyed my Liberian french fries once again.

CHAPTER 10

Elephant Tusk Band

We had been in Fisebu fourteen days and had become used to the routine. For some reason, the air was particularly oppressive one evening—it seemed to cling like glue as I walked—and I felt like I was breathing through a woolen blanket. That was the one thing I never got used to in Liberia—the humidity. I tolerated it, I lived in it, I worked in it, I slept in it, I played in it, but I never got used to it. None of us felt like playing bridge that night. Carol, Rick, and Dale took a flashlight and went for a walk. I couldn't move. All I wanted to do was camp out in front of the fan and pretend I was somewhere else—Alaska, the Swiss Alps, the Himalayas—anyplace where it was colder than here.

It was shortly after six. It was going to be a long evening. Off in the distance I could hear a faint sound of some kind of horn and the distant mumblings of people in a gathering. Something unusual was going on in the village tonight. I began to feel very alone and wished I had gone with the others. I had just begun to doze off when the door burst open, and Dale shouted, "Come on, Nancy! You're not going to want to miss this!" He grabbed the portable tape recorder, some batteries, and a cassette while I waited for my breathing to return to normal. "Hurry!" he screamed as I raced out, barely managing to close the door behind me. I forgot to lock it and was later thankful no one was in the mood to "borrow" anything that night.

His excitement was justified. The entire village was gathered around to experience one of Liberia's treasures—an elephant tusk band. Several of the villagers held torches aloft while the seven-member band played. All I could think was "It's true! Africa is just like they said it was!"

The band members were dressed in all of their tribal beauty. Shells and iron beads clanged together around long bobbing necks. Bracelets and beads adorned wrists and ankles; earrings dangled and flashed on heads that twisted and turned. Intricately patterned cloth was wrapped around loins and heads. Shiny, black, muscular bodies glistened with beads of sweat under the torches. Broad, callused, splay-toed feet pounded the ground in rhythm to the drums. A natural circular space formed to allow dancers to leap into the center and perform their gymnastic talents.

It was a magnificent sight. The gigantic elephant tusk horns, polished to a diamond sheen, were played frantically by intense men whose cheeks looked like they were going to burst under the pressure. The talking drums, squeezed tightly under strong arms, pounded and shouted like children having temper tantrums. Hand-hewn, tautly skinned drums in every size and shape were played in complicated rhythms by expert native hands. I was swept away in the totality of the moment. I couldn't help it. Everyone was moving. It was impossible to stand still. People were leaping one or two at a time into the center of the circle, as if on cue from some invisible conductor, to dance their organic rhythms.

All at once, three of the villagers came over, grabbed my arm, and pulled me into the circle. I danced like a madwoman possessed, doing movements I wouldn't have believed my body could do—transported, carried away by the music, the other dancers, and the moment. I was outside myself, watching another person. A person free, seized by abandon. I was a movement greater than the sum of its parts. The whole village was cheering, dancing, singing, chanting, and clapping. It was like no other sing-along in the world, and it was the freest I'd ever felt in my life.

Some years later, when I was studying acting in New York City, I was sitting in a class when the instructor said, "Most every actor can point to a singular moment when they knew they were hooked on performing. Some say it's that first rush of the applause, some say it's when they first had an emotional moment on stage, some say it's the thrill of playing someone else."

I danced nonstop for twenty minutes that night. When I finally did stop, I was dripping with sweat, and my hair was wilted and matted against my face. My neighbors rushed to me, whacking me on the back, touching my arms, slapping my hands, laughing their congratulations, and expressing their amazement. I had won my way into their hearts—and they into mine. I was hooked.

From then on, I was treated like one of the family. Every time I would run into someone or pass him on the street, he would greet me like a long-lost relative. He would slap my hand or touch my arms and exclaim loudly, "M'Nancy! How you keepin'?" If I hesitated for a moment too long, he would begin to recount the story of the elephant tusk band, laughing and proclaiming what a good dancer I was. Well, who wouldn't want to savor the moment? Dale caught it all on tape. What a shame there were no camcorders in 1965.

CHAPTER 11

Liberian Suntan

The month in Fisebu flew by. We said our good-byes to Carol and Rick, promised to visit each other (we never did), and loaded our duffels and my acquired artifacts into the hired taxi. We were being stationed in the town of Greenville, about 150 miles down the coast from Monrovia.

Greenville was a good-sized town with one high school and two elementary schools. Two other women PCVs had been there a year and were teaching at the missionary elementary school, and several Europeans (mostly English and Dutch) had small businesses in the area. All five of the Europeans were single men. Two more PCVs from our group would also be going to Greenville and teaching at the high school. I wondered who they would be and hoped that, by some miracle, it might be John and Virginia Lyon, but it wasn't.

The taxi driver hurtled along at lightning speed despite our pleadings to him to slow down, relax, and take it easy; we were in no hurry, we told him. It was useless, and we never fully relaxed on the entire journey along the unpaved road to Monrovia where we were to spend three days before our final posting in Greenville.

We were to gather and organize supplies and purchase what else we might want to take with us. Among our Peace Corps booty was a book locker with books on every imaginable subject. We had enjoyed Carol and Rick's book locker, so it was a thrill to have our very own. We knew we would have plenty of opportunities to enjoy the books over the next two years. Also included were some teaching manuals and some school supplies—composition books, newsprint paper, chalk, pencils, colored paper, crayons, and glue. We already had our medical manual and kit from the training that included a large box of gauze, bandages, first aid cream, antibiotic cream, and two giant aerosol cans of insect repellent. This was all taken by small plane to Greenville and would be there to greet us when we arrived.

We finished all of our shopping and packing on the first day so we had the remaining two days to enjoy the capital city on our own. We were thrilled to see that John and Virginia were staying at the hostel doing the same thing, so we decided to hang out together and go to the beach for the second day. I needed to go into town first, so the four of us decided to breakfast together at the Dukor Intercontinental Hotel.

Stepping out of the money bus into the hotel was like crossing the threshold of a time warp. A blast of delicious air-conditioning welcomed us into the lobby. A tall man in a black three-piece suit ushered us toward the back of the lobby, and we were met at the entrance to the restaurant by another tall man wearing spotless white gloves and a crisp white jacket, which contrasted majestically against his dark skin. He spoke flawless English, and we suspected he might have been educated abroad. He took us to our seats by the window overlooking a beautifully executed garden and the Olympic-sized swimming pool. It was 7:30 a.m., and people were already swimming, which made perfect sense in a country where the temperature rarely varies five degrees from eighty degrees Fahrenheit, night or day.

The waiter brought us clear ice water in frosty crystal glasses, which we were sorely tempted to drink, but we remembered the Peace Corps water warnings. In the environment of the Dukor Intercontinental it would have been easy to pretend we were anywhere in the world but in a third-world country in West Africa where everything we took into our bodies had to be consciously considered. In a way, we felt out of place. We were dressed appropriately for Peace Corps Volunteers, in our casual, comfortable, not particularly stylish, and definitely not trendy clothing. Most of the clientele were white Europeans dressed in the conservative, classically tailored, neutral-colored clothing so typical of old money. They were civil and formal and had a graceful, well-bred air, which communicated how they were to be treated. It was easy to see why they were automatically attended to. I'd never been in such close proximity with wealthy people, and I felt slightly shabby.

Years later, when I was an actress in New York City and making some pretty good money, I started going to Elizabeth Arden to get my hair done. The Elizabeth Arden Salon attracts wealthy women who are used to being catered to and fussed over. It was a pleasure to be treated with such deference. The cost was far beyond my budget, even though

I continued to frequent the place for several years. I was playing a part, trying to be something I wasn't, trying desperately to fit in. On my Elizabeth Arden day I would arrive at the salon dressed in my very best clothes—to have my hair done! My London Fog trench coat would hang humbly among the furs, and I affected a fake, friendly ease and tried not to do anything stupid. I was never comfortable there and very often had to scrape together enough money just to pay my hairdresser and hair washer their tips. My hairdresser made more money in tips than I made in wages!

The feeling of inferiority was not unlike the feeling of being at the Dukor that day, except that by virtue of being Peace Corps Volunteers, we had achieved our own unique status.

We thoroughly enjoyed our expensive breakfast of eggs Benedict, fresh local fruit, and strong coffee, and for an hour and a half I didn't once think about the humidity. We shared our previous month's experiences with John and Virginia and found out they would be teaching in a small inland village. Over the next two years, we met them once in Monrovia, and visited them once. We wrote a few letters back and forth and sent them a case of Club Beer as a gift, but our lives eventually drifted in different directions and we never saw or heard from them again.

At ten o'clock we took to the streets so I could buy a bathing suit. I had tried to find a bathing suit in Tacoma, but in December, you couldn't find anything resembling summer wear. I managed to find a Lebanese store that had a selection of one-piece suits, but none of the suits fit me on top, because of my size 32AA bra. I had always found it awkward to shop for bathing suits even in my own country but never blamed the designers for this problem—I always blamed my own body for not being the right size, so I didn't even bother going to other stores because I knew I'd find the same problem there too. The only solution was to buy padding to fill out the suit. I chose a black suit that was solid on top and bottom with a see-through mesh midriff. I put enough rubber padding in the bra to make the bustline look like a pointy Jane Russell. Obviously, the bust was not part of the body inside, but at least it filled out the suit. The only problem with the rubber pads was that they tended to slowly absorb water. When I was in the water, they would float like a balloon, but when I came out of the water, they sagged under the weight they had absorbed and dripped furiously. I couldn't do anything about the floating *in* the water, but I could remedy the sagging pads *out* of the water by pushing them together to expel the water, which I tried to do without anyone noticing.

It's safe to say I didn't spend much time in the water that day because what I really wanted to do was get a little suntan.

My experience of tanning in Alaska was lying out in the sun all day long and receiving only the slightest hint of color, so I was looking forward to finally getting a chance to achieve a healthy, well-bronzed, George Hamilton look. Although my husband didn't say as much, the amount of time he spent lying on the beach that day led me to believe he had the same romanticized idea of a suntan.

So while John and Virginia coated themselves in suntan lotion and frolicked in the Atlantic surf, we laid on our towels, baking. There was no such thing as sunblock. The purpose of lying in the sun was *to get a tan*. We basted ourselves in baby oil … it was cheaper and easier to get than suntan cream or commercial oils, and it performed the same function. Therefore, there we were, two lily-white, tender-skinned bodies, lying on a tropical beach, slathered in baby oil, baking on high in the noonday sun.

We were delighted when we began to see a pinkish glow appear on our exposed skin. My eyes have always been sensitive to the sun, so I wore sunglasses. Dale didn't. Every so often, we would get too hot and take a dip in the ocean. We would come out, slather ourselves in baby oil, and then lie on the beach again. John and Virginia commented several times on how pink we were getting and suggested that maybe we ought to come sit under their umbrella. We brushed off their offer, assuring them that we were fine and were glad to finally be getting some color. And anyway, being in Fisebu for the month, we had gotten a little tan on our faces and arms and were sure this was sufficient protection against a serious burn. A little burn would be good because it would turn into a deeper tan in a few days. We had it all under control.

Around three o'clock a perfect stranger came up to us and told us we were *very* red and we should get out of the sun immediately. He said that the tropical sun can burn the skin very quickly, and we looked like we were in for big trouble. The seriousness in his tone woke us up to really look at ourselves. When we pushed our suits aside to have a look, we were surprised at the sharp, sudden contrast. We woke up John and Virginia and started to pack up to leave. Only then did I notice I was a little tender when I moved.

We hopped a money bus back to the hostel, and I waited my turn for the shower. When I took off my suit and looked in the mirror, I was aghast. I looked like a red owl. I had never seen skin so red, and I knew I was in for a painful couple of days.

When I was a child, our family would often go to the lake in the summer, and once or twice I had come away with a burn. After a few hours, I could really see how bad it was going to be, and if it was bad, I got chills—and out would come the baking soda and Noxzema. The first night was always the worst because no matter what I did, I still had chills, and I could hardly stand anything touching my burned skin. I figured this would be one of those times.

By the time I got into the shower I was really feeling the pain. I knew it was still a few hours before the burn would really show up, and I was already more red than I'd ever been in my life. The warm water felt searing hot, and the shower drops felt like a million little mallets pounding against my skin. I couldn't stand even a cold shower, so I took a soft washcloth (even that felt like sand paper) and gently patted my skin. This kind of burn called for a baking soda poultice, but I was in no condition to trek to town to get some baking soda. I got Virginia to pat me down with Noxzema until I smelled like a walking eucalyptus tree. I felt ridiculous, but I didn't have to explain my circumstances to anyone—all they had to do was take one look at me, and they knew. I got many empathetic winces over the next few days.

That night, sleeping was impossible. I would say that I spent the night tossing and turning, but movement was out of the question. Every time I moved, it felt like someone lighting a match to my skin. And I had chills so badly I had to lie under no fewer than three blankets. Nobody knew much about the relationship of sun to skin cancer at that time, so the possibility didn't even occur to me.

It took about a week for me to feel better, but first I had to go through a few more stages. The next day was a continuation of the chills and pain stage. We didn't want to set foot outside in the sun because any heat was like a fire on our skin—even through our clothes. We did have to make one necessary trip to the market to get food, but the excursion plans we had for that day had to be postponed until two months later on our next visit to Monrovia because we were leaving for Greenville the following day.

By the next day tiny blisters had started to form. Our small plane carrying us to Greenville was leaving at noon, so we had no choice but to spend the morning gathering last-minute supplies and packing up our things. As we moved around and started to perspire, the blisters got bigger. Our skin was so damaged that the top layer would not allow the sweat to penetrate it, so the perspiration gathered below the surface inside the blisters, which got larger and larger the more we perspired. When the blisters got too large, they burst open, drenching our clothes with salty perspiration. Although this was initially cooling, the burst blisters revealed a new layer of skin underneath which, when exposed to the air and mixed with salt, stung like the dickens. Our wet clothes stuck to our raw skin, scraping against it as we moved. I was still wearing my tent dresses made out of polyester, which now felt more like plastic than cloth.

We managed somehow to get through the morning and finish all our preparations to leave for the small airstrip five miles outside of Monrovia where we would catch our three-seater plane to Greenville. Jack Reeder, the in-country Peace Corps Director, came to pick us up.

"What in God's name happened to you two?" he winced. "We'll stop by to see Comfort Butler before we go. She'll know what to do. She's our Liberian nurse here in Monrovia."

Well, I don't know whether it was Jack's instant paternal concern, the mention of going to see a nurse, or just the mere mention of her name—*Comfort*—but I started to cry. It was the kind of full, silent cry that comes out all at once with huge sighs and volumes of tears rushing from your eyes. The kind of cry that makes someone rush to you, putting their arms around you, and saying, "Oh, now, now, now, it's okay, it's all right. Shhh. Shhh. Everything's going to be fine." I was still sniffling fifteen minutes later when we arrived at the clinic.

Comfort Butler was everything a nurse should be—plump and pillowy, with a soft, relaxed, reassuring manner. She moved with a slow, graceful confidence that made me trust her immediately. I knew that no matter what she said, it would be the right thing, and whatever she told me to do, I would do. She was the kind of woman you knew had probably raised eight children simultaneously, attending to all their needs, without batting an eyelash. I wanted to stay with her forever.

She took a quick survey of our faces and went over to Dale first. His skin was even more burned than mine was; his entire chest and back were covered with blisters. If that wasn't enough, he hadn't been wearing his sunglasses, and his eyes were practically swollen shut; but throughout the entire ordeal, the only time he expressed any real pain was when I put Noxzema on his back.

"Um, um, um," Comfort said, as she looked us over again. "Too late for vinegar and baking soda."

Then she opened up a cabinet to reveal the most interesting array of items. On the left was a large assortment of the latest medications from Germany, England, Holland, and America. On the right the cabinet was chock-full of herbs, strange-looking liquids, brown and gray creams, and dried peppers. She took several containers from the right side of the cabinet and put them on the counter. She put a few dollops of each paste into a beaker. Then she put a combination of dried herbs into a mortar and ground them into a powder with a pestle. I was relieved to see she didn't put in any peppers. She combined the ingredients into another beaker and whipped them with a whisk. Sighing, she turned to us and said, "This will stop the pain."

She slowly and gently applied the foamy cream to all of our exposed skin. It was cool and soothing and seemed to literally absorb the burn right out of our skin. It was a miracle. We could even move a little without pain. How did she know how to do that? Most Liberians have very dark skin. Could it be that they burn too? "Yes," she said. "The dark skin provides some protection, but we burn too." I must have sounded terribly naive. I glanced at myself in the small mirror hanging on the door. I was an interesting shade of green, but I didn't care—I wasn't in pain.

She gave us a jar of the miracle mixture, and Jack took us straight back to the hostel, where we stayed put for the next three days, healing.

By the end of the third day, we were definitely bored and itching to get on our way—literally. We had no more pain, but our skin had begun to peel like onions and itch. Salty perspiration didn't allow us much relief from that, either. But at least we could move—wanted to move—to get our minds off the itching. Every chance we got, we were peeling each other's sloughing skin. Sometimes the skin would come off in huge maplike sheets, and other times we'd have to pick at it like monkeys looking for nits.

Jack picked us up again. "Well, you look much better. Let's try this again." We loaded up our things. As we were nearing the airstrip, he casually mentioned that all of our things might not fit into the small plane. We might have to leave a box or two behind, and it would be shipped to us within the next week or so. I had taken no care to separate necessities from other belongings. Once again, we held up our departure while we opened and rummaged through every box, pulling out the things we would need within the next two weeks. We did the right thing because we didn't see the other items arrive for a month.

CHAPTER 12

The Flight to Greenville

Firestone Rubber Plantation, Harbel

This was my very first time in a small plane, and it was exhilarating. Flying high enough to miss the trees but low enough to see everything clearly, we flew over one village after another. We flew along the crooked ocean coastline and watched the waves licking the shore. The sun shone on the lush, dense, tropical green forests surrounding each village. The pointy grass roofs of the mud-and-stick huts and patches of markets dotted the land as little stick figures went about their daily chores.

The tall British pilot was well tanned and dressed in crisp khaki, looking more like an elephant hunter than a pilot. The most direct route would have been to fly straight down the coast, but our pilot was proud of his adopted country and asked if we wanted the Cook's tour. We were elated. As we soared above the earth like the proverbial eagle, I suddenly understood why the bush pilots in Alaska became addicted to this kind of flying.

I had always wondered why, despite the phenomenal obstacles of weather, rugged mountain terrain, isolation, and poor survival odds, there is a certain breed of Alaskan bush pilot who can't get enough of the life. I figured that, aside from the risk, the spellbinding beauty was the real high. I was snapping pictures like crazy until I realized I didn't really want to experience the moment through the lens of a camera, so I put the camera away. We flew over various iron and diamond mines. We flew over the Firestone rubber plantation with its tall majestic rubber trees, our pilot giving us a tour guide's narration, shouting over the noise of the engine.

Then he did something that terrified me so much I was not able to appreciate the beauty of the situation. He swooped down, suddenly, close to the shore, and switched off the engine. I looked at Dale. His face was ashen and turning slightly green. I'm sure I must have looked the same to him. We grabbed each other's hand, squeezing until we cut off circulation. The pilot was merrily chatting away, not noticing the discomfort of his passengers. When he finally looked at us, he started up the engine immediately and took the plane to a higher altitude. It's a good thing he did that when he did because I'd always been prone to motion sickness as a youngster, frequently having to stop by the side of the road. This felt suspiciously like one of those times, and this plane was just too small to accommodate a case of car sickness. The color gradually returned to Dale's face, though his lips remained an ashen gray for some time.

After a few minutes the pilot said, "Do you want to stop for a while?"

Dale and I shouted, "No!" too quickly and the pilot laughed.

He said he didn't mean stop the engine again, but would we like to land somewhere and take a look around? Relieved, we asked if our stopping might inconvenience the Baptist missionary who was supposed to meet us at the Greenville airstrip and with whom we would be staying while the building of our house was being completed. The pilot told us not to worry about that because nobody ever came to the airstrip until the plane arrived anyway. I asked how they would know if the plane had arrived, and he said simply, "They can hear it." Then he added, "By the time we've landed, they're there."

We asked the pilot where we were going to stop, and he suggested the Firestone rubber plantation in Harbel. He had a friend who lived in an estate there and ran the plantation. They had a nice little airstrip, and we could refuel. If there was any indecision about where we should go, the refueling reason convinced us.

We landed so smoothly I hardly felt the plane touch down. We didn't have to wait more than two minutes before his friend showed up. He said he'd been out checking the trees near the airstrip when he'd heard our plane overhead. "You see," said the pilot in his perfect English accent, "that's the way of it here." As I glanced from one to the other, both dressed in safari khaki, I thought they looked remarkably alike, even down to the small space between their two front teeth.

There was something about the lilt of his English accent and magnificent use of language that, I must confess, left me feeling a little giddy. Then suddenly another feeling surfaced, and I realized I hadn't gone to the bathroom for three hours, which for me was some kind of record. I held my request until we got to the estate, then I asked our host politely if I might be able to use the bathroom. He looked at me with just the barest hint of puzzlement behind his eyes, pausing almost imperceptibly. Then, without missing a beat, he almost clicked his heels and said, "Certainly. If you'll just come this way."

He led me up two flights of a broad, winding staircase to the top floor of the house. I followed him down a long uncarpeted hallway and into a fairly large room at the very end. In the room was a gorgeous antique porcelain bathtub with four ornate legs and gold handles. Liberia is noted for its precious gold, and there is no mistaking real gold when you see it. In one corner of the room was the same style of sink, and beside the sink was a gold towel rack adorned with luxurious white towels. My host went over to a small cabinet and brought out a wrapped bar of fragrant soap, which he put into the gold soap dish holder beneath the handles on the tub. Then he placed a thick, soft bathmat beside the tub and motioned to the display of towels, like Monty Hall's girls showing you what's behind door number two. "You'll be all right, then?" he smiled politely.

I was speechless. "Oh!" he said, apologetically, "Ever so sorry, if you'll just come over and have a look." He motioned me over to the tub. He knelt down and demonstrated how to use the stopper for the drain. He turned the cold water on first, then the hot water, explaining that the water did tend to get rather hot, so it was best to turn the cold on first, then the hot, then when turning off, I should turn the hot off first, then the cold.

"Now then … if you have everything you need, I'll just leave you to it."

I don't know where my next insight came from, but in a flash I realized that the English don't say "bathroom" for "toilet." They say "water closet" for toilet and "bathroom" for bath. So here I was, standing in this elegant bathroom, with a very wealthy, very sophisticated English gentleman who had gone to great lengths to make me feel welcome, not once questioning my request to have a bath two minutes after my arrival at his luxurious home. At that moment, I could not have embarrassed him with the truth of the misunderstanding if my life had depended on it.

I paused, stood to my full five-foot-seven height, and said, "I'm thoroughly delighted. Everything is perfect—but I'll just need to use the water closet before I bathe."

"It's just next door." He indicated which direction as he left.

After I used the toilet, I had to decide what I was going to do. Should I wait a reasonable length of time and pretend I had taken a bath, or should I go downstairs and fess up to the misunderstanding?

That feeling of giddiness overtook me again, and I decided there was really only one right thing to do: I walked to the tub, grasped the rich gold handles, and turned the cold water on first, then the hot. Then I took my clothes off, slipped gently into the tub, and took the most relaxing bath I'd had in many months—soaking in the elegant fragrance of lavender bath buds and looking forward to using the body lotion in the crystal bottle on the shelf next to the fluffy white bath towels. I felt deliciously decadent.

A full hour later, I floated down the stairs, smiling from ear to ear. Dale looked at me with genuine concern, but our host smiled cheerily. "There, now, care for a drink?" He and the pilot were on their second. He set before me a refreshing-looking pink liquid with a twist of lime that tasted like sweet raspberry with a slight tartness. It hit the spot. I noticed Dale hadn't touched his—he just kept looking at his wife who, at that moment, he didn't seem to recognize. My goodness, what was a girl to do? I started to giggle, and I knew if I didn't stop right then, I wouldn't be able to, so I bit my tongue so hard I almost drew blood. My host asked me if I was all right, and I said "Perfect!" so loudly it startled me.

Just then, the French cook came in and announced, *"À la table,"* which meant that lunch was served. I took a deep breath and tried not to look in Dale's direction. Luckily, Dale and I were seated next to each other, so I didn't have to look at him if I didn't want to.

That lunch introduced me to goose pâté, baby lettuces topped with an unusual fruity dressing, and a fillet of sole with a light, lemon-butter sauce—a fare far beyond my range of culinary experience. I was used to bottled French, Italian, or bleu cheese dressing over iceberg lettuce, baked potato, and steak. My only experience of fish, up to this point, was baked halibut and breaded shrimp—except for the sumptuous Alaskan king salmon, which you couldn't avoid if you lived in Alaska.

After lunch and espresso, our pilot went to refuel while we toured the rubber plantation—rows of tall, thick trees with verdant green leaves, and the smell of burning rubber.

Dozens of Liberian workers wearing aprons and stocking caps hung high up in the trees like giant human fruit, their cleated shoes digging into the thick bark and ropes encircling their waists to prevent them from falling. Each worker had a sharp knife and was making a diagonal downward cut about one third the way around the trunk. Then he would hang a small cup at the base of the cut to catch the milky, malodorous latex that trickled from the tree. Each cup held one ounce of liquid, the amount extracted from a tree in a single tapping. One tapping took two days. After the first tapping, a thin strip of bark would be stripped from the bottom of the original cut for the second tapping. When the tree was tapped to the ground, the tree would be allowed to heal before a new tapping patch was started.

Our host chatted away, proudly displaying his plantation and pleased at our enthusiasm. He explained to us how the latex was strained, diluted with water, and treated with acid, which made the liquid latex turn into soft, pliable solid rubber. Then the rubber was pressed between giant rollers. (It made me think of when I was little and my mother would take the newly washed clothes and funnel them through the wringers on the washing machine until all the water was squeezed out and the clothes were pressed flat). After the rubber was rolled, it was air- or smoke-dried. By the time the tour was over, it was three o'clock, and I was eager to get to our new home. Our host thanked us for coming, as if *we* had done *him* the favor. He told us we were welcome anytime, and we invited him to visit us in Greenville, though we knew he'd never come.

Flying high above the trees again, I was remembering my bath. A faint rubber smell had replaced the lavender fragrance, but the luxurious experience remained with me throughout the rest of the flight, and I noticed that I was no longer itching. Dale never did ask me what had taken me so long.

Nobody spoke much during the forty minutes it took us to get to Greenville. Dale dozed, and I was tempted to, but the pilot had had a fair amount to drink, and I wanted to keep an eye on him to make sure he didn't fall asleep.

I took my camera out for our landing and arrival. The pilot obliged me by circling low over the town and pointing out the reverend's house, where we would be staying. Then he swooped over the long, narrow red dirt landing strip and banked to the left in order to show us the aerial view of the entire town of Greenville before we landed. It was almost romantic. Natives walking along the road with bundles on their heads, stopped to wave up at us. Scatterings of tin-roofed houses interspersed with the traditional mud-and-stick huts. We could see the gently curved sandy coast lined with dense palm trees—we could even see the coconuts on the trees.

Gliding over the center of town, we could see yellow-washed, hand-made brick storefronts, with flat checkerboard tin roofs lining the main road. Just off the main road was the high school that, from outward appearances, could have passed for any American high school. Not far from the high school was the Demonstration School, the elementary school where I would be working for the next two years. It looked great! Much more modern than I had imagined. Large, yellow bricks, tin roof, and even an outhouse!

This assignment was going to be easier than I thought, I breathed to myself. School was due to open in three weeks, so we'd have plenty of time to settle in. I would be able to meet my future neighbors, the principal of the school, and hopefully my fellow teachers. They could tell me all about the system and introduce me to the children, and maybe we could even plan to do some team teaching.

I was feeling less apprehensive with each moment. I remembered how Carol had set up her classroom in Fisebu and how effortless her teaching seemed. She had been the perfect role model—and she hadn't even had the benefit of a principal or other teachers to bounce things off. She had done it all alone. True—she had come into the Peace Corps with three years of teaching under her belt, but she had to start somewhere too.

CHAPTER 13

Student Teaching in America

My student teaching in a fourth grade class in Anchorage, Alaska was a glorious experience. My supervising teacher was a sixty-five-year-old career educator who had never had a student teacher. She admitted she was very nervous and set in her ways, and her principal had talked her into having a student teacher pretty much against her will. She had pure white hair, smelled like cigarettes, and spoke with a pronounced lisp. I could imagine the teasing she must have endured as a child, and I admired her honesty. Concern for her comfort quickly replaced whatever nervousness I felt. I was on the high edge of confident. I had aced all my education courses, which I found distinctly boring and abstract.

My enthusiasm was boundless, and I had always had a way with children—probably because I was such a child myself and could slip easily into their space. A couple of weeks into student teaching, I was taking complete charge of the class, and my supervising teacher was spending more and more time on cigarette breaks. The only drawback for her, she confessed, was that she was forced to smoke outside, and it was one of the coldest subzero winters Anchorage had seen in years. At odd times, I would look out the window and see puffs of smoke wafting from her little white Volkswagen, which looked for the all the world like an igloo in the snow, and her red-gloved hand occasionally flicking the ashes out the window. We shared a few good laughs over that one, and I loved her for her humanness. I aced student teaching too. She was retiring at the end of the year and said she was glad to have had the experience of a student teacher.

My college professor called me a "natural," and the principal offered me a job on the spot, which I would have taken, but I was already committed to going into the Peace Corps. Oh yes, I was going to be fine.

I wondered what Dale was feeling. His one-year teaching experience had been a disaster. He had graduated a year before me and had gotten a job teaching math at a local junior high school. He was clearly out of his element. His intellectual brand of pun-humor fell flat. His lanky, six-foot-five frame earned him the name Ichabod Crane. His thick glasses and formal, slightly stilted manner made him the brunt of cruel jokes and imitations. Those kids ate him alive. He became fidgety and eager to please, which gave the kids more fuel for insults.

Dale was a brilliant mathematician and a fine scholar, but it was all lost on these kids. He was terrified of them. So while I was having the time of my life teaching fourth graders, Dale was in despair and trying not to show it. I tried to give him pointers on how he could do things differently, but he told me that the things he tried never worked. I couldn't understand what could be so difficult. It seemed like the only thing we ever talked about was how horrible his classes were, and I was at a loss how to help him. Once I thought I heard him crying in the bathroom, but I could have been mistaken—or maybe I was just too afraid to let him be vulnerable. In any event, I never asked him, and that makes me sad. If he was apprehensive about teaching in Liberia, he never let on.

While we were in Monrovia, I had managed to hit up a couple of travel agencies for posters to decorate my classroom walls and had stocked up on as many school supplies as the Peace Corps would allow me to bring. I had taken a lot of glue and colored construction paper because I was good in arts and crafts and could teach the basics through visuals and hands-on techniques. Dale made sure he had stocked up on secondary textbooks and composition notebooks. Neither one of us had a clue about the abilities of our students, but Jack Reeder said that the high school was pretty well established and running smoothly, was better equipped than the elementary school, and had several Europeans teaching there. Two other PCVs from our group would also be teaching there.

He said that the Demonstration School was only two years old and could use an innovative teacher to pull it together. He said I would be the only PCV teaching there. There had been one or two before me, but they couldn't seem to make it work. I was pleased he thought so highly of me. I was too obtuse to see the implications of his statement.

He wasn't really complimenting me at all. He was giving me a pep talk.

I learned later that the top priority position was Dale's high school math and science placement. The high school was considered one of the best in the country. The students were not disrespectful junior high school kids—they were hardworking, serious young men headed for college. So what were they going to do with me? The Catholic elementary school already had two PCVs who had been there a year, and the two new PCVs from our group were teaching in the high school with Dale. The only other placement was the Demonstration School—where I could teach whatever I felt like teaching. This sounded like a good, creative, open door, but it was, in fact, a euphemism for "there's no curriculum, organization, or leadership."

The Demonstration School was built to be the elementary equivalent of the high school. The goal was to educate youngsters who intended to continue their education past the eighth grade. The principal was a very nice woman who was also a senator in the national legislature. Because she had been instrumental in getting the school built, she had been appointed the principal. Never mind that she had no experience in the education field. In any event, my youthful arrogance led me to interpret Jack's words as a compliment, and I let myself be flattered.

We circled the town once more and, as we approached the small landing strip, I noticed a large group of Liberians had gathered at one end, mostly children with broad, bright smiles. They waved and pointed in our direction. One person stood out among the sea of distended bellies and protruding belly buttons. He was much taller than the average Liberian male, and he was white. That must be the Southern Baptist missionary we would be staying with, Reverend Carpenter. I hoped he wouldn't be one of those Bible preaching, podium-pounding, fire-and-brimstone kinds of guys. I'd had my fill of that mentality both from my paternal Grandma's converted Catholicism and from the religious instruction I had taken during the year prior to my marriage.

CHAPTER 14

Religious Instruction

I had been engaged a year before I decided I wanted to be baptized, so I started accompanying Dale to his Lutheran church every Sunday. I had never been baptized due to the religious backgrounds of my parents. At the time my parents married, the Catholic Church still excommunicated you if you married someone from a different religion and didn't agree to raise your kids Catholic. Dad was Catholic, and Mom was Lutheran. Although Mom wasn't a practicing Lutheran, she wouldn't agree to raise her children Catholic. Dad married her anyway, and the church did its duty.

My father never set foot inside a Catholic church again—except twice: when his father died and when his mother died. Dad's sister said she thought Howard was deeply hurt because he couldn't attend the Catholic Church, and her frequent comments didn't particularly win my mother over. Dad never once mentioned missing going to the Catholic Church, though his faith and moral upbringing remained a constant throughout his life.

I went to Lutheran religious instruction once a week and listened to stately, Swedish Reverend Johansson preach his stern doctrine. Catholic dogmatism had nothing on him. He wasn't exactly an evangelist-type personality, so if you weren't paying close attention, you might assume he was tolerant. Big mistake. He just assumed everyone would, without question, believe what he was talking about. (Remember, he was the one who gave us the quiz on sex before he would marry us).

While his wife made yogurt from scratch, ten of us sat in a circle reading from the Bible and listening to Reverend Johansson interpret the scripture. We learned how Martin Luther left the Catholic faith because he sought freedom of interpretation and how he founded the Lutheran faith that was, of course, the one true faith. We learned how we must pray for the poor souls who believed in other religions or were not baptized because they surely needed help from all of us to get into heaven: what if some of them died before they could be baptized? We learned that there was no such thing as purgatory, but heaven and hell were certainly a fact. I listened faithfully, and there was nothing I couldn't live with—despite the exception I took to the one-true-faith idea and the heaven-and-hell idea.

Around the twelfth week it all took a different turn for me— that's the week the reverend hit on original sin—with an evangelical vengeance. All people were born in sin—that was the bottom line. Little babies, fresh from the womb, were sinners. Little babies, who had no knowledge of the world, who were helpless and dependent, who didn't even know who they were, were sinners, all. The reverend seemed to lump everything together at this point. Anyone who wasn't baptized was going to hell. Anyone who believed in one of those nonsectarian faiths (like Unitarianism) was in real trouble—they were going to the hottest part of hell. That was just the way things were, and there wasn't anything we could do about it! His voice found a completely new level.

Well, that was where *I* drew the line. I had tried to be so good my whole life—to do what my parents told me, to please my teachers, to work hard, to be kind to others, to share, to love. All of it made no difference whatsoever—I was born a sinner and would die a sinner— and the only thing that could save me was to be baptized into the Lutheran faith. As frightened as I was that this might be true, I rebelled in every fiber of my being.

I probed Reverend Johansson for a loophole. I questioned the whole concept of original sin in every way I could. I was center stage, but I couldn't help myself. I just couldn't accept the idea that a loving and benevolent God would stand for such a thing as original sin. Suddenly, the story of Adam and Eve was a fable, a cruel joke.

There was no going back. The reverend smiled condescendingly and wouldn't give an inch. The others in the group shifted uncomfortably. I had just lost my guarantee of getting into heaven. During refreshments I tried to seem nonchalant and unconcerned, and maybe it was my imagination that the others seemed to shy away from talking to me. Reverend Johansson smiled his usual impenetrable smile as if I had said nothing at all. When Dale came to pick me up, he asked me what was wrong. I told him why I couldn't go through with being baptized a Lutheran. He looked disappointed, but all he said was "Okay," and that was that. After we were married, we never went back to that church again.

CHAPTER 15

Arrival in Greenville

We landed smoothly and taxied toward the small group of children who were running to greet us. We hugged each other and walked down the steps to the waving arms and joyous calls of "Peace Corps! Peace Corps!" Reverend Carpenter smiled and waved, letting us bask in the fame of this first moment, while he watched from a distance. Well, this was it. This was, to me, the official beginning of our service in the Peace Corps. We had successfully passed the training, both in San Francisco and in Fisebu, and we were home at last. I glanced at Dale and saw tears in his eyes. His five-year dream had finally become a reality.

The children eagerly grabbed pieces of our luggage from the belly of the small plane, and, although I couldn't understand a word of what they were saying, it was clear that they were quibbling over who would carry what bag for us. The quibbling escalated rapidly until the reverend came over and broke it up. He said something in their tribal language, and they divided the pieces up quickly without another word. They were all smiles—there was no hint of lingering resentment among the lot—and soon our things were piled efficiently on top of, and into, every available space of the reverend's Land Rover.

Reverend Carpenter introduced himself as the Reverend John Mark Carpenter. Dale and I smiled, and I knew we were thinking the same thing: Jesus was a carpenter, John and Mark were disciples—all his parents would have had to do was to add the names Luke and Matthew, and they'd have it covered. I wondered if his wife's name was Mary.

Reverend Carpenter was a tall, impressively large man with a shock of black hair, firm handshake, open smile, and easy laughter. He wore a colorful African shirt and spoke in a cultured Georgia drawl, which measured each syllable before it slid smoothly from his mouth. His eyes listened to every word you said. His relaxed manner allowed for silences which, in less experienced hands, might have been uncomfortable. I could see why he was a minister—called to a profession that required empathy, compassion, and good listening skills. He had them all, and I knew if his family were anything like him, we would be friends for life, which turned out to be true, but we were only at the beginning of our long journey together.

I asked the reverend what language the children were speaking, and could he teach me? I had anticipated having to learn a tribal language during our Peace Corps training in San Francisco and was disappointed when that didn't happen. The trainers said it would be a waste of time learning any language because we could be placed anywhere in the country. Liberia is about the size of Tennessee, but no fewer than twenty-one languages are spoken there.

"Anyway," they said, "the national language is English, and that's what the leaders of the country wanted us to use."

Well, I didn't care—I was in their country, and I wanted to learn their language and would do that as soon as I got to where I was going.

Reverend Carpenter said the children were speaking English. I must have looked incredulous because he added, "It's Pidgin English. Your ear will get used to it in time." I had heard Pidgin English in Fisebu and learned to make out a few words here and there, but this Pidgin English had no resemblance to what I had heard there.

The reverend explained that, although most Liberians who live in towns speak Pidgin English, the regions have distinct dialects because of the differences in tribal languages. It was his advice that I try to master the Pidgin English and forget about the tribal languages, because even in a town the size of Greenville there were several languages spoken, and none of the languages had a written form. Oh, boy, this was going to be tricky, but I was glad I had the three weeks to let my ear get used to the Pidgin English before I had to teach. He said the natives understood our English better than we understood theirs. Small comfort.

As we drove along, the reverend said he was pleased we were going to be staying with him and his family. He said the way things were going, it would be three weeks (maybe longer) before our house would be finished and, once we got settled at his place, we would take a drive over to have a look at how it was coming along. He had been supervising the building of it. It was going to be the most beautiful Peace Corps house in the town, and he was sure we were going to love it.

I thought to myself, *How can a Peace Corps house be beautiful? What does he mean by that? Does he mean new? Large? Modern?* We weren't supposed to live like Americans—we were supposed to blend in—to live as close to indigenous as possible without jeopardizing our health. Beautiful was not part of the contract—and especially not "the most beautiful Peace Corps house in the town."

Two men PCVs from our Group VII had come straight to Greenville for their in-country training and were sharing a house with two second-year PCVs. It was a small two-bedroom house close to the center of town. One of the new PCVs (from our group) had recently petitioned for a vehicle. It was unusual for PCVs to have the use of a car, but his argument was that, since there were going to be eight PCVs living there and only the rare (usually nonworking) phone, and things were pretty spread out, a vehicle would certainly come in handy.

There were two female PCVs in Lexington, four miles away and across a river. What if an emergency occurred with one of them? We had to be able to be in close contact with each other for support. The small plane from Monrovia came to Greenville only every three days at most. The airstrip was five miles away, and, in order to get tickets, you had to walk to the airstrip a day in advance of your desired departure day. He had won his case, and a station wagon was being delivered to us the next day. We were all to share in its use.

This was not going to be like Fisebu at all. This was, by Liberian standards, a big city. I had been hoping for a nice quiet little village atmosphere where I could nestle into a romantic, primitive lifestyle and "get to really know the people."

I was a confirmed romantic. I remember when Dale and I had traveled the Alcan; we were invited into some of the homes of the Alaskan Native Americans. Even though Alaska had been a state for a few years, some of the villages in the hinterlands had remained uninitiated to the ways of white folk. We were treated to the warmth of the potbellied stove and observed some of the ways these sturdy people lived and survived in our northernmost state. We witnessed, firsthand, an ancient Indian woman weaving an elaborate Chilcat blanket from source materials.

Dale toting our suitcase to the airstrip, Greenville

"The art is dying out," she told us, "and our young people don't want to stay here. They want to go to Anchorage."

I thought of one particular street in downtown Anchorage—Fourth Avenue—where Indians and Eskimos often hung out. It was appropriately named "the longest bar in the world."

"I am the only one left in the village who knows how to make this," she said.

"It may never be finished."

I looked around at the trappings of her difficult life. The ulu and other crude tools for scraping seal hides and scaling and cutting salmon hung on the wall above the wood-burning stove. Birch logs, piled into one corner of the kitchen, were a testament to the cold, even on this early fall day. Four large buckets used for collecting snow when the water pipes froze were stacked neatly and accessibly in one corner, as a reminder that winter was not far off. Her life was hard work—a life of working in community in order to survive. Her face showed the marks of age and harsh, brutal winters. Her gnarled hands revealed the strength and stamina of her life that even Van Gogh would have loved to paint.

As she sat, deftly weaving the blanket with a swift, delicate touch, I wondered what could be so great about going to Anchorage. I was to see the strains of civilization on a primitive culture many times over the next two years, and I would often ask myself, "What is so great about being 'civilized'?"

The drive from the airstrip to the Carpenters' house was barren of houses. We were very close to the coastline and could see the ocean through clearings among the trunks of the coconut trees. Wow! Coconut trees—with real coconuts. The only coconuts I'd ever seen were without husks sitting in the produce section of a supermarket. It never occurred to me that these huge things actually grew on trees and we could simply walk over and pick them—if we could manage to climb the tree. I filed that away as something I was going to do. We turned into the long driveway that led to the Carpenters' house.

CHAPTER 16

The Carpenters

The Carpenters—Betty, Christopher, Nancy, John Mark, Kim. Missing: Mark

The large, white, two-story house, with its round pillars, sat stately among the palm trees. One of the palm trees was so close to the house, it reached over and fanned the roof with its enormous fronds. Its trunk looked like a thick snake. Orange and grapefruit trees graced the property. There was also another kind of tree with some kind of fruit that looked like giant footballs, which I learned later was a breadfruit tree. On one side of the house was a vegetable garden. A young Liberian man was picking some collard greens. He waved as we drove up and called to another young man who ran to meet us. The reverend introduced us, then told Samuel to take the bags into the house and put them in the guest room.

The unmistakable fragrance of freshly baked bread welcomed us into the house. We met the reverend's wife, Betty, in the kitchen. Her warm smile, round face, and blue eyes were framed by a shock of curly, blond hair. She apologized for not shaking our hands. Her arms were elbow-deep in flour as she sprinkled handfuls on a solid wood table and began plopping globs of raised dough onto it. Joseph, the tall, slim houseboy, was kneading and shaping the dough into loaves and filling more than a dozen bread pans. With the efficiency of a lion tamer, he whipped around, grabbed a thick towel, and removed four loaves of freshly baked bread from the oven.

Betty said, "Wait just a minute—I'll pour the coffee, and we can have some." She washed her hands, filled four cups with dark, rich coffee, and set them on one of the two empty tables in the corner of the enormous kitchen. Out of the kerosene refrigerator, she brought a jug of milk and a healthy tub of Danish butter. My mouth watered in anticipation of my tasty Danish butter melted on fresh bread, followed by dark roast Kenya coffee.

"Mark! Nan! Kim!" Betty called, and three children quickly appeared, smiling and smacking their lips. Though Mark was still a teenager (age 17), he was tall and built like his father, with the same easy manner of an old-fashioned, Southern gentleman. Nan (age 13) resembled her mother and had a grace of movement that made her look like she was gliding on ice. Kim was a spunky, spirited youngster (age 10), whose eyes darted from person to person, making it quite evident that she didn't miss a thing.

We sat down, the reverend said grace, and we proceeded to tear off chunks of bread, saturated them with great gobs of butter; within minutes we had devoured two loaves. I could have devoured an entire loaf by myself, but I didn't want to seem greedy. However, I noticed that no one else seemed to have the same problem of conscience.

"Once the bread is cool, it doesn't disappear nearly so fast," said Betty, "but it's hard to resist when it's hot."

My mouth was too full to answer.

"Monday is baking day," she said. "I find it helps to get it all done on one day, except for things like fresh biscuits, which can't be made ahead of time. But bread, cookies, cakes—they were all made today."

She had a family of five healthy eaters (and two houseboys) who were used to good Southern cooking, and she loved being the nurturing homemaker. I counted nearly a dozen loaves, not including the two we had inhaled. As soon as the bread cooled, it would be wrapped and put into the enormous kerosene refrigerator to be used during the week.

While Betty told the kids to finish their schoolwork, I went to the guest room to unpack, and Dale went with John Mark to check on a new church John was having built. The guest room was roomy with two single beds, which I pushed together to make one. Dale and I may not have been great sexual partners, but both of us loved to cuddle and be close, though the humidity eventually became a deterrent in that area too.

A short while later, Betty left the cleanup to the houseboy and called the kids together to check their home schooling lessons. She went from happy homemaker to schoolteacher in a flash, and the kids didn't flinch. Every few years the Carpenters got home leave, and the kids would attend their local school in Georgia, but they considered Liberia their real home, although I suspect that seventeen-year-old Mark found it the most difficult to be isolated from peers of his own culture. Homeschooling didn't allow for much peer interaction but there was very little choice in the matter because the schools in Liberia were far behind American schools, and the only Embassy school was in Monrovia.

I marveled at the way Betty slid from one domestic chore to another with the joy and ease of a gold-medal ice skater. It was surely her calling, and there was no hint that she longed to do anything else. I watched her like a hawk for some hidden, unfulfilled desire but found none. I admired the simplicity of it all and wished I could be so fluid. She appeared to have a happy marriage, she was a loving mother, a good teacher, a domestic genius, and even managed to help her husband in church activities. She had found her Shangri-la, and everything I was to see in the next two years would support this first impression.

Well, if she could be happy doing all that, why couldn't I? I would certainly try my best. I watched in admiration as she corrected the kids' English, math, social studies, and science. The children were at different levels and studying different things, based on the Georgia curriculum, and although Betty was not a trained teacher, she knew exactly what to do. She reminded me of Carol in Fisebu—it came naturally with no fear or apprehension. I thought of school starting in three weeks and felt butterflies in my stomach.

Dale returned from his brief outing with the reverend and joined us at the table. I noticed it wasn't long until he started chewing the inside of his cheek, but quit when Mark had a question about a new math concept that Betty couldn't explain and asked Dale if he could help. Dale explained it so calmly and clearly that even I understood it. Mark whizzed through the rest of his lesson, and Dale tried to act humble, but I could tell he was bursting with pride, and I thought he shouldn't try to pretend he wasn't.

When the lessons were finished, Nan grabbed two bananas and said to me, "Come on, I have something to show you."

Kindred spirits always seem to find each other. As we walked outside, Nan wanted to know everything about me. She told me she wanted to be a singer and an actress on Broadway or maybe a veterinarian in Liberia, she didn't know which. Her church back home had sent her some records of Broadway musicals, which she had played until they were almost worn out. Over the next months, the girls and I would sing and pantomime to those records many times. I told her I had majored in drama in high school and had been in many school plays; and the summer after college graduation I had played Alma in *Summer and Smoke* in a community theatre—and what I really wanted to be was an actress. She asked me if Dale would let me, and I said, "I don't know."

Then she asked me why I hadn't gone straight from college to New York to be an actress, and I said, "I don't know." But I did know.

I didn't go to New York to become an actress for the same reason I changed my major in college from theatre to teaching. Both of my parents warned me about the dangers of New York (remember, they had never been to New York), and my mom warned me about the insecurities of getting an acting job ("You *really* have to have talent") and to always have something to fall back on. My supportive maternal grandmother said I should go ahead and try it, but I must always remember to keep my clothes on. My paternal grandmother said I needed to get my head out of the clouds, and who did I think I was anyway? My paternal aunt just laughed.

My acting professor/advisor in college said I was very sensitive and had good instincts, but when I tried out for two different plays he was directing, he didn't cast me in either one. I was particularly crushed when he cast somebody else as Emily in *Our Town*, a role that I had played in high school and for which I was perfectly suited. I summoned the courage to ask him why he hadn't cast me, setting myself up for a broken heart. He took me into his private office.

Being the charismatic drama king that he was, he explained how painful his decision had been. It was between me and another girl. He wanted me to understand that he was deeply torn. He said he liked me better, I was the better actress, I was more suited to the role, but ultimately he was forced to choose the other girl. I couldn't understand who had forced him to choose the other girl. What was he talking about? If he liked me better, why didn't I get the part? What was wrong with me? I was young, sensitive, and unfamiliar with the ways of the theatre, and he was acting as if he had some dark secret he couldn't tell me.

I was like a sponge. At that time, I had no idea how to separate my person from the criticism. I asked him what he meant.

He leaned forward with tears in his eyes and foreboding in his voice: "Well, dear, you have a voice problem."

I took it as a death sentence.

"Your voice is thin and nasal, and I'm afraid it won't project."

I gulped hard and told him I had no trouble being heard in my high school plays.

He smiled condescendingly and said, "Well ... high school plays ..."

Then he told me a long story of how he'd had a Southern accent when he started out as an actor, and it had taken him six months of intensive training to speak standard American. My problem, however, was slightly different. He had been born with a rich vocal quality, but my voice would take years of disciplined effort to overcome. He held me. This man was my idol, and I adored him. He was a father figure, a creative genius, a strong, sensitive man who knew how to woo—I was in love with him and trusted everything he said. I was crushed. My fate was sealed. I left his office with a large lump in my throat and couldn't wait to get to my dorm room so people couldn't see me crying.

Nan pointed and told me to look up. There, sitting perched on the roof of the house, looking down at us, was an enormous chimpanzee. I gasped, and Nan laughed, "That's Big Boy, my chimp." She made some clicking sounds and held up the bananas. Slowly he turned around and, grabbing hold of the trunk of the enormous palm tree, climbed backward to the ground and lumbered over to us. I noticed a long, thick rope was fastened to a collar around his neck and attached to the top of a large cage on the ground. Big Boy took the bananas and plopped down on the ground to have his snack. He threw the banana peels over his shoulder and shoved the second banana in his already full mouth. Cheeks bulging, he looked at Nan for more, and we both laughed.

I thought, *Darwin was right—this is a relative.* He looked and acted entirely too much like my own species to deny it. Nan introduced him to me and told him to shake my hand. I held my breath while my brother reached out. His hand was twice the size of mine, and Nan told me to move slowly. As my hand touched his, he let out a squawk, and I jumped a mile. He turned and bounded away to scale the coconut tree and find his favorite place on the roof. "He's real sweet, but he has a mean streak, so when you come outside, just check where he is before you go walking around. I'm the only one that can handle him when he gets in one of his moods. I think he wants to mate, and that's why he gets mean."

I assured her I'd be very careful.

"He won't try any funny business, he just gets moody—and he's strong—you have to let him know who is boss and stand your ground. Even Daddy doesn't go near him when he gets like that. But he lets me handle him—he knows who his mama is. When he first came to us, Kim was afraid of him, and he sensed it. He doesn't like her and bites her every chance he gets. Poor Kim. She can't even go near him. He doesn't really hurt her; he's just being a meanie."

I asked her how they happened to get him. "We were at the airport one day and a missionary, who had been teaching in the country, was attempting to take his chimp on the plane with him to his new fly-in post. He was having a heck of a time, and the more he pushed for it the more the airline said, 'No way!' The man looked desperate. His flight was about to take off. We were standing there watching him and feeling more and more sorry for the man and his beloved pet. The man was looking around for some sign of hope when he saw us—and that was it! I knew right from the start that he would be my chimp. Big Boy adopted me immediately. Kim has a chimp too. She's just a baby, and her name's Abigail."

I thought of my childhood pets. As a child, I'd had an Irish setter named Chammy and a parakeet named Bimbo. Our pet resource was the local pet store and the neighbors' free puppies. When you live in Liberia, your pet options expand considerably. Nan and Kim loved animals, and I was to meet many an unusual pet over the next two years, but the chimps were my favorites.

We found Kim in her room trying to finish her homework under the watchful eye of Abigail. Abigail was a typical toddler, curious and into everything. I couldn't see how Kim could get any work done at all. Abigail and Big Boy had large cages outside, but Abigail wanted to spend most of her time with her "mommy" inside the house. Kim adored her little baby, but Kim was ten years old, and Abigail had needs that were very close to those of a human baby.

It was time for her diaper to be changed, so Kim locked the door and grabbed a fresh one. As soon as Abigail saw what was going to happen, she tried to make a run for it. Finding the door locked, she screamed and ran under the bed.

Kim scrambled over to the bed and pulled her out and slapped her hands and scolded, "Bad girl, bad girl!"

Abigail wailed. I felt distinctly uncomfortable and wanted to tell her to stop it, but it wasn't my chimp, so I had to bite my tongue.

"She hates to have her diaper changed, but she's not potty trained, and she wants to stay inside, so we have to keep one on her."

Kim managed to get Abigail over on her back, Nan held her down, and Abigail continued to scream, but somehow the diaper was successfully changed. I managed a relieved, somewhat ironic, smile. In the blink of an eye, Kim was tickling Abigail until Abigail's lips rolled back and she was shrieking with laughter.

It was getting late, and the reverend was ready to take us to meet the other PCVs in town. The three of us got into the Land Rover and headed for town. Our new house was on the way, so we stopped off to check it out. From the outside it looked like a small, modern ranch-style house made of yellow-washed cinder block. I was shocked at how Stateside it looked. I didn't know how my romantic expectations and this house were going to reconcile. Nevertheless, I oohed and ahhed appropriately as the reverend toured us through the large kitchen, larger living room, bathroom with white porcelain fixtures and indoor plumbing, large master bedroom, one spare bedroom inside, and one spare bedroom attached to the covered porch area outside our front door. Wow! The entire house was painted and looked ready to be occupied.

Outside the back door was an elevated water tank to catch rainwater. Since it hadn't rained for months, it was dry. There was a running stream not too far behind our house, so there would always be plenty of water, and that's why they decided to put the house there.

There were a couple of drawbacks, the reverend explained. First, the mosquitoes. They always found their way to the water, so we'd have to be sure to spray our bedroom every night before retiring.

I noticed a well-worn path going from the main road past our house not far from our front door. The path led to a small opening in the tropical growth, and I could barely see the running stream through the trees. This was the second drawback. The reverend said that the neighbors had been taking this route to the water ever since he had cleared the property. He had explained to them that, once the new PCVs moved in, they could no longer use that path. He said we would have to be firm about it, or we'd have a steady stream of visitors walking by our house every day at dawn and dusk. My mood brightened. We were going to be right at the hub of neighborhood activity—I wouldn't dream of saying a word to my neighbors about the path!

I told the reverend the house already looked ready to be lived in, and he told us he had to install the rest of the pump attached to the underground well beside the water tank or we wouldn't have any water. That would take about week because there was a holiday coming up, and he couldn't get workers. The job itself wouldn't take that long. He said we'd have to adjust to Liberian time, and it could be very frustrating at times.

The other things he was waiting for were the large items that were to be shipped from the Peace Corps warehouse in Monrovia: kerosene refrigerator, stove, beds, water filter, a card table, and four folding chairs. Anything else we wanted in the way of furniture, we'd have to buy ourselves.

He said some of the local Lebanese and Dutch and German stores had furniture, but he didn't see why we should pay top dollar for imported goods when we could get them from Liberians. "They make fine wicker furniture out of local materials, and it's really cheap. You just have to ask around—lots of people make it, and occasionally you can find some at the market." I asked when the stuff from Monrovia was due to arrive.

He chuckled, "They're on Liberian time, too. Sometimes I think they're on Liberian time more than the Liberians are. All they have to do is pack it up and get it to the airport. There won't be that much, so they should be able to get it all on one flight. The first day we'll be able to work on the pump is Wednesday, but that job should only take one day at the most. So maybe, just maybe, Thursday."

Now I was really excited. I asked if there was any way we could call them and get them to bring the stuff on tomorrow's plane. He said he'd been trying all morning but couldn't get through. "The phone system is not the best here, as you can imagine." He'd keep trying, though. Dale was chewing the inside of his cheek. While we were chatting, several people from neighboring houses had come out to have a look at the new PCVs and wave to the reverend.

After a few minutes, satisfied that we'd seen enough, the reverend hustled us into the Land Rover. He said the market would already be closed so we could explore the town tomorrow. We headed for the Peace Corps house just off Front Street.

We could smell the aroma of Liberian cooking as we approached their door, but there was something oddly familiar about this particular dish. Perhaps it was something Carol had cooked in Fisebu. Suddenly it came to me. I had smelled that same aroma at the Peace Corps hostel in Monrovia. I remember, specifically, because it was when I was first experiencing the symptoms of morning sickness from the pill. I gulped hard at the memory.

Precisely at that moment, the door flew open and standing there, with apron on and ladle in hand, was none other than Steve Wilson. I literally gasped. "Hi!" he said. "Come on in. I'm just cooking dinner. Would you like a beer?"

Dale and I said, "Sure," and our Baptist reverend said, "Pass."

Steve wiped his brow and whipped out two cold ones. "Glass or bottle?" he asked.

We noticed the beer was Heineken and said, "Bottle's fine."

Steve cooked, and we sat at the table outside the kitchen door sipping our beer and listening to every detail of Steve's life since he'd arrived in Greenville a month ago. He hardly paused to draw breath until his three roommates came in and he had to stop to introduce us. The two veteran PCVs seemed nice enough and pretty much into doing their own thing. The other PCV from our group was easygoing Stan from New York. We took the first opportunity to excuse ourselves, wished them a good dinner, and said we'd probably see them at market tomorrow.

It was 5:40 p.m. and beginning to turn dusk as we turned into the reverend's driveway. A majestic purple hue engulfed us, and a kind of hush fell over everything. It felt like a magic spell. The sun was closing its eyes and slipping into a peaceful sleep. Then, within minutes—darkness. I'd never seen such darkness, even in the long Alaskan winters when the sun rose at 9:30 a.m. and set at 2:30 p.m. I remember taking walks in Fisebu, but the huts were close together, and there was always a fire burning somewhere or the odd kerosene lantern lighting our way. Except for the faint glow coming from the side of the Carpenters' house, there was no light. Looking into the distance from where we'd come was like looking into a black hole. It felt eerie.

Then I noticed a familiar aroma coming from the kitchen—a smell that transported me Stateside in a whiff. Betty had decided that, after a month of being in the country, we were ready for a taste of home. She broke into her special store of foods, and we enjoyed a sumptuous dinner of Southern fried chicken, mashed potatoes, collard greens, biscuits, gravy, and the official drink of the South—iced tea. Dessert was cherry pie. Except for the humidity and the collard greens (a first for us), we could have been home. After dinner we listened to Broadway show tunes on the hi-fi, and the Carpenters eagerly shared some of their Liberian adventures.

CHAPTER 17

Turkish Coffee

The reverend had finally gotten hold of the PCV office in Monrovia. They were one step ahead of us—we would receive the rest of our goods the next day.

The Peace Corps had given us a sum of money to purchase household items from local stores, so Dale and I got up at 5:00 a.m. and were ready to walk to town by dawn. In Liberia, the time of the rising and setting of the sun never varied—you could set your watch by it, and we often did. Most Liberians could look at the sun and tell approximately what time of day it was at almost any moment, but we never got the hang of it except for the obvious rising and setting of the sun at both sixes (6:00 a.m. and 6:00 p.m.).

The reverend said he'd be happy to drive us to town, but we wanted to walk, not only for the pleasure of savoring our new town but to get a sense of how long it would take us to walk to work each day. What we didn't count on was the "necessity" of stopping to meet every neighbor as we passed their houses, as well as chatting with every person we met along the road. We enjoyed every second of the time getting there. Although our ears weren't yet accustomed to their Pidgin English, I managed to understand that they were eager to meet us and welcome us to Greenville.

We learned the elaborate Liberian handshake, which consisted of shaking the front of your partner's hand, as we do in America, then moving the hands upright and shaking again, then down, then up (this could be repeated any number of times, depending on the enthusiasm of the participants). The shake ended by sliding the hands away from each other culminating in a loud snapping together of middle fingers and thumbs. All of this had to be done with a great dramatic flair.

Many of our neighbors promised to bring us gifts of food and baskets. Mrs. Witherspoon, who lived directly across the street from our new house, said she would get us fish from the shore. I told her that would be great but to wait a few days until we moved in. Nearly every person commented on our beautiful new house and promised to visit us as soon as we moved in. They had been using the path to get water and were keeping track of its progress. Almost half of the people we spoke to said they had a brother or cousin working on our house. I thought this seemed a little exaggerated until I found out that almost everyone in Liberia seemed to be related in some way—if only distantly—and that they take this connection very seriously. There was frequent mention of cousins, brothers, sisters, aunts, uncles, and cousins once or twice removed.

By the time we reached town, it was eight thirty, and the market was in full swing. We weaved in and out among the country cloth and cardboard boxes spread with all sorts of unusual food and goods, but we were interested mostly in acquiring household items, so after a time we headed for the stores on Front Street.

A young, handsome Lebanese man (Kahlil), who lived upstairs with his pregnant wife (Jemma), owned the first store we entered. He engaged us in conversation for at least five minutes and then asked us, "Will you take some coffee?" It was a question, but his manner brooked no refusal.

Coffee was the last thing I wanted. I was sweating profusely from the humidity, my polyester blouse was doing what it does, and I would have preferred a cold, frosty beverage. Dale was wearing one of the 100 percent cotton shirts his mother had made for him and didn't seem to be sweating nearly as much as I was. He smiled and said, "Sure, we'd love some."

The Lebanese man looked unusually pleased. He took out a tiny metal cup with a long, thin handle. In it, he put a large spoonful of fresh, finely-ground coffee and a large spoonful of sugar. Grasping the cup by the end of the long handle, he held it over a concentrated flame (somewhat like the Bunsen burners we used in high school chemistry class) until the coffee mixture boiled. It only took about a minute. As the mixture was just about to froth over the top, he removed it from the flame. When the foam receded, he repeated the heating process two more times. Then he poured it lovingly into the tiniest coffee cups I had ever seen. He slipped in a slice of fresh lemon rind and gave me the cup. Then he repeated the same procedure for Dale.

I lifted the tiny cup to my mouth, holding the handle between my thumb and first finger, like a child's teacup. I took a small sip and rolled the thick liquid around in my mouth to savor the full-bodied flavor of the bittersweet Turkish blend. I wasn't used to drinking such strong coffee, and after a few sips I could feel an unmistakable buzz.

The cup was still half full. I'd had enough, but I didn't want to insult the Lebanese proprietor, who was watching me intently, so I took a final, large mouthful. I didn't realize that, with Turkish coffee, you don't drink it all the way down the cup because the finely saturated grounds quickly settle to the bottom, leaving a strong, glutinous residue, which was now rolling around in my mouth. I was stuck. I couldn't spit it out for fear of insulting the proprietor. The only other alternative was to swallow it. I looked at Dale, who had somehow managed to escape my dilemma by sipping very slowly. I gathered my courage and swallowed the grounds in one gulp.

By the time I handed the cup back, my hand was quivering from the caffeine. I wish I could say that the experience cured me from the coffee habit, but America's favorite legal addictive stimulant is still my favorite beverage. When I learned to drink Turkish coffee the way it was intended, it became a pleasant, social ritual. But standing there in the Lebanese store, I still had one more hurdle to jump.

We handed our cups back to the proprietor. He asked if we'd like another cup, and I said, "No, thank you, that was delicious."

Then, being the good, conscientious American that he was, Dale asked him, "How much for the coffee?" The proprietor's shocked expression told us we had done something very wrong, but we didn't know what. Was he insulted that we didn't want another cup? Did he see I had swallowed nearly all the grounds at the bottom of the cup— what? The silence seemed to go on forever.

Finally, Dale said, "Well, we have to go and do some marketing." He reached into his pocket, pulled out his wallet, and asked again, "How much do we owe you?"

The proprietor's deep brown eyes widened to show the whites all the way around. "Nothing! I made it for you. It is a gift!" We had insulted him in the worst possible way by offering to pay him for his hospitality, and we spent the next few minutes apologizing profusely, then accepting another cup of his generosity.

I moved beyond buzz. We chatted about our countries, our customs and traditions. We prattled on about our families, our hopes, dreams, and goals for our futures. We talked about our religions—their similarities and their differences, our holidays, food, education, and marriages. We exchanged invitations to dinner and promised to come into his store whenever we came to town, which, as it turned out, was almost daily. Before we left his store—I had no idea what time it was—we had purchased Turkish coffee, sugar, demitasse cups and saucers, and a long-handled metal cup.

We exchanged the European good-bye—double-cheeked kisses all around—and carried our treasures out into the street. We strolled to the edge of town, greeting everyone we met along the way. Then we stopped, looked at each other, and burst out laughing. We had come to town to load up on supplies for our house and all we came away with was the accoutrements for making Turkish coffee. What would we tell the Carpenters?

We quickly agreed that our experience with our Lebanese friend was far more valuable than anything we could have purchased for the house. Looking at our watches, we noticed it was already 2:00 p.m., and I was uncomfortably hot and hungry so we decided to head for home to share our story with the Carpenters.

CHAPTER 18

Letters From Home and Moving In

The next day was all excitement. The anticipation of goodies from Monrovia was fun for everyone. Not only was our stuff arriving by plane, we anticipated getting some mail from home, and the Carpenter children often received toys from their Baptist mission in Georgia. It had been over four weeks since I'd had any mail from home, and I longed to read what was going on with my faraway family.

I received ten letters. I inhaled them, absorbing every detail of the life I had left just a few short weeks ago. Nan and Kim Carpenter at my feet, I read aloud the entire ten letters to their rapt attention.

My older sister, Ginger, had begun spending more and more time inside her house. It had actually started shortly after the Alaskan earthquake in March of 1964. I had come home from college the day before for the Easter holidays. It was Good Friday and Ginger was at work in town when the quake hit. I remember feeling the first rumblings and then Mom screaming at us to stand in the doorway. My mom, my younger sister Pam, and I squeezed into the doorway and watched the violent shaking of the earth in every direction.

Parked cars on our street were being tossed to and fro like toddlers' toys. Standing lamps fell to the floor, and kitchen cabinets swung open, strewing their contents across the floor. Dishes flew out of the cupboards, and the refrigerator gave birth to milk, eggs, leftovers, and everything else in its belly. The dachshunds had found refuge under various chairs; the parakeet's cage had clanged to the ground, and Bimbo was squawking his protest. Mom started running around trying to keep the cupboards closed, and Pam was rescuing Bimbo from being squished by flying pots and pans. I was still holding up the doorframe.

The quake registered 8.7 on the Richter scale and lasted three and a half minutes. When it was over, we knew we had just survived a major disaster. Where was Dad, and what about Ginger? All phones were dead; there was no electricity or water. Mom thought quickly to get the transistor radio, and after a few moments of silence, the reports began. Dad drove up within a few minutes and raced into the house. The radio said that the downtown area and the area on the inlet were hit the hardest. The suburb of Spenard, where we lived, was hit the least. We had to find Ginger. The music store where she worked was on Fourth Avenue, and the report said that Fourth Avenue had been completely destroyed by the quake. Mom looked stunned, and Dad said he was going to go look for her, and we should stay put.

A full hour later, Ginger drove up. She had been teaching a guitar lesson to an eleven-year-old boy when the quake hit. She took the boy outside on the street and held him close as people ran frantically in every direction, like in an old Godzilla movie.

Then, as if in slow motion, she watched all the buildings on the opposite side of Fourth Avenue fall to the ground, like so many dominoes. The street parted like the Red Sea, snapping its lashing jaws and swallowing the tumbling structures one at a time. The newest five-story structure, JCPenney, crumbled to the ground like so many pick-up sticks. After the quake subsided, she waited for the boy's parents to arrive, then managed to find her car down the hill, unharmed, amid the rubble of other cars. Driving the usual way home would have taken a cool ten minutes, but the quake had left gaping crevices in every street so that wherever she turned, she was confronted with the fear of falling into the earth under the street. It took her an hour to find a safe way home.

Now, more than a year later, she was becoming increasingly afraid to go outside. By the time another year had passed, she wasn't going outside at all. Nobody knew how to diagnose the problem, so responses to her behavior ranged from "Snap out of it—you're being silly" to Dad's advice to her husband :"Don't let her get away with this, you spoil her." Even through years of therapy, her complete self-confinement lasted over two years. And it took many more years to battle the fearful feelings. Ten years later, she was diagnosed, appropriately, as having post-traumatic stress syndrome, which, left untreated, unacknowledged, and invalidated, had led to agoraphobia. Now, with proper medication, she has been symptom-free for over twenty years.

My younger sister was a senior in high school, captain of the cheerleading squad, and clearly a popular beauty. Though we were five years apart in age, we had been close growing up. During the time I was away at college, our lives drifted in different directions, so when I saw the picture of her enclosed with the letter to me in Liberia, I saw someone I really didn't know anymore and was eager to read all about her.

Dad and Mom were in their early forties and in the prime of their lives. Two of their chicks had already left the nest, and the third was about ready to fly. Their early years of marriage had been fraught with struggle. Both Mom and Dad had come from poor families, had married during the Depression, had had their first child when Mom was barely nineteen, and another within a year and a half. Then Dad was drafted to fight in World War II in Europe, while Mom was left to raise two kids on her own.

When Dad returned home, he was given back his job as a manager of a Safeway store, and he worked twelve hours a day, six days a week. Though many women were beginning to work, it was still the age of the stay-at-home mom, and that is just what Mom did. They both worked very hard to make ends meet.

After we moved to Alaska, Dad began taking half of Saturdays off—then whole Saturdays. They bought a cabin on a lake two hours drive from Anchorage and spent every weekend there, summer or winter. They boated, water-skied, fished, and hiked in summer and rode snowmobiles, went snowshoeing or ice skating, and played board games around the potbellied stove in winter. They got to know all the cabin owners and formed fast friendships, some of which have lasted to this day.

Things seemed to be moving so fast at home, while my life in Liberia, with each new breath and fresh sensation, was taking its own sweet time. I had only been in the country a little over a month, but it felt like much longer, and nothing about my life in Liberia seemed even remotely connected to the lives in the letters.

Our less than primitive house, Greenville

We moved into our new house about a week later. Steve had managed to get control of the Peace Corps station wagon and was keeping it at his house and holding on to it for his own personal use. If we wanted to use it, we would have to convince him that our needs were more important than his. He consented to lend us the vehicle when we moved the heavier items into our house, but refused when we wanted to use it for hauling smaller household goods purchased from town.

"Steve, we need to use the car today."

"Why?"

"We need to buy a lot of household goods to stock our house."

"Like what?"

"Pots, pans, dishes, et cetera."

"Have a boy carry them for you."

"But the car is supposed to be available to us to do that sort of thing."

"Well, I need the car today. What about the reverend's car?"

"We've been imposing on the reverend for two weeks. Every time we want to use the Peace Corps car, you need it for something else."

Steve laughed his horselaugh and said he couldn't help it if our schedules conflicted—he had to drive other people around too—and besides, the reverend wouldn't mind. It was obvious that our attempts to gain use of the car were always going to be met with this kind of runaround, and the conflict it created wasn't worth it.

Steve was right about one thing. The Carpenters' generosity was boundless. After they helped us move the Peace Corps furnishings into the house, we knew the first order of business was to boil and filter water to drink. We had already drunk about a gallon of water that morning during the moving process, and the reverend left us with another gallon to tide us over. If we ran out before boiling and filtering could be completed, we'd have to walk the mile to the Carpenters' house to get more water, and that could be a dangerous health hazard in the midday sun for two already dehydrated foreigners.

The neighbor children watched us pump water from our well into the barrel above. Each one wanted a turn, and soon the water was dribbling over the top, and they were running back and forth underneath to catch the drips and play in the overflow. We invited them inside and explained the miracles of indoor plumbing and the relationship of the running faucet to the pump outside. Then, with gleeful anticipation, one after another they turned on the faucet and watched the water pour forth. We filled several large kettles and put them on the stove to boil. It took forever for the large kettles to begin to boil—well over forty minutes.

By the time the water had boiled the required twenty minutes, the water filter was assembled, and the kerosene refrigerator was already cold. It took another thirty minutes for a few inches of water to seep through the chalky filter. By that time we were so thirsty we could hardly stand it. We had long ago consumed the spare gallon of water the reverend had left us, most of which had sweated right out of us. We had been told that we really shouldn't drink the first supply of water from a brand-new filter because the first run should be used to clean and prepare the filter. They said it probably wouldn't hurt us, but the initial chalky taste was enough to make you puke. My thirst took precedence, and I forced it down anyway.

They were right—it made me puke. I lay down, weakened by dehydration and thirst, while Dale braved the trek to town to load up on bottled soda. While he was gone, the reverend stopped by with another gallon of cool, boiled, filtered water. We ended up having to let two runs go through the filter before the water was fit to drink.

And I could still taste the chalk, but it was less if you chilled the water. The reverend said we'd better have dinner with them, and we happily agreed. Though I ate, all I really wanted was water and more water. After dinner we walked the mile back home with only a small flashlight guiding our way. The metronome of our padding feet was the only sound we heard in the pitch-black African night.

The first night in our new home I fell into bed and slept heavily and without covers for about thirty minutes. The buzzing of mosquitoes around my ears awakened me. The Peace Corps warnings also buzzed in my ears: *AVOID MOSQUITOES*. Even though we were taking our malaria pills regularly, it was still possible to get malaria.

We got out of bed and began rummaging through our stuff to find the two aerosol cans of Shelltox bug spray. We closed the bedroom door, held our breath, and heavily sprayed every inch of the room. Then we closed the door, ran into the living room, and waited. We figured ten minutes would be enough time for the mosquitoes to meet their maker and for the spray to dissipate. We could still smell the spray when we returned to the bedroom, but it didn't bother us that much. We slept the rest of the night undisturbed. Not even the loud purring of the fan kept us awake. After that, we took to spraying our bedroom in the same way every night just before retiring. Looking back on it, I wonder we didn't get brain damage from inhaling that strong stuff for nearly two years. Maybe we did. But one thing we didn't get was malaria.

CHAPTER 19

Charlies, Curtains, and Dresses

The house seemed enormous with our meager allotment of Peace Corps furnishings, the rooms echoing with emptiness. I'm a person who likes being surrounded by soft cushions, cloth, and colors. I like to feel snug but not crowded. I definitely needed more furniture, curtains, and tchotchkes to make me feel more at home. Instead of worrying about my first day of school, I set about making our house into a home. I was in heaven. I went to the stores, loaded up on sewing supplies, then to the market and loaded up on food. I put out the word for a sewing machine and wicker furniture.

Within a few days I had a sewing machine, and within a week, a "Charlie" showed up with a wicker couch and three chairs. A Charlie is the Liberian equivalent of a traveling salesman. Charlies travel all around West Africa selling their wares door to door. This Charlie had come from Sierra Leone. He had a large covered pickup truck full of ebony and ivory carvings, musical instruments and drums, thick rolls of hand-woven, hand-dyed country cloth, a wide variety of metal trinkets, jewelry, and furniture. American dollars went a long way.

I was ecologically and spiritually ignorant of the consequences of supporting the white hunters killing animals for tusks, horns, hides, and furs. The Charlie took his time. After I had purchased the couch and three chairs for a total of twenty-five dollars, he took a large fold of African cloth and spread it on the ground. Then the carpetbags came out. Handling each item like a fragile egg, he unwrapped the newspaper-covered artifacts and placed them gently on the cloth. The yard was already full of curious neighbors, with more arriving each moment. One by one, the Dutch, German, and English businessmen and the other PCVs showed up with purses in hand to have a look. Steve and his roommates were the last to arrive in the Peace Corps station wagon. It reminded me of putting bird seed in a feeder and watching as one bird, then another, and soon a whole flock would be there, as if by some magical communication.

I wasn't interested in anything but the hand-made, hand-carved items. I wasn't interested in owning any visual art that I couldn't touch and smell, and I wanted mostly things I could use or wear. I bought baskets, cloth, beaded jewelry, pouch bags, large grass carrying bags, a dozen small iron figurines representing Liberians in every possible activity, a talking drum, and two carvings—one out of elephant tusk, and one out of rich ebony, both of which sit on my shelf today, triggering memories as I write this book.

Bargaining was in full swing, and none of the PCVs or Europeans walked away empty-handed. It was a good time, and the Charlie made a killing. With his truck nearly empty, he was heading back to his sources to stock up again. He and other Charlies were frequent visitors in our town and often used our yard as a base of operations, but business was never quite as good as it had been on that initial visit.

The next order of business was to make curtains. We had an ample number of windows that let in the light of day that I love so much, but the naked windows were also an invitation for unexpected faces to appear at any time of night or day. Since our house was beside the water path, the faces inevitably filled the windows at both sixes and at other odd times of day.

"G'mahnin', M'Nancy! How you keepin'?" would often sound through the window, shocking me out of some private moment.

Eventually, I came to realize that this custom of looking in the windows of my house was not any kind of lewd voyeurism, but I was a curiosity, and it was a way of entering my life—of making a connection. I began to feel protected—looked after—but if I wanted any kind of privacy, I would have to make curtains. After nearly a week, I finally had enough sense to fashion makeshift curtains out of towels and sheets and a couple of nails, but this offended my aesthetic sensibilities. I've always felt that a home is a reflection of the people living there, and the hanging sheet design was certainly no accurate reflection of me.

By the end of the following day, I had made curtains for five of the ten windows, and the next day I had finished them all. Then I set about making myself a completely new wardrobe using only 100 percent cotton material. I had brought with me a few basic Simplicity patterns: tent dress, sleeveless blouse, skirt, Bermuda shorts, and man's shirt. It was not the custom for women or girls to wear slacks or shorts of any kind. Dresses and skirts were the only acceptable attire, and since I was representing the United States, I was expected to abide by the custom. My Bermuda shorts would have to wait until our safari to East Africa.

It took me about two hours to cut and sew a dress or skirt, and about one and a half hours for a blouse, start to finish. When I finished the curtains and set about making the clothes, I realized that, unless I wanted to spend the morning in town purchasing more cloth, I would have to make my clothes out of the same variety of cloth as the curtains. I was on such a roll, I decided to keep sewing. I chuckled all the while as I thought how I was going to look like the von Trapp children wearing their curtains. When I told the Carpenter girls the story of *The Sound of Music*, I was careful not to leave out that part so they could laugh along with me.

The curtains did help with the privacy problem—when they were drawn—but when they were open, the friendly faces were a given. Sometimes, even when the curtains were drawn, those familiar voices would echo "G'mahnin', M'Nancy, G'mahnin', Mistah Dell" as they passed by on their way to get water.

There was barely a week left until school opened, and I still had a lot to do to get the house running smoothly and in order before I started working full time. I had already met Mrs. Carter, the principal, and many of the children who would be in my class. I would be teaching a class of upper-elementary children ranging in age from eight to thirteen, with a wide range of abilities and skills. My student teaching in Alaska was done with a homogeneous grouping, both of age and ability, so this broad grouping was going to be a challenge, and I was more than a little nervous. I remembered my father's pet name for me was "worrywart," because I was always imagining the "what if" scenario. I had planned a number of diagnostic activities that would get me through the first week, after which I would know more about what to do with them.

CHAPTER 20

David and Ralph

Ralph, the Rhodesian ridgeback, in foreground

David was the first of many guests who would stay at our house over the next two years. Since we had the biggest and most modern Peace Corps house in town, we were naturally the "hotel of choice" for any Americans, Peace Corps visitors, or U.S. military who might be passing through.

David was the only PCV in a small village about three hours drive up-country from Greenville. He was well into his second year of service and wanted to re-up for another year. He had started out in Greenville but had found it much too metropolitan for his taste. He was short and muscular, drank black coffee by the gallon, chain-smoked nonfiltered Camels, and showed a mouthful of saliva and yellow teeth when he talked. His fingers wore permanent brown and yellow stains. He was an intellectual and could talk endlessly about any subject from Descartes to jazz. He and Dale hit it off immediately.

He showed up on our doorstep one day with a small duffel and large, tan dog and introduced himself. His dog was a Rhodesian ridgeback, a majestic looking dog with the same strong, lean build as a large boxer, but he had the unique characteristic of a long ridge of hair on his back that grew in the opposite direction from the rest of the hair and which, when the dog became agitated, stood straight up on edge. The dog's name was Ralph. That seemed like an unusual name for a dog so, naturally, I asked how he came by it. David said he had gotten the dog in Monrovia when he was just a puppy. He was taking him home in a cab, and Ralph got sick and barfed all over the back seat. The puking noise he made sounded like "Ralph," so that's how he got his name. Needless to say, I loved that dog from that moment on.

David told us that the only reason he had come to Greenville at all was to introduce us to someone who wanted a job as a houseboy. This young man had been David's houseboy, and when David moved up-country he had gotten him a job with another PCV. The other PCV had finished his tour and gone home, so the boy was once again unemployed. David sang his praises so much we would have been foolish not to hire him: honest, strong, hard worker, bright, good sense of humor, speaks good English.

We met Robert Isaac the next day, and within minutes we knew it was a match. Even though David's mission was complete, we invited him and Ralph to stay with us a few more days. Intellectual discussions over Johnny Walker Red went far into the night, and David told us fascinating stories about his first two years in Liberia. But the "city" was not for him, so two days later he was happily on his way back to the bush. We visited him once or twice.

His house was wall-to-wall books and full-to-the-brim ashtrays, but his main interest was the Liberians who lived in the bush. We had been given strict Peace Corps warnings not to get involved in Liberian politics. This was a foreign country, and despite its strong allegiance to America, if things got rough, it might be tricky. There were two distinct groups in Liberia—the indigenous people and the Americo-Liberians.

The Americo-Liberians were the richer, ruling class, and the larger group of indigenous people was kept pretty much under their control. Although the country was peaceful under President Tubman's long benevolent dictatorship, there were the occasional harbingers of discontent.

David was outspoken and didn't give a hoot about the warnings. At the end of his service, he became a little too vocal an activist for the indigenous sector and was told to back off. We were, after all, invited guests in the country—there to serve them and not to cause strife. Even though he was living with the indigenous people, his charge was to serve the needs of government.

After his tour of duty, he remained in Liberia under his own steam, and we eventually lost track of him.

CHAPTER 21

The First Day of School

Richelieu, Joseph, Fred

The night before the first day of school, the butterflies in my stomach had taken up permanent residence. After a fitful sleep, I got up at 4:30 a.m. and made some coffee.

I was totally prepared for school. My supplies were ready—bundled so they'd be easy to carry. My 100 percent cotton dress was ironed and ready to wear, my lunch was packed and waiting in the kerosene refrigerator. I had spent hours planning various activities to "break the ice" and diagnostic exercises to evaluate the academic levels of my students.

107

Shortly after my arrival in Greenville, Mrs. Carter, the principal, had taken me to visit the school. There was no private place to store any supplies I might need. There was one locked room that everybody used; I was certainly welcome to leave things there, and she would get me a key. I thanked her, and then she calmly advised me to carry what I needed with me because everybody had a key to that room.

I wasn't thrilled about having to tote all my supplies to and from school every day, so I said I would put my name on everything and asked whether she thought it would be safe to leave them in the room.

She said, "You can leave them, but whatever is in that room is community property."

She unlocked the room to show me its contents. It contained a few composition books, heavily mildewed from the humidity; chalk; and a variety of American texts from the 1950s, also mildewed. There were only a few copies of each grade level and subject: reading, social studies, math, science, and spelling. She said there used to be a lot more books but they tended to disappear.

I thumbed through the yellowed pages of stories about Father, Mother, Dick, Jane, Spot, and Puff taking a drive to see Grandmother, who lived in a perfectly appointed suburban house with a white picket fence and a garden full of neatly tended flowers. I wondered what any of this had to do with Liberia. The history books weren't any better.

Then I had something like a "Helen Keller" moment—when she finally understands that the word *water* stands for the thing. My heart began to race as I came to the realization that everything I'd ever been taught was from the point of view of white middle-class thinking. I truly hadn't realized until that moment how skewed and one-dimensional American textbooks were. I managed to get through four years of an intensely "maverick" four-year liberal arts college in Alaska without realizing that. All those poignant questions asked by my PhD professors went right over my head—until that moment, sitting in that dingy little room in a country halfway across the world. I had taken off the rose-colored glasses for but an instant, and I knew I would never see the world quite the same way again. Over the next two years, this revelation would lead me to review and question every perception I'd ever had in my twenty-one years.

I sat there in the early morning sipping my coffee and staring blankly at the three full bookshelves from our book locker. I hadn't had a chance to really examine or categorize the wide variety of books yet. Through my early morning gaze, a small turquoise-bound book caught my eye, and I pulled it from the shelf: *Liberian Folklore* by Doris Banks Henries. I flipped to the first page and within half an hour had devoured the entire book. I'll never know why the trainers hadn't called our immediate attention to this little gem of a book.

I would use this book as a springboard for teaching reading, spelling, and language arts. The subject matter was familiar, and it was written in story narrative, a form organic to Liberians. I could incorporate acting, music, and art, and it would be perfectly suited to all ages and ability levels. This single little book opened the door to a direction in my teaching that has served me to this day.

I couldn't wait to get to school. Dale's school was very close to mine, so he helped me carry my pack of supplies. He suggested that I leave my supplies at his school at the end of each day and pick them up on my way to school each morning. He had a file cabinet and a closet that only he had access to.

As I approached my school, I double-checked my watch. There wasn't a single soul around. School was supposed to start at eight o'clock and it was 7:45. Where was everybody? Does Liberian time also apply to the hour school starts? Dale's school consistently started on time. Eight o'clock rolled around, then 8:30. I concluded I must have made a mistake. Carrying my supplies, I walked to the principal's house, and the houseboy answered the door. He informed me that Mrs. Carter was in Monrovia in Congress and would be back next week. School, of course, was closed until she returned.

Somehow, everyone seemed to know this but me. Then I remembered I had heard about Congress being in session but didn't think for a second that school would be affected by it. The high school was in full swing, as were the other schools—only the Demonstration School was affected.

I was feeling let down, with time to kill, so I stopped off for a cup of Turkish coffee and a chat with my Lebanese friends. They were quite familiar with the goings-on at the Demonstration School and told me it was closed more often than it was open. Holidays were proclaimed for every conceivable reason from birthdays to headaches, and certainly, Congress was one of the more significant reasons.

I quickly deduced that I would have much more time on my hands than I had originally thought and mentally ran down a list of things I could do to fill it. There was just so much home decorating you could do, and once it was done, it was done. Visiting the Carpenters was always fun, but they were also busy with their own lives. Reading was great but I couldn't sit still for too long without feeling antsy. Sewing was fun, but cloth costs money, and I'd already spent more than my allotment to get the curtains done and my wardrobe in shape. Baking bread and cooking meant I would be sweating my brains out, a prospect that didn't thrill me. I had no idea I was a writer until much later in life, so the thought of writing didn't occur to me.

I'd never been a person to be bored. Even as a teenager, I don't recall expressing the plaintive "I'm bored," call of many of my peers. I always managed to find something to do, and my imagination consistently erred on the side of activity.

I remember my father's advice, "Don't think too much. Always have something to do, something to look forward to. The secret of happiness is to keep busy."

My father passed away at age sixty-six from heart failure. In the twenty years since he's been gone, I've had time to learn that he had a genetic tendency to depression, and he tried to control it by staying busy. In his later years, he sought comfort through alcohol, but all I saw was moodiness and a drinking problem. My father fought his "disability" in the only acceptable way a man of his generation and background felt he could. Getting help was a sign of weakness. Therapy was out of the question, medication for depression was too radical an option, and as the sole breadwinner, he had to be strong for his family—all women.

I adored my father, so it was understandable that my way of coping was to stay busy and try not to think. But before my two years in the Peace Corps were up, the demon of depression would force me to look head-on at that way of coping.

I went back home and dove into organizing my bookshelves. Afterward, I pulled the first of many books and read it from beginning to end in three hours. This began my love affair with reading which, up to that time, had been a minor pastime. I pulled the next appealing one from the shelf, poured myself a sixth cup of coffee, and began reading Ayn Rand's *The Fountainhead*. Though I'd heard students talking about it in college, it was a little too radical for my taste, so I had managed to escape reading it.

By the time Dale got home, I was a good way into it, but welcomed the interruption. This was the longest time I'd ever spent at one stretch just reading. Dale had already heard about the postponement of my school opening. He had met two young students dressed in blue school uniforms who asked him where their teacher was. He queried them about their teacher and found out they meant me. I was glad to know I wasn't the only one that didn't know school was postponed, and he said, "Oh, they knew, all right, but they were looking for you so they could show you their brand-new school uniforms and new composition books. I invited them to visit you at home, but I guess they didn't show up, huh?" I told him I had spent a good two hours with Kahlil and Jemma at their store before I came home so they may have come during that time.

Suddenly, two little faces appeared at the window and called, "Mistah Dell? Mistah Dell?"

Dale turned to me and said, "There they are!"

Richelieu and Joseph were brothers but looked like twins. Richelieu was the older and was the spokesman for the two. He was thirteen, looked eight, and acted forty. Mature and poised, he introduced himself and his brother. They still wore their school uniforms and had composition books with them. I complimented them on their natty appearance and their conscientiousness in already having their notebooks in hand.

Richelieu accepted the praise graciously, like a politician in an election year. Then, articulating each word slowly, he said, "Yes, thank you M'Nancy, but … we have one very serious problem. The problem is pencils. We have no pencils. You must please give us one pencil."

It was not a question. It was a request of such serious proportions that I couldn't possibly refuse, for to refuse would have been denying the last request of a dying man.

"Of course! You must have pencils." I immediately gave each of them a brand-new pencil.

111

Fingering the pencils lovingly, Richelieu said, "Oh, M'Nancy, these pencils are too splendid, just *too* splendid. Thank you very *very* much for the pencils." I wondered where he learned to talk like that. He enunciated each word perfectly from the first consonant to the last and, even though he pronounced the words with his tribal accent, I could understand everything he said.

I asked him why I hadn't had the pleasure of meeting him before today. "I was staying with my father in Monrovia. He is a government official, but now I am staying with my mother who lives not far from here." I invited them to stay for an American-style dinner of canned roast beef with gravy over rice, biscuits with Danish butter, and fresh fruit salad. The biggest hit was the baby marshmallows in the fruit salad. I happily gave them the leftovers they asked for, to take home to their mother for her dinner.

CHAPTER 22

The Bananas

The next morning I was up at sunrise with Dale, slipped on a tent dress, shook out my shoes to get rid of any unwanted crawlies that usually found a bed there during the night, and made breakfast. We were already used to farina and fruit as breakfast staples. This morning I fixed some canned Danish bacon and fresh bread.

After breakfast and washup, I opened the curtains and noticed Richelieu and Joseph sitting on our porch watching our neighbors on one of their many trips to the stream for water. I asked them how long they'd been there, and they said since sunrise. They wanted to accompany me to the market, but they had an important request first. To Richelieu, every request was of utmost importance, so I stopped what I was doing and invited them in. His request was that he be allowed to pump water for me every day for a small fee of twenty-five cents a week.

I pondered the request, examining him with feigned furrowed brow, while mumbling, "Hmmm … hmmm." Then I asked, "Will you alone be doing the pumping every day?"

He said, "Oh, yes, every single day, except on the days that Joseph will be doing the pumping."

"Ah," I said, "I see. And on those days that Joseph will be doing the pumping, will he be fairly compensated for his trouble?"

Richelieu straightened his spine and smiled, pleased with the negotiation procedure and his obvious understanding of the big words. "Oh, yes, M'Nancy, for he will be the one doing the work." I looked at Joseph, who was bursting with pride that he had become the center of the conversation.

"And Joseph," I said, "do you find this negotiation satisfactory to you?"

"Oh, yes, M'Nancy, this negotiation is most satisfactory." He smiled.

"All right then," I said, "I will expect my water tank to be full every day, and you will receive twenty-five cents every Friday." They stood, smiling, and we shook hands, Liberian style, on the bargain. I told them I was going to go to market. I didn't need anything, really, but I had time on my hands, and I enjoyed the market experience. We walked together, and while I stopped off for a cup of Turkish coffee and a visit, the two of them went on to the market, saying they would perhaps see me there.

Market, Greenville

There was always something new to see at the market. Today it was the bananas. There were always bananas—single bananas, piled high into pyramids—bananas that sold two for one cent. But today, one of the vendors had brought an entire bough of bananas to sell. There must have been a couple of hundred bananas on that bough. Since they were green, I inquired whether they were bananas or plantains and was assured they were bananas. I was told to pull off what I wanted.

The novelty of an entire bough of bananas was too much for me. It was like a family, and I couldn't bear to separate the siblings. I paid the man a dollar for the lot, then went to locate Richelieu and Joseph, who carried them to the house and hung them on the porch to ripen. I was mentally planning what I would do with so many bananas ripening all at once. I would make a couple dozen loaves of banana bread and store them in the Carpenters' large refrigerator. We could eat off them for a long time. I would give some loaves to the Carpenters and save a few for gifts. Of course, we would mash bananas and put it in our morning farina and have some in our daily fruit salads. Maybe I would give some to the neighbors too; Mrs. Witherspoon occasionally palavered for fish for me, and it would be a nice gesture in return.

Soon I would learn about a simple lesson in giving. Not everything is given to get something in return, and not everything that's received needs to be repaid. The bananas taught me that.

It was a fun experience to awaken each morning and see the dark green bananas beginning to ripen, day by day, into a rich sunflower yellow. Each day neighbors passed by to say hello and commented on the beautiful bough of bananas hanging on my porch, telling me just exactly how many days it would be until they were just right to eat.

"Five more day, M'Nancy, they be fine."

"Only three more day, M'Nancy."

Finally everyone agreed that the bananas would be perfect the next day. My mouth watered in anticipation of the first bite of the first banana.

The next day I awoke with the 6:00 a.m. sun just as I did every day. I went out onto the porch, my mouth fell open, and I froze. There before me was the huge bough ... with stems empty, not one single banana left. I couldn't believe my eyes and I couldn't believe I had been robbed. I had made no enemies. Why would someone come along and steal my beautiful bananas, the bananas I had nurtured and waited so long for? The answer came soon enough.

All day long, as I went about my daily chores in the village, my neighbors came up to me and thanked me for the delicious bananas. Soon I began to chuckle and feel more euphoric with each new "thank you," as I realized that these people from this "primitive" culture knew far more about giving and receiving than I did. They knew that it is in the sharing where the greatest reward is realized. How could I have learned this if I hadn't "given" them my coveted bananas?

CHAPTER 23

The First Day of School—Again

Two more weeks had slipped by, and now I was really ready to start school. Dale had already been teaching a month and loved it. The other PCVs were comfortably ensconced in their respective schools, and I had yet to begin my first day. Richelieu was keeping me abreast of Mrs. Carter's political activities in Monrovia, so I knew she was to return tomorrow, and school would begin the next day. My nervousness had long ago been replaced by eagerness.

When I showed up at school, I was pleased to see many youngsters (90 percent boys) waiting outside the school, dressed in their clean, pressed, royal blue school uniforms. The boys wore shorts and shirts, and the girls wore dresses. Elaborate plaited hair adorned the head of each girl. Most of the children wore molded plastic or rubber sandals. Some of the boys had on their Sunday-best leather oxfords, which were too narrow for their wide feet, which caused the shoes to gape at the opening, giving them a flattened appearance. Since most of the shoes had no laces, the tongues stood straight up in mock salute.

One by one, the other teachers arrived and introduced themselves. It began to look like I might be the only female teacher, another first for me, having come from a Stateside elementary school community made up almost entirely of women.

Mrs. Carter was the last to arrive, with two boys carrying four large, heavy bags. She unlocked the door and let us in. There were seven teachers in all—five men and two women. My class consisted of twelve children—ten boys and two girls, ranging in age from ten to thirteen, Richelieu being the only thirteen-year-old. Mrs. Carter told me I would be teaching fourth through sixth grades in one room. She dug deep into one of the bags and pulled out one book at each grade level of math, science, English, and history and handed them ceremoniously to each teacher. The students looked on in great anticipation. She told

Mrs. Carter

us she had brought them from Monrovia, and they were our official textbooks.

Richelieu walked over to me and caressed the new books. "Oh, M'Nancy. These books are too splendid, just *too* splendid."

And indeed they were. They were the most recent editions of Scott Foresman texts from America. The pages were still crisp on the inside where the mildew spores hadn't yet taken hold. The aroma was positively transporting. I reveled in it for several moments. But I had my work cut out for me. This was the official text, and I assumed I was required to teach from it. I scanned the table of contents and flipped through the English book, but I already knew that it would contain nothing relevant to the Liberian culture. Computational math was the only common language in any of the books. New or old, the books would have to be adapted if I was to teach anything of use to my students. But in the meantime, here I was, it was the first day of school, and my students were looking at me, eager to begin. I took a deep breath and went inside, the children trailing after me like ducklings.

Over the next few weeks I had very little spare time. When I wasn't actually at the job, I was learning Pidgin English and preparing teaching materials. The Liberian teachers taught by rote and recitation. They copied directly from the text onto a blackboard, and the children would imitate as the teacher pointed to and said each word. I couldn't do this. I knew the students didn't know what any of it meant, but they were good at memorizing. I knew that even the teachers had sketchy knowledge. I painstakingly translated and adapted the texts into simpler language and burned the midnight oil making carbon copies for the students. The math was easier.

Mrs. Carter didn't seem to be too concerned about much of anything. She mostly sat in her cubby of an office and did her knitting. I certainly had my doubts about what I was doing there. Nobody seemed to care one way or the other how teaching was done and even though I was trying to be a model for good teaching methods—nobody noticed. No one attempted to observe, ask questions, or learn from me. Each day the other teachers came in and copied irrelevant text onto the board, and the students chanted their recitations. Each day after school I translated the text into what I felt was more closely related to the Liberian experience, made copies by hand, and created as many visual aids as my time would allow. And each day my students asked me if they could copy and memorize. I felt like I was tap-dancing in place.

After only a couple of months of teaching, I was beginning to hate my job. The way I was working was inefficient and unappreciated. No matter what I did, the texts were irrelevant, and I simply didn't know enough about their life experience to adapt them effectively. I was carrying armloads of materials back and forth every day and had no time to do much of anything except struggle through preparations far into the night.

Should I do what the other teachers did? Nobody would think twice about it if I did. Mrs. Carter often commented to me that I was working too hard and I should slow down. I was insulted that she didn't seem impressed by my sweat and toil, but after a time I decided that she was right—I was working too hard. I was working hard—but I wasn't working very smart. I didn't know what to do, and I felt demoralized and alone. Dale had no advice to offer me, and the other PCVs were too involved in their own school routines to pay much attention to me. The seasoned PCVs simply shrugged their shoulders as if to say, "Well, I've seen it all before—it's no surprise to me."

That was when I began to realize that I wasn't going to save the world. John F. Kennedy's words rang hollow: "You're there to help the underprivileged, to teach, to help them to help themselves. It's the hardest job you'll ever love." Well, I didn't love it. What was I going to do? I'd always been a doer but I didn't have a clue what I was going to do about this. Time moved unbearably slowly.

Teaching some of my students out of my home, Greenville

One morning, a few months later, while I was sipping my coffee and thinking down the road to the next year and a half, a feeling of intense anxiety seized me. I wanted to run—to escape. My heart was pounding, and, though I was breathing fine, I felt like I was suffocating.

I was terrified and began racing around trying to alleviate the panicky feeling. I woke up Dale and told him what was happening to me, but he became confused and unable to help me. The whole thing lasted only a couple of minutes but it seemed like an eternity. I went to school somewhat shaken. I decided to take the next day off. It would be nice to hang out in front of the fan, read a good book, and forget about school for one day.

I was used to getting up with the sun now, so even though I set my alarm for much later, I woke up anyway. I'd have to leave the curtains drawn until the morning water rush hour was over, then I'd enjoy a relaxing day reading, writing some letters home, maybe doing a little sewing.

It had been two weeks since I'd received mail from home, but it seemed longer. When I thought about home, I became teary. I was homesick. That's probably what yesterday was all about—I was just homesick. What day was it anyway? Friday. The end of April 1966. Spring in the United States. In Tacoma, the tulips and daffodils would be in bloom. We'd be going to the daffodil parade in Puyallup—dozens of huge floats made entirely of daffodils. The weather would be warm one day and cool the next—mercurial spring. Not at all like the absolute dependability of the weather here—eternal dog days of summer. Same. Always the same. I hadn't seen a flower in months. There were no flowers in Greenville. Anchorage would still have snow on the ground, and, if it was Sunday and the sun was out, Mom and Dad would be at the golf course, dressed in their sealskin parkas, playing a fast nine with their fluorescent green golf balls. Or maybe they would be ice-skating or sipping hot chocolate by a bonfire on the frozen lake.

What would I talk about in a letter? I didn't feel like writing anything. I was lonely and discouraged, and what could they say anyway, from halfway across the world? When I had gone through a bout of depression in college, they felt so helpless that all they said was "What is the matter with you? What have we done wrong?" I decided to save the letter writing for another day.

When the morning water-bearers were mostly finished, I opened the curtains, grabbed a book and sat in front of the fan to have a good read. I was about twenty pages into the book when there was a knock at the door. I was usually at work by this time, so who would be knocking now?

I peeked out the window at the same moment Richelieu peeked in, with Joseph beside him, and it scared me half to death. "G'mahnin', M'Nancy! How you keepin'?"

"Richelieu," I said, "what are you doing here? You should be in school!"

"We heard you were at home, and we came to see about your malaria," he said.

"But I don't have malaria," I said.

He looked perplexed. "What is the meaning of this?" he said. "You do not have fever?" He sounded so officious, I almost laughed.

"No, I do not have fever." I took on his tone. "I am very tired, so I decided to stay home and rest today," I reassured him.

"Are you certain you do not have fever? The class is very worried about you and told me to come to you." Richelieu had established his position as spokesman for the entire class and reveled in it. "You must rest, M'Nancy."

"For true," I said. "I am going to rest. Thank you for checking on me. Tell everyone not to worry. I do not have fever."

"I see, M'Nancy." He paused to consider. "Then—we will stay and help you rest," he opened the door and motioned for Joseph to have a seat.

"Richelieu," I said, "you should be in school."

He drew a slow, deep breath. "Yes, we should be in school. But M'Nancy, we do not have our teacher. You are *here*," he gestured.

"Yes, that's true," I said. "I am here. And when other teachers are absent, the students join other classes for the day."

His eyes opened wide and he said, as if stating the obvious, "But M'Nancy. You are the best teacher. It would be impossible to join another class."

"Impossible?"

"Yes," he reiterated. "It would not be practical at present."

"Ah," I paused. It was useless to get into an analytical discussion with Richelieu. He was way too good at it. "Richelieu," I said, "what do you want to be when you grow up?"

With great flare and certainty, he said, "Oh, M'Nancy, I will be a politician, of course."

"Perfect," I said. "I think you will make an excellent politician."

"Oh, indeed, M'Nancy. Indeed I will," he mused. "All right, M'Nancy. I'm coming to go now." He motioned to Joseph, and they left.

I realized that, during the course of our conversation, I hadn't felt the least bit lonely. In fact, I felt uplifted. I sat down once again to read my book. I needed a break and I was determined to have it. My father's voice deep inside me said I was avoiding the issue, and the thought gave me some discomfort. My father was a confrontational problem solver. A take-the-bull-by-the-horns, face-your-problems-head-on kind of guy. And my mother was evasive—an expert at avoidance. I fluctuated between the two like a Jekyll and Hyde, and not feeling entirely comfortable with either one. I had not yet begun to find my balance, my own way of dealing. The balance would come eventually, but only after many years of experiencing the results of going too far one way or the other.

I had just settled into the book again when I heard Richelieu's familiar voice: "M'Nancy! We are here."

I realized in a split second I was going to have to be firm and really take charge here, or I would never get any privacy. I jumped up quickly and opened the door with authority, ready to show him who was boss. There, standing before me, were the serious faces of every student in my class.

"They have to come see for themselves, M'Nancy." He looked at them. "You see our teacher does not have fever."

The look of relief on their faces made my heart melt. I invited them in. They huddled together like a group tied by a rope. I took them on a tour through the house. What interested them most was the water filter. I explained the whole process of boiling and filtering water to kill germs that mainly cause runny tummy (amebic dysentery). I could see they were utterly fascinated at the idea of something you couldn't see causing such violence in their bodies. They asked me question after question, over and over. They wanted to taste the magic water and carefully rolled it around in their mouths like expert wine tasters.

When they couldn't taste any difference between filtered and unfiltered water, they asked me again to tell them about the invisible germs.

Richelieu took them outside to demonstrate the water pump, and of course all the children had to try it until, finally, the water was overflowing and they were running back and forth underneath it. I was having a great time! It was just what the doctor ordered. The water filter was the best lesson I'd ever taught.

Then it hit me. Why not teach some days out of my home? What better way could I teach them about what was really needed—health and hygiene? We would put the teaching to practical use—we could practice it right here—washing hands before handling food, boiling and filtering water, brushing teeth. We could go to the market, they would show me what they used for hygiene and cooking, and I would create lessons using the items they could afford and have access to. It would be an experiential, hands-on educational approach, and that excited me! And I would be teaching something useful.

Mrs. Carter approved my request without hesitation and asked if she or other teachers could join us occasionally. I was thrilled, and the children felt so special. Richelieu took credit for the whole idea, and I let him.

When Dale came home from school that afternoon, he was surprised to find me bustling around and in such high spirits. He reminded me that Monday was a school holiday and suggested maybe it was time to make an R & R trip to Monrovia. We could eat in nice air-conditioned restaurants, see a movie, and go sightseeing. He could walk to the airstrip today to get the Government Travel Requests. We could take the small plane tomorrow and come back Monday. Of course, we couldn't afford to stay at the Dukor Intercontinental, so the hostel would have to do. It seemed like a century since we'd been in Monrovia.

The director had said to let him know when we would be in Monrovia so we could have a chat about how things were going. We managed to get through to him later that day and he invited us to stay at his place. There were some other PCVs from our group in Monrovia but they were singles staying at the hostel, and he thought we might like the option of a private room. It would be nice to stay in an air-conditioned house on the hill overlooking the city. He said that he or his wife would pick us up at the airport but asked why we hadn't flown in with Steve today on the missionary plane. We told him we didn't even know Steve was going.

"Don't you guys talk to each other in Greenville?" he asked. Steve's girlfriend had come in from the States, so he had flown in to meet her. "They're staying at the Dukor for the weekend. I wonder he didn't tell you."

"Well," said Dale, "we're not real close with Steve."

"But you share the car. Don't you share the car?"

"Well, yes, I guess so," said Dale. "But Steve holds the reins pretty tight, so unless we need it for an emergency, we don't bother."

"That sounds like Steve, all right," said Jack. "But you know you guys are just as entitled to keep it at your place," he said. "I don't really care one way or the other, but you have to speak up if you need it. It wasn't meant to be anybody's personal vehicle."

"I know he helps the girls in Lexington across the river, carrying them where they want to go and hauling groceries and such," said Dale. "He seems to be very generous with his time and trouble for the singles, as long as he's in the driver's seat. But we rub each other the wrong way."

"Well, okay. Whatever. But if you need it—just speak up. I'll remind him that the use of the car is supposed to be shared."

CHAPTER 24

R & R

Monrovia

The Carpenters drove us to the landing strip and asked us to pick up a few things for them in Monrovia. I wanted to get a gift for them and one for Kahlil and Jemma. I also wanted to rummage through the Peace Corps warehouse and pack up a few more school supplies to send to Greenville.

The plane showed up promptly at 7:00 a.m., and we were on our way.

Jack met us at the airport. "Well, you look a little different than the last time I saw you. You even have a little bit of color."

"From walking around," I assured him. "We haven't been doing any sunbathing since the last fiasco, though the beach in Greenville is nice. We go there to watch the sunset sometimes. It's not far from the Carpenter's place."

"How do you like the Carpenters?"

"I don't know what we'd do without them," I said. "They're our family. Our home away from home. Did you know that Betty's pregnant?"

"No kidding," he said. "What's that, number four? Are they going home to have it?"

"Nope. They're having it in Liberia. She'll come to Monrovia when she gets close to term." I thought of how they still must have enjoyed sex after sixteen years. I knew that something definitely had to give in my marriage, but I couldn't think about that now. It scared me too much. I would avoid the issue for another six years.

"You just missed John and Virginia," said Jack. "They were here last weekend."

The view from Jack and Evelyn's house was beautiful. We could see the entire city from their manicured, palm-lined street. Sumptuous plants adorned the screened-in patio. A hammock rippled gently in the breeze. We dropped our bags, and the houseboy met us on the porch with some fresh-squeezed lemonade and a tin of tea biscuits. I headed straight for the hammock and barely managed to get there before Dale. As I plopped into the soft cushions, Jack said he was going into town in about twenty minutes if we wanted a ride.

A heavy black-and-white cat came lumbering out of the house, jumped up on the hammock, and sat on my stomach, purring loudly. I was immediately smitten. Jack said she had recently had a batch of kittens, and ever since then she had become an affection junkie. I asked where her kittens were, and he said he had given away all but one—a little black-and-white male.

Dale looked at me and knew what I was thinking. "Oh-oh," he said.

Jack jumped up to look for the kitten. In a flash, he was back holding the furry little rascal in the palms of his hands. Dale started to express his objections, but it was too late—the kitten was mine, and I'd already named him Mac Cat. Jack chuckled as Dale merely shrugged.

Jack showed us to our room. "Another of your group is staying here for a few days," he said. "Sarah Thompson. She comes into Monrovia pretty often. She's teaching in Fisebu with Carol."

God, I thought. *I wish I were there.* I tried to imagine how Carol had managed to set up that entire school from scratch, by herself. In my eyes, she was a genius.

"How does she like it in Fisebu? Does she like working with Carol?"

"Well, she's kind of a loner. A very independent sort—used to doing things her own way. She probably would have been happier in a post by herself, or here in Monrovia. You'll see her later."

I remembered Sarah. She was one of the group from New York City. They socialized mainly with each other, and they always seemed so strong, self-assured, if not on the jaded side. Sarah was a tall, thin redhead who smoked and drank heavily and had moved to New York after living in Boston for fourteen years. She still spoke with a strong Boston accent, though in every other way she was a big-city New Yorker. It would be interesting to talk to her about Fisebu.

The Sound of Music was playing in the movie theatre. I thought what a shame the Carpenter girls weren't here—it would be a dream come true for them. How could I tell them I'd just seen *The Sound of Music* for the third time?

Evelyn pulled out a bundle of indigenous tie-dyed fabric she had purchased from a lady in an obscure part of town. It was the same lady I was going to visit the first days in Liberia when I got sick from the birth control pills and never made it. That would be number one on my to-do list. Evelyn said to plan to spend some time there to watch how she did it. I don't remember any such thing as tie-dye in the States until the late sixties, and I have a theory that it was introduced and became popular as a result of returned PCVs from Africa. I don't know if this is true, but it surely happened simultaneously. I know that when we came back and I did tie-dyeing with my fourth grade class in Tacoma, nobody had ever seen or heard about it before. Woodstock popularized it, and although the fad has pretty much run its course, elaborately tie-dyed garments are still available in the small tourist town of Woodstock and in parts of the West Village (Greenwich Village) in New York City.

Of course, I would have loved to eat a meal or two at the Dukor, but I couldn't bear the thought of running into Steve. Evelyn gave us a list of places to go in the city. She asked if we were going to spend any time at the beach. We all laughed. We would drop by and give our regards to Comfort Butler while we were here.

About 3:00 p.m. we took a taxi back to Jack's to change clothes and relax before going out to dinner. I knew I was going to order a T-bone steak, a baked potato with sour cream and chives, and a large green salad for starters. I didn't care how much it cost; it had been over four months since I'd had fresh beef of any kind, and my mouth was primed. I was basically a meat and potatoes eater and had not yet discovered other forms of protein, and I wasn't particularly fond of fish.

Humming the songs from *The Sound of Music*, I unpacked a couple of dresses to hang out the wrinkles and then took a nap. I awoke about an hour later with a stuffy nose from the air-conditioning. Dale had already gotten up, and I smelled cigarette smoke and could hear voices in the other room. Sarah must be here, I thought.

I dressed and walked toward the living room. Dale and Jack were there with Sarah. She was visibly upset and looked like she'd been crying. I lingered, wondering if I should go in. That's when I noticed how disheveled she looked. She saw me standing there and motioned that it was okay to join them.

She was in the middle of telling them that she had been raped. She had gone to the beach alone to sunbathe and read. There were many people there, but she had gotten too warm and decided to go for a walk along the water's edge. She wandered onto an isolated area of the beach and sat down for a while to soak in its beauty and stillness. That's when he came upon her.

At first she was startled by his sudden appearance, but when he asked her for a cigarette, she felt better. After he lit up, however, he didn't leave, and that made her feel uncomfortable. Sensing danger, she got up and started to walk quickly back toward the populated beach; that was when he grabbed her. When she struggled, he pulled a knife. Then he forced her down on her stomach and raped her. Her instincts told her to be still or he would really hurt her. After he finished, she continued to lie still, her eyes nearly closed.

When she heard him run into the bushes, she opened her eyes, grabbed her panties, and ran. Then she opened her clutched hand to reveal the panties.

A chill ran through me. Jack offered her a scotch, and she took it straight. He said his wife was still in town, so would I mind accompanying them to take Sarah to the doctor? Of course I wouldn't mind. I was shaken, but I tried not to show it. This wasn't about me— it was about Sarah. We stopped off at the police station first, and she told her story all over again.

While the doctor examined Sarah, Jack and I sat in the waiting room. "Do you think they'll catch the guy?" I asked.

"I doubt it," he said. "Why in the hell was she walking along the beach alone, anyway?"

"What do you think will happen?" I asked.

"Well, she was able to give a good description of the guy, but it's pretty basic here. It's not likely they'll catch him, but they'll scout in the same area for a while. Maybe he'll surface again—return to the scene of the crime sort of idea."

"God, it's awful," I said. "What a devastating thing."

"Yeah, it's not good," he said. "But she's been around, you know. She's not innocent. It's not like she's a virgin or anything." I blinked hard, and my insides turned cold, but all I said was "Uh-huh." I couldn't pinpoint the source of my feelings or find any words to say. I just knew that what he had said was terribly wrong. But that was the thinking of the times. Rape was a sex crime. And even if she had been a virgin, sooner or later she would probably have sex anyway—just a matter of time, so it would be a moot point eventually.

His words were etched into me forever, but I was unable to articulate my discomfort until one day, many years later, I heard someone say, "Rape is not a sex crime, it is a crime of violence and violation." Years of anger came pouring out, and I wept for Sarah, for the violence she experienced; I wept for Jack and his ignorance; and I wept for myself and the years it took me to finally "get it." I'd been holding on too tight to see beneath the accepted definition of the day. And finally, I wept for all women down through the ages who have had to survive such violation without the dignity of validation or support.

Sarah was given penicillin for treatment of VD and something called a "morning after" pill for prevention of pregnancy. The doctor said she wasn't injured, just shaken up a bit. He told her to go home and rest, and she'd be all right in the morning. If something like that had happened to me, I couldn't fathom being all right in the morning for many mornings to come.

"When I was in there," she said, "the doctor asked me if I had led him on." She laughed too loudly. I could hardly breathe.

"She's strong," I told Dale at dinner. "I guess it's true what they say about living in New York. If you can make it there, you can make it anywhere." I wanted to be that strong.

Sarah was already asleep when we got back to Jack's at 9:00 p.m. Evelyn said Sarah seemed fine, and she was going back to Fisebu tomorrow morning. I set my alarm early because I wanted to say good-bye to her.

Evelyn offered us a nightcap. As I sat on the couch, I looked around and I realized this was the first opportunity I'd had to really take in the surroundings. I asked Evelyn to take us on a tour of the house. It had the elegant look of the tropics without being ostentatious. Neutral colors for walls, curtains, and bed coverings. But the artwork, sculpture, and accent pieces were the bold African prints and designs of Liberia and neighboring Sierra Leone and Ivory Coast, as well as the cross-continent countries of Kenya, Uganda, and Tanzania.

Everything was spotless and well placed but not so neat as to make you feel unwelcome. It was decorative without being cluttered. I felt it was a nice blend of rustic and modern Africa. Each of the rooms had its own flavor, while all being part of a piece. I almost felt like I was back home, and I fell asleep feeling nostalgic. At three o'clock in the morning, I got up to go the bathroom, and when I flipped on the light, I saw two giant cockroaches copulating on the toothbrushes. The illusion of being back home was quickly shattered. When I got back to Greenville, I began storing our toothbrushes in a container.

The next morning we ate breakfast with Sarah at the Dukor Intercontinental and swam in the pool for an hour (we didn't run into Steve). Later I had fun rummaging through the Peace Corps warehouse and packed up two big boxes of supplies to take with us on the plane. We stopped by the Peace Corps mailroom and retrieved five letters from home and a box from Dale's mom that had been sitting there for nearly three weeks. Whatever was inside was broken into a million pieces. When we opened it, we found plastic bags full of cookie crumbs packed in popcorn. The enclosed letter explained how she had heard that popcorn made good packing material, so she thought she'd try it out. The cookie crumbs were stale, but since the bugs hadn't found their way inside, we ate them anyway. The popcorn was soggy.

We asked Jack why they hadn't sent the box to us by small plane when it had arrived, and he said we were probably lucky to get it at all. He suggested we might want to tip the Liberian working in the Peace Corps mailroom to insure future deliveries. I have to chuckle as I write this, sitting in my New York City apartment, thinking of the many people I have to tip (mail carriers, building superintendents, doormen, cabdrivers) simply to ensure normal service. This would not be the first time I would find similarities between Liberia and New York City.

Dale and I were concerned about the thirteen rolls of film we had developed into slides, recording our first impressions of Liberia. They were sitting in an airtight military box with silica gel packets. We had shown them to our neighbors in Greenville to delighted squeals and shrieks of laughter. We were worried about their fading from the humidity and heat but were afraid to send them home for fear they would never get there. Jack assured us that most of the stuff sent from here to the United States did reach its destination—it was the incoming stuff that is opened and stolen. We thought how awful we would feel if our very first impressions of Liberia and our experiences in Fisebu, which we so carefully captured on slides, were lost to the pilfering of mailroom employees.

We returned to the mailroom, slipped the attendant two dollars, and told him we would be sending a package home and would appreciate his personal attention to the matter. We hoped that his broad smile meant "I'll be happy to see to it" and not "Great! Goodies for me." When we got back to Greenville, we packed up our slides and sent them home—but they never arrived. The next time we were in Monrovia, we checked at the mailroom and asked to see our two-dollar friend, but we were told that they'd caught him tampering with the mail and fired him. Every picture we took from then on we kept with us and have them to this day. Even some forty-five years later, there has been only minimal fading, and every single picture was taken with the inexpensive Instamatic camera of the day. I have some fine picture memories, but as I sit and write this memoir, I wonder what those lost pictures of my first impressions might have triggered.

CHAPTER 25

Mac Cat

Mac Cat hanging out in his favorite underwear drawer

We had to figure out how to get Mac Cat back to Greenville on the plane. The plane had no provisions for transporting animals, and there was no such thing as the Sherpa bags of today. We scoured Monrovia for any kind of pet carrier but found none. The only alternative we could think of was a cardboard box I could hold on my lap. We punched holes for air and put in a soft blanket to try to make it as comfortable as possible. The moment we put Mac inside the box he went berserk. He flailed around inside, clawing at the box, wailing and trying to get out. I tried to comfort him by talking softly to him. The drive to the airport was torture.

My heart was breaking for him. Just when I was ready to give him back to Jack, he became quiet. I took that as a good sign and boarded the plane. He was quiet until we began taxiing down the runway, then he started up again. It occurred to me that he might not be getting enough air so I stuck my thumbs through the air holes in the sides of the box to make them larger. He seemed to quiet down after that and I continued to talk soothingly to him. After he'd been quiet for a time, I thought I'd peek inside to see if he was all right. I slowly opened one flap of the top.

As soon as I did, he lurched forward and shot halfway out of the box before I was able to grab him. He was fighting for dear life, and before I could push him back in the box and close the lid, one of his sharp claws dug into my thumb at the fleshy point where it joined my hand—reaching clear down to the bone. It didn't really hurt except for the initial skin puncture, and it wasn't even bleeding, but by the time we reached Greenville, my thumb was completely numb. Mac Cat was calm for the rest of the flight. John Mark and the two girls drove us back to our house, and all of us were thrilled to see a frisky cat leap from the box and shake himself out in his new home. I opened a can of mackerel, and we watched, in disbelief, as he devoured the whole thing. A few minutes later, he threw up. "Well," I laughed, "I guess he's officially mine now."

Over the next few days, Mac Cat adjusted beautifully, finding his favorite spots in the house and running freely outside. My thumb, however, was still numb, and that was beginning to concern me. I could still move it, but I couldn't feel a thing. The puncture wound, still visible, never bled. I looked through the Peace Corps Medical Manual but found nothing about cat claw puncture wounds. Rusty nail puncture wounds require tetanus shots.

Then I started to think: rabies. I opened the Peace Corps Manual and read: *Rabies is a viral disease of animals and humans that can be spread through a bite or a scratch. If the virus reaches your central nervous system, it causes inflammation of the brain and is nearly always fatal. The earliest symptom is a fever, followed in a few days by violent mouth and throat spasms. These spasms are made worse by the sight of water (hydrophobia). The incubation period for rabies is usually one to three months.*

133

Mac Cat hadn't bitten me but his claw had dug all the way to the bone. I knew he hadn't had any animal shots, because that sort of thing wasn't done in Liberia.

Rabies was not a pretty thing to read about, and the treatment sounded ghastly: fourteen shots in the stomach over fourteen consecutive days. But the alternative was madness followed by death. We called Comfort Butler. She told us that the claw probably hit a nerve, and as long as I could still move the thumb and it didn't hurt, the feeling would probably return eventually. She told me to watch the cat for any strange behavior such as aggression alternating with extreme fear, or anything else that seemed out of the ordinary.

I felt much better until Mac Cat decided to disappear the next day.

Two days later he was still gone, so I placed another call to Comfort. She told me to call Jack Reeder and get to Monrovia immediately. She would call the doctor. The small plane wasn't due for another two days, so Dale ran to Steve's for the car to go look for the reverend while I threw a bunch of things in a duffel bag. The reverend often knew of private missionary flights going in and out, and we would try to thumb a ride on one of those to Monrovia.

Steve and Dale drove up in the station wagon. Steve seemed genuinely concerned and offered to drive us around to look for the reverend. Dale rolled his eyes as he walked past me to the bedroom. I told Steve I thought it was a nice gesture but said that wouldn't be necessary; we were perfectly capable of driving a car.

Then he told us why he thought it would be better if he drove us: We weren't used to driving in the country, and we weren't used to the station wagon's idiosyncrasies. (This is where he reminded us of Dale's accident on the way to Fisebu.) He reminded us that we were stressed out and worried and might not be able to keep our mind on the road.

We assured him that we'd be fine. We had both driven since we were sixteen, in all kinds of weather and all manner of road conditions, and this was hardly a marathon—we were just going to look for the reverend, who, we were told, had gone to Juarzon, a few hours north of Greenville. We had driven down the Alcan Highway so he shouldn't worry about us, we'd be fine.

"Well!" he said. "Did you once consider that I would have to be without a car for the day?"

That silenced me. I looked at him a long moment without even a hint of judgment. Then I got up and made him a cup of Turkish coffee. As we sat sipping, I quietly told him we'd drive him back to his place before we left. I could see something in him had changed. I think he must have heard himself and realized how selfish he'd sounded. At that moment, I felt only compassion for him. While Dale packed, Steve and I talked about his stay in Monrovia, his time with his girlfriend, and his feelings about being separated from her. I told him about our crumbled cookies and popcorn, and we laughed about copulating cockroaches on toothbrushes.

"Do you play bridge?" he asked.

"Sort of. We learned in Fisebu, but we're not very accomplished."

He said, "I've been avoiding learning it, but I think there's no way around it here—I'll have to, sooner or later.

"Yeah," I laughed. "The Europeans around here are serious players. We've played with them quite a few times, and they're mostly pretty patient with us. Hans is the tough one, the Dutchman. He can really put you down. You just have to take it on the chin with him."

"Hey," he said. "How about I get a fourth, and you and Dale can teach me what you know?"

"Sure thing," I said. I felt wonderful. If not for my concern about the rabies, it would have been a perfect moment. Dale emerged, surprised to see us laughing like old buddies.

"Okay" I said. "We'd better get going." I got some food from the refrigerator while Dale closed the windows and pulled the curtains.

Just then I thought I heard a meow at the back door. I froze. There it was again. I rushed to open the door, and who should be standing there but Mac Cat himself.

"Well, lookie here!" I shouted. I opened the screen door, and Mac Cat sauntered in, rubbing himself on my leg and purring loudly.

"Well, he sure doesn't look rabid to me," Steve said.

"Thank God," I sighed.

The next evening Steve and Judith (one of the single PCVs from across the river in Lexington) joined us for an evening of bridge and Johnny Walker Red. By the time the evening was over, the Johnny

Walker bottle was empty, and we didn't care if we played bridge or not. We sat around laughing at everything and reminiscing about the relevance of our Peace Corps training in San Francisco.

We kept a vigilant eye on Mac Cat over the next weeks. He stayed close to home, and since he showed no signs of unusual behavior, I never had to have the rabies shots.

Mac was the epitome of the cat who comes and goes as he pleases. As Mac Cat grew into a healthy, unaltered male, he would frequently spend a few days away from home. He usually returned from his outings at sunrise looking skinny and scruffy, with a few new battle scars. We'd be awakened by Mac's soft meows underneath our window and know he had returned home for his much needed R & R. Then he would spend the next few days eating, sleeping, and nursing his wounds. Mac was never a very doting pet, but at these times he was particularly affectionate and allowed me to pick him up and pet him as much as I wanted to.

One day I left the top drawer of my bureau open, and he found his way inside. When I went to close it, I saw him snugly nestled in among my underwear. I thought, *What a cute accident*, and left the drawer open another time to see if he would go in there again. He did. He was so adorable that I never bothered to close the drawer again, and it became his favorite place to hang out. I did, however, move my underwear to a different location and put a soft blanket in its place. We'd enjoy each other's company for a few weeks—then, without warning, he'd be gone again.

One morning about 3:00 a.m., after Mac had been gone for four days, we heard loud cat wailings that sounded exactly like a baby's plaintive cry. I knew immediately that Mac had been injured. I jumped out of bed and threw open the back door, expecting to see him dying on the doorstep. I looked down but I didn't see him. I squinted through the screen door, but it was pitch black out, and Mac was a black cat. I called his name softly a few times. Nothing.

I made the assumption that it must have been another cat and was about ready to close the door when I heard another forlorn cry. I looked up and saw Mac Cat, attached to the screen door, spread eagle, and his belly pressed against the screen, wailing his protest. In an effort to get closer to our bedroom window, he had climbed up high and one of his claws had gotten stuck in the mesh screen. He let me release his claw and lift him off the screen. I carried him inside and set him down to inspect my furry warrior.

He was a sorry sight. He had really gotten into it this time. He had little nicks and scratches, he was limping, and he had a nasty cut over his left eye, which had become infected and caked with blood. He offered no resistance when I cleaned the wounds and applied antiseptic ointment. He offered only mild resistance when I pulled a pointy thorn from his foot. After his first aid session, he quickly found his favorite spot in the bureau drawer and slept for three days, waking only to eat and relieve himself.

After that, Mac never strayed very far away from home. He spent his time either on the porch or inside the house, curled up on the furniture or in his drawer. He became a regular participant in our twice-weekly school sessions at the house. At first the children were nervous around him. They were used to cats being wild and skittish and were afraid of being scratched or bitten. But Mac was a perfect gentleman and became the darling mascot of my class. They marveled as I opened cans of mackerel for him. Feeding animals was one thing—but fish! Most of the children ate canned mackerel only as a special treat and were aghast that I would feed such "caviar" to a cat.

They began to have a kind of reverence for Mac that he seemed to understand and revel in. He met people at the door, purring and rubbing against them. He loved being picked up and petted and held. He was the king, and he knew it. Many a time I would smile to hear little voices outside the window, "M'Nancy, we have come to play with the Mac Cat."

CHAPTER 26

Puppy Crisis

One day Robert came in with a message from PCV Cindy Aiken, saying she had a puppy crisis. One of her neighbors had brought over a box of five four-week old puppies, and they were dying. Two others had already died. When we got there, the five little puppies and the mother were curled together in the box. The mother seemed healthy, but the pups were skin and bones. I assumed they weren't getting enough milk, but the mother's teats were full, and the pups were nursing voraciously.

The mother was a tan-colored mutt mix, and all the pups were spotted like Guernsey cows. Cindy told us to look closer. I bent down and was just about to pick one up when I saw the cow spots moving. The spots were actually swarms of fleas and they were literally sucking the lifeblood out of the pups. Cindy wanted us to help her bathe the puppies to try to save their lives. The mother didn't seem upset when we took the pups one by one, bathed them and scraped off the fleas. Then we towel dried them thoroughly and applied Vaseline to the bloody lesions. Keeping the pups wrapped in blankets secluded from the mother, we listened to their hungry whimpers as we bathed and dried their mother. Then we sprayed the entire floor area to kill whatever fleas had managed to escape the bath. We found a large new box and clean blanket and reunited them. The pups, once again, took up their voracious sucking.

Cindy told the neighbor she would care for them for a few weeks, but she couldn't keep them. As it turned out, only one of the pups survived the ordeal, and Cindy agreed to keep it. It grew into a healthy, unruly dog you couldn't help but love.

Unfortunately, some months later, Robert Isaac came to us with another plea for help from Cindy. It seems that her dog had gotten hold of two three-week-old kittens and was tossing them around like old dishrags. Cindy managed to rescue them from his grasp, but their stomachs were ripped open, exposing their intestines. The solution was left to Dale, who filled a bucket with water and drowned the poor creatures. I'm sure he was devastated but steeled himself for our sake. It must have been traumatic for him, but all I could selfishly relate to was my own anguish.

CHAPTER 27

Husking Rice

Robert Isaac, our houseboy, Greenville

During my month in Fisebu, I had vowed to learn how to husk rice. I was at the market one morning and noticed a beautiful mortar and pestle. The mortar was roughly carved on the outside and smoothly finished on the inside. I bought the mortar for two dollars and the pestle for one, and a woman at the market thought I had paid far too much. I hired someone to carry it to my house while I carried the twenty-pound bag of crude rice and large, flat rice basket I'd just paid twenty-five cents for (the same woman thought *that* was a bargain). I remembered how easy it had seemed when I watched it being done in

Fisebu, and if I wanted to fit in and live like the natives, this was a good way to begin. This was going to be fun.

There seemed to be a custom in our town that you set your mortar and pestle right outside your front door. I'm not sure why this was the case, but I guessed it was because most people spent a good deal of time pounding and sifting rice and could wave to passersby or socialize with neighbors as they worked. Nevertheless, I wasn't about to break custom, so I set mine up in the same way. All my neighbors would see me working as they passed, and it couldn't hurt public relations. The mortar and pestle sitting in front of my door did not go unnoticed by a single person. "Ah, M'Nancy, you gwain to pound rice!"

"G'mahnin', M'Nancy, it be a fine mortar!"

"Good, M'Nancy, make you strong!" The comments continued.

"How you keepin', M'Nancy? You need help to pound rice?" I assured them that this was something I was going to do easily on my own. At that moment, however, I did have a fleeting thought about my tendency to idealism. So as not to make a fool of myself, I waited until Robert showed up so he could refresh my memory of how it was done. The Demonstration School was on holiday that day, so I had everything set up and ready to go when Robert arrived after his school day.

He was thrilled when he saw the mortar and pestle. He was always pleased to be able to demonstrate his expertise at anything, particularly physically. He took off his shirt, revealing his torso. It was masculine and muscular, and he looked older than his sixteen years. His white perfect teeth gleamed as he smiled broadly at me. He was used to the effect he had on American PCVs, who couldn't begin to match his physique or physical prowess.

Robert had been a houseboy for PCVs since the first group arrived in-country in 1962. He was all that David said he was—a hard worker, who learned quickly, had a gregarious personality and a good sense of humor—and understood Americans.

The Peace Corps encouraged us to hire houseboys for three reasons. First, we would need the help, since washing sheets and clothes by hand, toting water, and a multitude of other chores would require strength and endurance we wouldn't have. Second, the twelve dollars a month we would pay him would put him through school, buy his clothes and supply him with food. And third, we could teach him about hygiene and tutor him in his academics.

What they didn't tell us was that Robert would become indispensable to us. He would teach us far more than we ever taught him. We grew very attached to him and extremely fond of his easy ways and missed him terribly when we returned home. We continued to write and send him money for some years. The last I heard, he was teaching at the college in Monrovia, but that was before the coup of Samuel Doe. We haven't heard from him since, and fear he may have been one of the many casualties.

Robert rubbed his hands together and got ready to demonstrate the task at hand. I chuckled at him, thinking he was being a bit dramatic, and he laughed out loud at me saying, "Okay, M'Nancy, you watch!"

He scooped out a couple of canfuls of rice and threw them into the mortar. Then he took the pestle and began to beat the rice, coming down hard, his arm muscles flexing in the afternoon sun. The husks separated easily under the pounding pressure of the heavy five-foot-long pestle. It was not difficult. It might take some practice to build up my strength, but if thirty-five-year-old Mrs. Witherspoon across the road with five kids could do it, surely I could too.

When all the husks were loose from the rice, Robert used his large hands to scoop it into the flat rice basket I had bought. Then, with expert deftness, he shook and tossed the rice again and again high into the air, letting the breeze blow away the husks. After a few minutes, all the husks had disappeared. All that was left was the white rice and a few bugs. When we got around to cooking the rice, all we had to do was put it in a bucket of water, and the bugs would float to the top to be skimmed off.

Now it was my turn. The thought suddenly occurred to me that quite often, when Robert showed me how to do something, he left off telling me an important detail or two, possibly because he thought it was obvious and I could see it for myself. But after a few such lessons, I quickly deduced it was probably that he wanted to have a good belly laugh at my expense. It was sort of a little game we played. I allowed him that pleasure because it gave me a good laugh as well, and I love a good laugh more than anything in the world.

Taking my cue, I scooped two canfuls of rice into the mortar. Realizing I would have to find my own way of holding the pestle, I lifted it and stuck it into the mortar to get the feel of it. With some effort, I began to lift and pound. After a time, I could see the husks beginning to separate from the rice, and this gave me the encouragement I needed to keep going. Admittedly, the task was becoming increasingly arduous. However, I remained undaunted until the last of the husks was divorced from its mate.

Robert applauded as sweat dripped from my forehead, stinging my eyes. Several neighbors had already gathered to watch and cheer me on. The hard part was over, so I took my bows. Then I lifted the mortar and put the contents into the rice basket. Gently shaking the basket to get feel of it, I confidently tossed the contents into the air. More than a little rice landed on the ground. I shook the basket a few more times to get a better sense of the weight and tossed a little higher. A few husks flew away, but most stayed right where they were.

Robert coached me on, saying I needed to throw the rice *much* higher, keeping it in the air longer so the husks could catch the breeze. Third time's a charm. Once again, I confidently shook the basket back and forth like a gold panner working his claim. Then I threw the contents high in the air. It was beautiful! A sight to behold. The rice almost stopped in midair! Then, just as it was on its way down, a hearty gust of wind came up, blowing the entire lot of husks all over my sweaty face, into my hair, nose, and eyes and into my smiling mouth! It surprised me so much that I dropped the basket, leaving the rice no place to go but down. I wiped my eyes, spitting the husks from my mouth, and assured everyone I was all right.

Without missing a beat, Robert said, "Oh, I forgot to tell you, M'Nancy, stay upwind!" Then he slapped his knees and howled.

The others followed suit. It was a story that would greet me wherever I went. After our laughter subsided, I wondered what exotic deadly tropical disease I might get from swallowing unwashed rice husks and a few stray bugs.

CHAPTER 28

Chicken and Chop

My neighbors, Greenville

The first time Robert cooked us a Liberian meal was unforgettable. Robert had been our dinner guest two or three times before he offered to make us a *real* Liberian dinner (they called it "chop"). We had no idea he could cook, but after this first meal, he became our mentor of in-country cooking techniques and cuisine. On the morning our dinner was to take place, Robert told me I would need to obtain a chicken for the meal. None of the Liberian or Lebanese stores in town sold fresh meat, so I asked him where I could find a chicken.

He pointed to the surrounding huts and said, "There!" He said Mrs. Witherspoon across the road had five chickens, Mrs. Jefferson had three, Mrs. Washington had four, et cetera, as he pointed around at all our neighbors. Of course we had seen chickens in the yards of all our neighbors and would occasionally be given the gift of an egg or two, but we would never think to swipe one of their chickens for our evening meal. Robert didn't seem to understand our concern. We told him we would gladly pay for a chicken, to which he laughed, "Oh—then no problem, M'Nancy!"

After school, I paid a visit to Mrs. Witherspoon and her five chickens. I asked her if she would be willing to sell one of her chickens to me. She asked me which one I wanted, and I pointed to the largest, plumpest looking one. With much dramatic emphasis, she told me she could never sell that one because it was her best laying hen.

"Of course," I sympathized, "I wouldn't think of taking that one."

The next one I pointed out was *much too young*. The third was older but *still laid eggs once in a while*. The fourth was *the only rooster*—

"No way, M'Nancy!"

The final choice didn't look like it had an ounce of meat on it, had been pecked by the others until most of its feathers were missing, but she assured me it could run like the wind. I couldn't help noticing how muscular (and probably sinewy) it was.

"*That* chicken," beamed Mrs. Witherspoon, "make the best chop," She congratulated me on my choice.

When I asked her how much, she countered with, "Fah dollar!"

It was the definitive statement that told me the process of palavering had begun.

Liberians enjoy a good palaver more than anything—second only to laughter. I think the reason it is second only to laughter is because a good palaver session is always followed by a good hearty laugh on both sides.

The process goes something like this. After she quotes her initial price, I react with a highly dramatic feigned "heart attack" and profound amazement that she could ask such an exorbitant price for such a worthless piece of goods.

Then she demands to know why it is so worthless, after which I elaborately list all of the worthless qualities of the item: Her legs are too skinny, and she's missing two claws. Her feathers have all but been plucked out, and her skin shows through. She is obviously skin and bones, and she looks like she's ready to die any minute. She looks sick—probably is sick—is unfit to eat, and we'd probably have to throw her away anyway.

When she is satisfied with the list, she interrupts, "Okay, okay! How much you want to pay?"

I counter with a definitive, ridiculously low offer of twenty-five cents.

The scream and "heart attack" reaction on her part is followed by a list of the chicken's *good* qualities: She survived *two* rainy seasons. No dog could ever catch her—she runs too fast. Her remaining feathers are healthy and a beautiful color! Skinny chickens always taste the best—all meat—no fat!

Then it's my turn again. "Okay! Fifty cents!"

This second monetary offer is her cue to change tactics.

"Oh, M'Nancy! I have five children to feed. I need to buy rice. You muh please help me to buy mah rice!"

This is where I always give in.

We finally settle on a price of two dollars, which I know is a very healthy sum for a chicken. When I hand her the money, she slaps my hand with great flare, and we both laugh uproariously at the deal she has put over on me. It is well worth it.

After the chicken palaver is complete, it is quite another thing to round up my purchase. I know I have to maintain an impersonal detachment to my chicken, or I'll never be able to have it killed. It is difficult enough having palavered over the chicken—doing so has already made it somewhat personal.

While I stand there looking at the chicken, Mrs. Witherspoon stands there fingering her two dollars. She isn't going anywhere, and I know she is waiting for the second act where I will be the performer and she the audience. (If I paused and thought it through, I might come to my senses long enough to know I should let Robert catch the chicken or ask her if she would mind catching it.) But pride is a funny thing, and, anyway, I want to have the experience of catching my first chicken.

I take a few tentative steps in the direction of the chicken. The chicken takes just as many tentative steps away from me. Oh boy, this is not going to be that easy. Mrs. Witherspoon is smiling. It's too late now. The worst thing that can happen is that I will make a fool of myself, and I've already done that enough times to know the payoff will be in laughter, and what more could a natural performer ask for than a captive audience?

I wonder where the rest of my neighbors are—they usually show up at times like these. No doubt they will be here shortly.

Suddenly, I am determined to catch that scrawny little beastie. I give a good fast dash toward the chicken, which lets out a gravelly squawk and is gone. I don't know how those other chickens know which one of them I am after because they keep right on pecking the ground—they never move an inch.

Then I try the fake-food-in-the-hand–"Here, Chickie, Chickie" technique. She is curious enough to come within range, but when I reach for her, she escapes like a fox in the woods. I try this technique at least a dozen times before I give up.

During this procedure, two or three other neighbors show up, greet me cheerily, and then stay to "chat" with Mrs. Witherspoon. Nobody offers to help me—it is too good a show.

I'd have to say right now that I love slapstick comedy. I can't imagine anything funnier than a middle-class white girl, wearing an above-the-knee tent dress and sandals, with a short bouffant hairdo, trying to catch a scrawny, pathetic looking runaway chicken.

I chase that chicken from one end of the yard to the other, around the hut, through the hut, tripping, falling, and getting up. My tent dress clings to me, my hair is wet and limp, and my legs, arms, and face are covered with red dirt patterned with dripping sweat—but I never *once* lay a hand on that chicken!

Finally, exhausted, I sit on the ground and laugh with my neighbors. Then I say, "Okay, Mrs. Witherspoon, *you* catch it!"

She replies, "No mi'ya, M'Nancy," (translation: "Sure, no problem"), and with one swift movement, she scoops up that chicken, feathers flying, and plops it in my arms.

I am dumbfounded, say thank you, and start to walk away. After a few steps, I realize I don't have anywhere to keep the damn thing, and I am not about to keep it in my house. Although chickens run free, they seem to know the boundaries of their own yard, and I am certain that my chicken will not remain in my unfamiliar yard.

I turn and ask her if I can leave the chicken in her yard until Robert comes. "Sure, M'Nancy, no mi'ya!"

I let the chicken go, thank her, and calmly walk back across the road.

It wasn't over yet. Yes, we'd all had our laugh, and I had given them another great story to tell, but I knew, with smug satisfaction, that chicken would be in the pot by nightfall.

An hour later Robert came to cook dinner. He went across the road, grabbed the chicken on the first try, and was back in a flash. I didn't tell him of my afternoon adventure. Then he took a handful of rice and fed the chicken. I couldn't believe that Robert thought the rice would fatten the chicken up in the short time she had left before her demise, so I asked him why he was feeding the chicken at this final hour.

He chuckled through his wide, toothy grin, like he was holding some magic secret. "You will see, M'Nancy, you will see."

I also knew he wasn't feeding the chicken out of some altruistic motive. When it came to animals, the Liberian people were not prone to acts of kindness. It was a common sight to see dogs and cats being kicked or beaten. I often wondered why animals would stick around someone who didn't feed them and who physically hurt them, unless it was their nearest proximity to garbage. The justification Robert gave for why they don't feed their domestic dogs and cats was "If you feed them, they will steal. Just watch them—you see—they steal."

"Maybe they steal because they're hungry," I countered, but I couldn't convince him that if an animal is well fed, it has no need to steal food.

After the chicken had eaten its fill, I waited for the next step. Robert asked me if I wanted to watch him wring the chicken's neck, but I told him I'd pass that one up and quickly turned heel and went inside. After the deed was done and the chicken had been plucked, Robert brought it inside to show me why he had given her the rice. With one quick slice, he opened up the chicken and carefully removed the stomach. Then he perforated the membrane, exposing the pocket of undigested rice. "See, M'Nancy, what do you think of that!" He slapped his knee and laughed at his amazing magic trick. I felt ill and the thought passed my mind that someday I'd become a vegetarian.

Next came the preparation of the palm butter. Palm nuts are about the size of large dates, bright orange with black tips, and are found growing in large clusters high up on palm nut trees. A palm butter dinner in Liberia is the equivalent of a Sunday roast beef dinner back home. Robert had instructed me to get plenty of good red hot peppers, too. He was satisfied with the dozen or so he saw on the counter next to the basket of palm nuts. I was tempted to tell him to go easy on the peppers tonight, but I promised myself earlier that I was going to let Robert do the cooking without benefit of my input. I really wanted to enjoy this dinner in authentic Liberian style.

Robert put the palm nuts in a large pot, covered them with water, and turned on the stove. You had to boil the palm nuts a good long time to soften them up. While the palm nuts boiled, Robert rinsed and skimmed bugs off six cups of rice. I quickly calculated that six cups of raw rice would yield twelve cups cooked. There was only going to be the three of us for dinner. Then I realized, of course, that Liberians eat rice for breakfast, lunch, and dinner, so twelve cups might barely last one day. And of course, Robert would be happy to take the leftovers for tomorrow. With the rice and palm nuts boiling away, the kitchen became extremely steamy and hot. It didn't bother Robert in the least— he refused a fan, stripped to his shorts and happily continued cooking. I wanted to watch everything he did, but I could only tolerate five minutes at a time, so I kept running back and forth from the kitchen to the chair in front of the living room fan.

When the palm nuts were soft enough, Robert drained off the water and set them aside to cool. Then he cut up the chicken and put it in a pot of water to boil until the meat fell off the bone. Then he got out the fixings for making corn bread. This he whipped together in about three minutes (not counting the time it took to strain the weevils out of the corn flour) and popped it into the oven.

So we were having rice, corn bread, chicken, and palm butter for dinner. I mentally scanned my list of the basic food groups and realized we were a little short in the fruits and vegetables groups. I slotted the palm butter into the vegetable group (although I hadn't the slightest idea where it belonged) and wondered if I should slice up the fresh pineapple for our dessert. I remembered my vow of noninterference, so I decided to leave it whole, but I put it in plain sight on the table—just in case. Dairy was always a problem, but we did have a little mixed powdered milk in the refrigerator. You couldn't stock up on too much powdered milk all at once because, no matter how you stored it— open or not—it would always sport those little worms that were the same color as the powder. They were small enough to slip through the strainer, so you had to spread the powdered milk out on a layer of waxed paper and let your fingers do the sifting. It's still a mystery how bugs and worms just show up in sealed goods. Even in America I sometimes find little black bugs in freshly opened cereal if the box has been sitting around a while. I refuse to entertain the idea that the eggs were already in there waiting to hatch.

Once cool, the skin of the palm nuts can be caressed off (similar to the way a tomato skin can be rubbed off after a tomato is set in boiling water for about a minute). The pulp is pulled open and the pit removed, and then the pulp is ready to be mashed and pressed until it resembles the color and texture of straw. When the mixture is pressed through a strainer and the pulp is removed, what's left is a dark, mustard-colored potage about the consistency of soft butter. Thus the derivative, "palm butter." Then the mixture is put back into the pot with whole red peppers and simmered for about forty minutes. I knew the palm butter would be on the hot side, but I didn't how hot. Robert had put in all twelve peppers!

Peppers are the one crop everybody grows. In Liberia, you could never have too many peppers. The pepper was a staple in many ways. In food, of course, it was used as the primary seasoning. With a few exceptions such as fruit and farina, the pepper was used liberally in everything.

Years later, when I became a vegetarian (yes, I really did) and was deeply involved in spiritual and holistic practices, I read in countless books about the therapeutic uses and properties of red pepper. It is good for digestion; it's good for colon cleansing; it's good for circulation; it burns fat, so it helps you keep your weight down—the list goes on. Incidentally, none of the books expressed a common concern that hot peppers create stomach ulcers. In my study of herbs and herbal remedies, cayenne pepper is a standard remedy for sinusitis. You grind it up powder-fine and inhale it. Since my Achilles heel is sinus problems,

I tried it a few times, but the reaction was so extreme and unpleasant, I stopped doing it—but it did unclog my sinuses.

Anyway, the Liberians already knew all about the properties of red pepper and used it for practically everything. They ingested enough of it daily to kill off any living organism, they inhaled it for colds and stuffiness, they used it as an enema (I was appalled), and they rubbed it in open wounds and sores. Pharmaceutical remedies were impractical or not available, and the pepper did manage to keep wounds clean of parasites, but that's another story.

While the palm butter made love with the peppers, the rice boiled to twice its size, and the corn bread baked along, I set the table in the living room. The cooking odors were making my mouth water.

As Robert took the bread from the oven, turned off the rice, and added the chicken to the palm butter, he yelled, "Chop be ready in fah minute, M'Nancy!" I put on a clean tent dress and filled the glasses with fresh, cold, filtered water. Robert cut the corn bread, placed the entire twelve cups of rice in an enormous bowl, ladled the thick palm butter into another bowl, and we were ready to sit down to the table.

Then he did something that baffled me. He took a sweatshirt out of his bag and put it on. On top of the usual heat and humidity, the baking and boiling had raised the temperature in the house at least another five degrees. He was shiny with sweat, and here he was putting on a fleecy sweatshirt! I simply didn't know what to say. This time I'd keep my mouth shut and my eyes open. Dale had been licking his chops for an hour and, true to form, had easily endured the kitchen temperatures the entire time, but even he was baffled at Robert's behavior.

Robert piled his plate with more rice than I'd ever seen on one dinner plate before. He scooped two or three large ladles of palm butter on it, carefully topped it with three plump red peppers, then rubbed his hands together and smiled at us. Dale followed Robert's lead and piled his plate full. I took two small spoonfuls of rice and a polite amount of palm butter, being careful not to scoop any peppers onto my plate.

Robert took a heaping spoonful and slid it into his mouth. He was pleased with his creation, saying it was the best chop he had ever tasted, and took another heaping bite. Dale took a healthy spoonful, chewed quickly and swallowed, "Um, very good." His eyes shone wet as he drank some water and took a square of corn bread.

Just then a strong childhood memory surfaced. When I was growing up, I wanted to be just like Dad. He was my hero. Everybody said I looked like him, and I secretly believed that I was his favorite of the three of us girls. He even told me that once, but after he passed away and I shared that with Mom, she said, "Nancy, I think he told that to all of you," but I never believed her—I still think I was his favorite.

One of my dad's favorite dishes was fried, breaded oysters—raw oysters, dipped in raw egg, rolled in crushed saltines and fried in Crisco. I desperately wanted to please my dad, so I pretended for years that it was also my favorite dish. We were the only two in our family who ate them, and it quickly became a special event.

At nine years of age, I smiled and ate oyster after oyster and asked for more. Sometimes I could barely choke them down. Occasionally he would glance at me sideways and say, "You don't really like these, do you?"

To which I always replied, "I do too," and asked for more.

As I sat in anticipation of taking my first bite of palm butter, I told myself I didn't have to please anybody—it was okay not to like it. Actually, I couldn't have hidden my reaction if I'd wanted to. I took a small bite—certainly enough to get a good taste. Almost immediately my mouth was on fire. I gasped in air, chewed quickly, and swallowed, and my throat caught on fire. I swear I could feel the fire all the way down my esophagus and into my stomach, but I knew that was ridiculous. I thought my flair for drama had finally gotten the better of me, so I inhaled a few more times and reached for the water. It was then I learned that the fire from peppers is not alleviated by water. After the initial swallow, the fire seemed to grow in intensity. Robert handed me some corn bread and instructed me to eat it immediately. He seemed genuinely concerned at my involuntary distress—he had really wanted me to enjoy his perfect Liberian dinner. Our intentions were in alignment because after a few swallows of bread I was ready for another taste.

The second spoonful wasn't such a shock. I took plain rice and just the tiniest amount of palm butter. Though it was still fiery, I could actually taste the flavor this time. It was delicious. There's really no way to describe it. I suppose the nearest equivalent, in my experience, is a buttery spaghetti sauce, sans the tartness of the tomato, but the taste is really unique unto itself. It ultimately became one of our favorite dishes, though I would always make a slightly milder version for myself, and when we returned to the States, we managed to smuggle a couple of jars in our satchels.

When I moved to New York and realized the truth of the familiar saying, "You can find anything in New York if you look hard enough," I began my endless search for palm nuts. I guess the exception proves the rule because, in the thirty-two years I lived in New York, I never found any.

Robert was relieved that I had found a way to eat the chop so he began to chow down in earnest. Watching him and Dale eat was awe-inspiring. Robert savored every large juicy mouthful, frequently groaning with pleasure. In between my small courageous mouthfuls, I noticed his forehead starting to drip. He occasionally wiped it with the sleeve of his sweatshirt and continued to enjoy his burning feast. Every so often he would meet my amazed gaze and smile, his large, perfect white teeth gleaming against his black skin. I enjoyed watching him as much as I enjoyed the taste of the palm butter.

Finally, at one point, he let out a "Whew!" like he'd just run the marathon in hundred-degree weather, and I could stand it no longer. "Robert," I said, "why on earth don't you take off your sweatshirt?"

"Oh, M'Nancy," he laughed, "the hot is the best part—to see if you can take the peppers in your body." So I deduced this was some sort of challenge to Robert, which, on reflection, fit his personality perfectly.

On the other hand, Dale was suffering. His steely smile was a dead giveaway. He was not enjoying his predicament, but he would never admit defeat. To him, this was not so much a challenge, but a test, and probably, I surmised, had a great deal to do with competition and self-esteem.

Dale was not a quitter, which is one of the many qualities I admired about him. One time in high school he was asked to be the piano soloist with the community orchestra. He spent months practicing daily under self-imposed hardship conditions. He sat at the piano dressed in two sets of long johns, a woolen hat and muffler, warm insulated boots, and the heat turned up, practicing for hours. He must have been in agony but never complained. On the day of the performance, he wore only a tuxedo, light socks, and shoes—no underwear. Under the hot, glaring stage lights, he performed the entire Gershwin's *Rhapsody in Blue*, flawlessly, from beginning to end, as calm and cool as an Alaskan spring day.

I watched the two of them, in awe, as they consumed nearly three-quarters of the rice and palm butter with tears streaming down their faces. My pineapple, ripe to perfection, hit the spot for me. After that Robert often cooked his Liberian specialties for us but he was careful not to put too many peppers in my share.

CHAPTER 29

Country Wife

Dale was a regular churchgoer growing up and missed it when we stopped cold turkey after we got married. I was always drawn to the idea of going to church. My paternal grandmother took my sisters and me to her Catholic Church when we stayed over, but I found it too inflexible, and it scared me to be told I was such a sinner. As we walked down the long aisle to our pew in front, a bleeding Jesus stared down at me from his place on the enormous wooden cross. The nails through his hands and feet made me slightly sick.

My grandmother was the epitome of a good Catholic convert—full of righteousness and judgment. One damning word from her could make my blood run cold. She seemed to know if you were even thinking sinful thoughts. She always lit a candle for my father to be let out of the purgatory she knew he'd end up in and saw it as her Catholic duty to take us to church whenever she could. If she couldn't save my father, maybe she could save us. My father was the only one of her three children to marry outside the faith, and this was a thorn in her side till the day she died. My mother was the one who encouraged a reluctant son to visit his mother, remembered her birthday, planned holidays to include the grandparents, took care of them when they were ill, and brought us kids to visit with great frequency. But Mom wouldn't convert, and that was the one unforgivable sin Grandma couldn't overlook.

I went to a few Protestant Sunday schools from time to time, but they never lasted long, and I was never comfortable with the dogma, though I enjoyed coloring pictures in the Sunday school booklets and getting stars on my homework. Once, the teacher said she would give a new Bible to every child who memorized the Ten Commandments. I was absent the following week because of a headache (I had forgotten to study my Ten Commandments).

The following week the teacher forgot I was absent, so when she passed out the Bibles, I got one anyway. I took the Bible and felt guilty for the sin of omission, but my fear of ridicule was stronger than my fear of lying, so I kept my mouth shut. My thought was to memorize the Ten Commandments when I got home. But when I got home, everyone made such a fuss about how I'd earned a new Bible I forgot about my promise to myself. By the end of the day I think I'd convinced myself I really had memorized the Ten Commandments in earnest (I still don't know them).

My maternal grandmother had converted from being a Lutheran to being a Jehovah's Witness. Dad forbade her to talk about her religion with us, but that's like telling a bee not to buzz. Being a witness to the words of Jehovah—sharing the words and the message—was her church's platform. This created a real dilemma for Dad. Having a Lutheran mother-in-law was bad enough, but having a Jehovah's Witness was the worst of all possible scenarios. Dad considered it a religion of the lower classes—the downtrodden—the poor, who hid behind the teachings of Revelation to excuse their condition. My Jehovah's Witness grandma preached against the sin of arrogance and the worship of pagan gods. And what could be more pagan than Catholic idolatry with its Christmas, Easter, gift giving, worshipping Jesus on the cross, and even that Pope—who does he think he is anyway?

Once, when my maternal Grandma stayed with us for a whole week while my parents went on vacation, Dad made it clear we weren't to believe anything Grandma said about religion. This was a tough one because I loved my grandma dearly, and she was the only one in my family who seemed to really understand my creative soul. So I listened to everything she said with an open heart, but after a week I could no more believe in her religious dogma than anyone else's. They all sounded the same to me. My last try at organized religion was when I tried to become a Lutheran to please Dale.

Reverend Carpenter was always inviting us to come to his church on Sunday. Dale almost always went, and I almost always didn't, but this didn't seem to upset the Carpenters. I was forever welcome in their home and was a real favorite with the girls.

One particular Saturday the reverend made a special plea for both of us to come to church the next day because something profoundly special was going to take place. A bright young Liberian man, who had recently become a Christian, was discovered to have two wives. The reverend convinced the man that he must give up his country wife. The man had gone through serious turmoil—torn between his Christian beliefs and his country juju beliefs.

The reverend had been standing by him, in friendship, to help him see his confusion and the error of his ways. Finally, the man had agreed to give up not only his country wife, but his juju objects (fetishes) as well. This was the Sunday that, in front of a congregation of witnesses, the man was giving his wife back to her father. Even I couldn't stay away from this one.

The singing had just begun when we arrived at the church and took a seat in the front row. Liberians have an innate ability to harmonize with each other. They play their voices like musical instruments in an orchestra, creating dissonant sound vibrations I've never heard from the human voice before—all on perfect pitch. You didn't just listen to the singing—you experienced it in every fiber of your body. There was no sleeping in this church.

The reverend began his sermon on the subject of serving two masters. Soon he was on an impassioned roll, telling the story of the young man and his struggle with his marriage to two wives. He reached a fever pitch when he spoke of the young man seeing the light and Jesus coming into his heart to raise him from the sin of bigamy. He ended softly with tears in his eyes, thanking Jesus for saving us poor sinners and being grateful that it's never too late to repent.

Then he raised his hands for silence. A hush fell over the congregation, and the reverend called the young man to the front. Then he called the young country wife and her father to the front. I gasped audibly—she was a good eight months pregnant! As the reverend preached on about God's will and right decisions, my eyes were riveted on the young girl's face—sad and serious—as someone translated the reverend's words into her native language. When the young man took her hands and gave her back to her father, she looked at the ground, almost like she was ashamed. I had to bite my tongue to keep from crying.

At lunch with the Carpenters I couldn't help asking the question, "Why didn't he give up the Christian wife who wasn't pregnant?" But the reverend seemed puzzled by my question, and I realized, at that moment, that was just the way things were.

CHAPTER **30**

Bush Hike

The next Sunday the reverend was set to go on a bush hike. One of his Liberian protégés had a church in a small village about a day's walk from Greenville. He invited us to go along. There would be six of us: John Mark, Dale, two Liberian men to carry supplies, one Liberian man to cut bush, and me. I was relieved to hear that Liberian guides were accompanying us. Each would carry a machete and could save us from the many dangers that lurk in the bush.

Every Liberian past the age of two knows how to use a machete. You can get them at any market, cheap as dirt. They are kept razor sharp and are used for everything from cooking to weed whacking. I watched Robert chop chickens, whack open coconuts, and deftly blaze the bark off a cassava root. He taught me how to use it, and it eventually became the most valuable implement in my kitchen. Even so, when I saw it hanging there, I would occasionally flash back to the meat cleavers used in all the horror movies I saw as a teenager.

One day around dusk, I was strolling back from the Carpenters' house when I saw a huge stick in the middle of the road. As I got closer, I realized it was a large cassava root—about three feet long and a good eight inches in diameter. Obviously, someone had dropped it off the load on her head, but it wasn't like any Liberian to leave food lying around. A couple of my neighbors were walking a few feet behind me, so as I approached the cassava root, I turned and pointed it out to them. They shouted and ran to me, one of them pushing me aside and the other one screaming, "Snake! Snake!" In less than an instant, three men came running from their huts waving machetes and converged on the snake, chopping its head off in one swift blow.

It took two men to hold the stick that lifted up the limp body of the headless cassava snake. When my breathing returned to normal, I remembered from reading in the Peace Corps manual that the cassava

159

snake is one of the most deadly and dangerous of all the snakes in Liberia. Because it moves so slowly, it is not able to get out of the way and will strike first. Its bite is fatal within minutes. I got weak in the knees and started to tremble. I thanked my neighbors for saving my life, and they offered me the gift of the dead snake. I politely refused. As my saviors walked me home, eager to share the story with my husband, I thought: *Another great use for the machete.*

Slightly before dawn, Dale and I met the reverend at his place. The early morning breeze held the promise of a pleasant beginning. We could get in a good four hours of hiking before the moisture would saturate the air in the sun's scorching heat. I didn't have to look at a thermometer—I knew it was eighty-five degrees, but somehow it felt cooler this morning. The reverend said it was coming on to rainy season, which may have accounted for the cooler feeling in the air, and he wanted to get this hike in before the season started.

The young man we were going to see had trained with the reverend before going back to his bush village to preach the word and teach English. No white people had ever been to his village, and only a few of the villagers had ever even seen a white man. There was no reason for them to travel to Greenville, and there was far too much to do at home to think about satisfying a curiosity. It probably never even occurred to most of them to be curious about white people.

"His story is very interesting," said the reverend. "Johnson was born in the village and lived there until he was ten, when he left to seek his fortune. He ended up on the streets of Monrovia. An American missionary traveling in Liberia found him and brought him to the American embassy. He was cute and charming, and they took him in. He worked at the embassy school, and they let him sit in on classes there. He was a fast study and learned English in a matter of months. Took to it like a duck to water."

I asked how Johnson got his name. "When he was studying at the embassy school, he became fascinated with memorizing the names of American presidents. Shortly thereafter, he changed his name to Andrew Johnson. The Americans couldn't pronounce his tribal name anyway, so they willingly called him by his new name. He wanted to be called by his full name—Andrew Johnson—but Americans kept shortening it to Andrew. Finally, he agreed to be called by only one name, but he insisted the name be Johnson."

Before Johnson reached the age of eighteen, he was working for the Liberian government as a tax collector. His job was to go into the hinterland villages and collect the mandatory five-dollar hut tax. About the only time a village saw a stranger from Monrovia was when the tax collector came around.

Each person who owned a hut had to pay the government five dollars a year. There was no benefit to the hut owner as far as I could see. Nobody came to fix a road, nobody came to maintain a water supply, nobody came bearing promises of better living conditions. About the only use I could see for the government extracting money was to provide its America-Liberian government officials with a better standard of living. How on earth they were able to collect it is beyond me. Most of the villagers didn't even use government issue money. Their mode of exchange for goods was long, twisted pieces of iron country money that they carried in an unwieldy bunch tied with a rope and hanging from their waist. An entire bundle of country money wouldn't be worth fifty cents but could sustain a bush family for a long time. If the tax collector collected ten bundles for each hut, he'd need a truck to carry it all back to Monrovia.

The steady whacking sound of the machetes cutting bush became a kind of metronome against the monotony of the burning heat. Within an hour of starting out, we were drenched in our own perspiration, and by the time the sun burned through, we felt like we were swimming in syrup. Sweatbands made of country cloth were frequently removed and squeezed out, and I had long ago stopped pulling at my tent dress to keep it from clinging. My padded bra adhered to me like two suction cups, and although I was miserably hot and my real bra size was 32AA, I refused to give up the padding. My culture's standard of beauty for women included full breasts, and I wasn't about to be out of fashion, even in tropical Africa. (In 1970, when I moved to New York City, the women's movement was in full swing, and it was the fashion to wear see-through tops without a bra, so I courageously disposed of all my bras. That experience of freedom was the first of many that opened a crack to let a ray of light shine through my little prison windows. But that freedom was still seven years down the road, and I was oblivious to such a thought as I trudged along in the bush that day.)

My JCPenney hiking boots were cutting into my ankles—even with heavy socks—so I was relieved when the reverend called for a break. I loosened my laces, and one of our Liberian guides made a poultice out of leaves and mud and applied it to my ankles. I had brought sandals, but wearing them in the bush was not an option. Only our guides wore open-toed shoes in the wild. The machete cleared away much of the tangled foliage but was not subtle enough to handle the many crawlies that rested beneath it. Africa is teeming with an endless variety of bug life so adapted to its environment as to be invisible to the most discerning eye.

Going to the bathroom was even trickier, and I had visions of invisible snakes leaping up and biting me on my exposed derriere, but our guides were kind enough to scout out sites for me. They assured me they were snake-free but said to keep an eye out for sneaky spiders. Needless to say, I didn't spend any more time squatting than absolutely necessary.

After two more hours and another rest stop we came to our first village—a dusty clearing in the midst of heavy jungle. As we walked into the open, wide-eyed children and curious adults poured from their huts, crowding around us and talking excitedly. The guides, speaking in their native tongue, explained who we were and where we were going.

There was no refusing their hospitality for the night—the only problem was who would be the lucky hosts. They debated the problem for a good thirty minutes, and the agitation of the participants was exceeded only by the winner's elation. It was decided that they would split us up and spread the wealth, but Dale and I insisted on being together. Finally, we were taken on a tour of the huts and allowed to choose our accommodations, but there was really no decision—we would stay in the chief's house—the largest and most elegant hut in the village.

It had three rather spacious rooms, a tin roof, and a dirt floor. The chief and his first wife would stay in one room, the reverend in another, and Dale and I in the third. What luck! This was going to be fun. Our room had a bed slightly wider than a twin but shorter in length and a grass mat resting on the floor next to it. By the village standards, it was the Plaza. I was delighted. A private bedroom! We dropped our duffels on the floor. I heard a dry crunching sound as I sat on the bed and felt the hard wooden frame against my buttocks. The mattress was a sort of giant pillowcase stuffed with dry grass.

In those days, I could sleep anywhere if I was tired enough—and I was certainly tired enough—but it wouldn't be dark for another two hours, and I wanted to explore the village in the daylight, so I wiped the sweat off my body and put on a clean dress. My bra clung to me and was wet on the inside but still dry outside, so I didn't bother to change it: a fresh one would be wet in two minutes anyway. My small hand mirror revealed that my short hair was still teased and sprayed nicely on top, though a little sweaty around the edges. A fresh dose of deodorant, a little lipstick, and I was ready to go.

When I emerged from the hut, I noticed a large circle of men sitting on country stools with Dale and the reverend among them and one empty stool for me. In the split second I stood there looking around at the circle of men waiting patiently for me, I understood the concept of power. I had a feeling that was strangely familiar but that I couldn't quite put my finger on.

Then it hit me. As far back as I could remember, my father was always waiting for my mother. The cries of "Connie! Aren't you ready yet?" rang through the house. Then, more agitated: "Connie! Come on! Get the lead out! Let's get a move on, we're going to be late!" But all that followed was Mom's deafening silence or quiet humming.

Dad was the aggressor—the one with the obvious power—the ruler—the patriarch. Mom was the receptor, the nurturer, the passive one in the relationship. Dad could be verbally caustic and often used cruel sarcasm, but he was never physically abusive, and they had an agreement never to argue in front of the children. I think it was more difficult for Dad to keep that agreement, and I now think that many times his anger was redirected at my older sister and me. He was the one who gave us the spankings that Mom said we deserved.

Mom shouted at us far more than Dad, but his outbursts were scarier because I always felt the potential of physical punishment, and sometimes the spankings were severe. The occasional swat from Mom merely hurt our pride; yelling at us was her primary way of trying to maintain control.

The mystery of it was that my parents almost never yelled at each other. I perceived my mother as the submissive one and Dad as the powerful one because of their differences in style. But now, as I walked slowly toward my stool, I felt the power my mother must have felt by making Dad wait for her, and I understood the meaning of what I later would come to identify as passive-aggressive behavior.

I took my place in the circle. I felt conspicuously female. There wasn't another woman in sight. Whatever was going to take place was clearly an event of great importance and honor, and all such events naturally excluded women. I didn't fit into the Liberian definition of a woman because I was a foreigner and Peace Corps.

In America, the subtle (or not so subtle) exclusion of women was so integrated into my upbringing that I'd never even noticed it. But here I saw everything with fresh eyes, and once you see, you can never go back.

The timing was perfect. It was one of the most volatile and awakening times in American history. It was the beginning of the women's movement, the Kennedy brothers had begun their ascent to power and were being systematically killed off, followed by the assassination of Dr. Martin Luther King Jr., and the Vietnam war was in full swing. The Peace Corps was in its infancy, and I was also an infant on my own journey of self-discovery that was slowly easing the pressure of my conservative upbringing.

The ceremony was about to begin. The chief untied the string on a small cloth pouch, revealing a handful of nuts that looked like palm nuts, only pink. I glanced at the reverend for an explanation. "They're kola nuts—they're unbearably bitter—and they're a narcotic, so don't take much—just a little bite. It's an honor. They'll be offended if you refuse."

"What will it do?" I asked.

The reverend chuckled. "It's not like you'll go berserk or anything, but you might feel a little euphoric. It's not a bad feeling."

The wide use of drugs as recreation was just beginning in the United States, but Anchorage, Alaska was about five years behind the times.

The most I'd ever done in college was smoke cigarettes. I wouldn't be introduced to marijuana until I moved to New York and began my acting career in 1972, and I wouldn't try cocaine until 1978 when I did a show in Los Angeles, and the whole cast was floating around on it. Fortunately, experimentation with these drugs was cursory because I didn't like the odd feelings of being out of control.

I was nervous as I watched each person take a large bite of the kola nut. You weren't supposed to grimace at its sour taste. The reverend showed no facial reaction, and Dale was as stoic as ever. When it came to me, I took the smallest bite I could without refusing altogether, and my tongue shriveled up so fast that my eyes closed and my head shook involuntarily. I looked around for disapproving glances, but I saw only the gap-toothed grin of one of the older men. I grinned back, and he slapped his knee and laughed soundlessly.

Nobody spoke for a long time. I was waiting for the euphoria to kick in and was vaguely disappointed when nothing happened. I asked Dale if he felt anything, and he said, "No, do you?" I looked around, and it did seem that the colors were more vibrant—they seemed almost translucent, like thick liquid, but it could have just been the power of suggestion and my willingness to be susceptible, because Dale said he doubted I'd had enough of the kola nut to feel anything. He may have been right, but after decades of living with my reactions to all manner of stimuli, I realize that everybody is different, and I could very well have had a reaction to the stimulant in the nut.

After the circle broke, the children seemed to come out of nowhere, crowding around me and touching my hands and arms. They were fascinated by my golden-blond hair and begged to touch it. At first they were tentative, touching and pulling back, exploring the texture and rubbing the strands between their fingers. As they got bolder, they began stroking my entire head until the teasing fell away, and I was left with my hair hanging limply around my face. After a few moments I didn't care because they were giggling and having so much fun, but when they wanted to cut pieces of it as souvenirs, it stopped being fun.

The reverend came to my rescue with firm admonishing words, which, if they didn't understand his meaning, couldn't possibly be mistaken in their tone. I understood the children's curiosity because I had never touched the hair of a black person. I assumed, because it was closely napped to the head and tightly curled or elaborately plaited, that it would feel coarse and wiry. But one day for an art lesson, I was making papier-mâché puppets with my students and asked for volunteers to donate some hair. I cut a little bit of hair from several kids and was surprised to feel how cushiony it felt—not wiry at all, but soft and furry. And I thought: *Another stereotype shattered.*

Our host killed a chicken in our honor, and we had a sumptuous dinner of rice, chicken, palm butter, collard greens, fried plantains, and fresh oranges. For dessert, the children offered us great hunks of sugar cane. Their stained teeth revealed their fondness for this treat and predicted their eventual tooth loss. There was no way to sterilize the canes, and the children had been handling them lovingly with unwashed hands, so I kindly refused the treat, saying I was on a diet. They laughed heartily at the strange concept of a diet. Dale, however, decided to try it and said it tasted great. We would be back in Greenville by the time his runny tummy hit.

When it was dark and all the dishes were washed and dirt floors swept, Dale and I took our flashlight and found a bushy spot on the edge of the village to relieve ourselves. I hoped I wouldn't have to get up in the middle of the night. When we returned to the hut, we noticed someone had placed a large covered soup tureen on the floor beside our bed. It was made of white porcelain and decorated with little pink flowers. It looked like the bone china cups my mother collected. I was intrigued. I thought perhaps it was a gift. I lifted it carefully and, before I placed it on the stool beside the bed, I looked at the bottom and read: "Bone China. England." It was heavy and bulky and, if it was a gift, I didn't see how we'd manage to carry it back. And how on earth did they get it? I wouldn't disturb anyone tonight—the mystery would be solved in the morning.

Dale stayed awake for a while and read by flashlight, while I fell asleep immediately and slept soundly until the middle of the night when I was awakened by a scratching sound somewhere in the room. I lay frozen in the pitch black, trying to figure out where the sound was coming from. It seemed to be all around me. I imagined all sorts of crawlies running across the floor, and childhood thoughts of alligators under the bed made me curl into a ball, making sure my hands and feet were as far away from the edge of the bed as possible. It was impossible to go back to sleep—and where had Dale left the flashlight?

My common sense told me he left it on the only piece of furniture in the room. I reached over to the small stool and felt the soup tureen. Continuing my blind search, I grasped the flashlight and turned it on. Shining the beam along the floor revealed nothing but packed dirt. I moved the light up the wall, scouring every inch of the packed mud and stick. The noise continued, so whatever was making the sound was bold enough to be undaunted by the light. Africa was teeming with exotic animals, and I couldn't imagine what manner of creature was sharing our space. Even my childhood fantasies didn't encompass this one.

My light traveled along the crooked edge of the ceiling and landed on one of the small tree-trunk beams. There, unmistakably, were two shiny red eyes staring back at me. I gasped soundlessly and clutched Dale's arm. He woke up with a start. We followed the light beam, where two more eyes appeared. Braving the discovery, I moved the light across beam after beam, all of which had pairs of red eyes staring at us. After about a century I asked Dale what he thought they were. He said, "Rats." I shuddered, keeping the light glued to the eyes, as if the light, itself, was a shield. Soon, the creatures' curious stares turned to boredom and they began skittering along the round narrow beams, scratching their way back and forth. I watched as the enormous rats ran their races, hopping over each other to continue their journey. Dale didn't seem at all nervous—in fact, he chuckled in amusement.

"What's so funny?" I asked.

"Well, the reverend told me about the traveling rats before we came. I decided not to tell you because I thought you might sleep right through and not notice them. I didn't want you to lie awake all night." I had mixed feelings: on the one hand I was annoyed that he thought he had to keep something from me, like I was a child, and on the other hand, I did stay awake the rest of the night—watching little red eyes dart back and forth. I was afraid to go to sleep because I slept with my mouth open, and I couldn't bear the thought of a rat falling on my face.

In the not too distant past, Dale and I had visited a leper colony and had seen, firsthand, the results of rats nibbling on flesh. I had learned that rats were attracted by the smell of rotting flesh on the lepers, and because the lepers couldn't feel anything in the diseased parts of their flesh, the rats could nibble away throughout the night. They assured me that rats didn't eat living flesh of humans, but I wasn't taking any chances. By first light, my flashlight batteries were dead, and the rats had gone back to wherever they went in the daylight. Relieved, and strangely not the least bit tired, I woke Dale up to accompany me to the bushes.

When we returned, the reverend was up. He had brought out our store of coffee and was putting some into the boiling water. It smelled delicious, and I got a flashback memory of my paternal grandmother sucking fresh coffee through a sugar cube between her front teeth. My grandmother had false teeth. Then I thought of the children sucking on their sugar cane. The reverend poured us a cup of coffee and said, "Sugar?"

I said "No!" too quickly.

"Oh," he said. "The chief wants to know why you didn't use the chamber pot he put in your room."

"What's a chamber pot?" I asked.

"It's that beautiful porcelain bowl with the lid," he said. "You use it instead of going to the bushes."

"Oh!" I said, embarrassed. "It's so beautiful. But it seems out of place—I couldn't figure out what it was doing there. And where in the world did he get something like that?"

"The chief said he sent someone to Monrovia to fetch them when he heard the president was going to be coming through the village last year, and he only brings them out for very special guests."

Before we continued on our journey, I made sure I left my calling card in the chamber pot as a matter of courtesy. Actually, using that same chamber pot was as close as I ever got to meeting the president of Liberia.

We reached our destination village in only an hour and a half. I took off my boots and put on my sandals. My ankles were still hurting from the day before, so the guide applied another poultice, which made me feel like I had an ice pack strapped to my ankles. The cooling effect was immediate. We tried not to scratch mosquito bites, and I decided to take a long nap in the afternoon just in case we were visited once again by red-eyed rats during the night.

Our accommodations at Johnson's hut weren't quite so elegant as the night before—and no chamber pot. Our spare set of batteries was in the flashlight, and I knew I'd have to conserve them for our trips to the bushes. I thought once again how fortunate men are to have their plumbing on the outside and how much less cumbersome and infrequent are those trips to the bushes. Many Liberian men didn't even bother to go to the bushes; they just found a spot and turned their back. Modesty never seemed to be an issue. I never got used to passing the occasional man on the way to school, urinating by the side of the road. I would always avert my eyes, but they would wave with their free hand and shout, "G'mahnin', M'Nancy!" In all fairness, I have to say that I frequently saw Liberian women lifting their lappa skirts as well and squatting wherever.

After my midday nap, I wanted to go exploring. There wasn't much to explore, but the children were delighted to show me around. I was given a tour of every hut in the village and offered all manner of food, most of which I refused, seeing as how even cooked food can be contaminated from handling. After visiting the fifth hut, I felt my experience was being thwarted by my own fear. I had come to Liberia wanting to "live like the natives," and to be sure, that was naive thinking because, after a few bouts of diarrhea, I realized my body was in no way prepared to meet that challenge. So I'd begun to be scrupulously careful to the extent that I was isolating myself from the very experience I wanted to have. I decided to throw care to the winds and sample whatever I was offered and let my body do what it would. The only thing I didn't do was drink the water, but Club beer was plentiful, even in this little village, so I had a little party all my own.

I had a beer at every hut. While much of the beer sweated right out of me, and I had eaten a substantial amount of food, by the time I had finished "visiting," I was quite tipsy and trying desperately not to show it. I felt very friendly. I let the children touch my hair, and I even cut off pieces of it for them to keep. A heated debate began over the color of my skin. Yes, my legs are white, yes, my arms are white, but how about the rest of me?

Reassuring them was simply not enough. Their strong insistence convinced me to show them my stomach to prove, without a doubt, that I was white all over. I did this with such dramatic flair that they were falling on the ground with laughter, and so was I. Dale was watching in amazement, and once again that look of "Who is this person?" crossed his face, which was met with my usual reaction—more laughter.

The reverend had tears rolling down his cheeks, and finally so did Dale. The beer wore off, but the experience didn't, and when we left for Greenville the next day, the children begged us to come back and play with them. I learned a good lesson—everything in life involves some risk, and being too careful is just as unhealthy as not being careful enough.

The hike back home seemed to fly by. My ankles were still raw, but I had become anesthetized to the pain. The steady whacking of the machete and trampling boots on tropical earth, even the sweat rolling down my body, added to my feeling of strength. I hadn't exercised so much since the Peace Corps training, and it felt great—my body had reached a sort of threshold where I felt like I could walk forever.

After four hours we took a short break, but I kept moving because I didn't want to lose momentum. Dale kept encouraging me to sit but I assured him I was fine, and the reverend sided with me, saying he felt the same way and often did when he went bush hiking. It was a natural high, and I recognized it as the same feeling I'd had after dancing to the elephant tusk band in Fisebu. I was to experience this feeling countless times throughout my life—whenever I moved beyond what I thought were my limits— physically, psychologically, mentally, or spiritually.

CHAPTER 31

Big Boy

We arrived home shortly before dusk to the happy meows of Mac Cat at the Carpenters' front door. Betty and the girls were putting dinner on the table, and the aroma reminded us that we were famished. A quick washup and a change of clothes, and then we sat down to eat our fill. After dinner the stories began, and we laughed our way through the theatrical telling of the kola nuts, rats in the night, cutting pieces of my blond hair as souvenirs, the exposing of my white tummy, and the presidential chamber pot.

There was a brief silence, and then Betty said that something very sad had happened while we were away. Nan left the table and went to her room while Betty told the story. Just before dusk one evening, Nancy had put on a favorite record of Al Hirt's trumpet music. A group of children had been passing by and started dancing to it. Big Boy, Nan's chimp, was also fond of the music and, as was his usual behavior, had climbed to the top of his cage to join in the dancing. Big Boy was an energetic dancer and always stole the show with his comical antics.

As the music continued, more children showed up to dance and sing. Soon the focus shifted away from Big Boy to the twenty or so children and their acrobatic dancing. Shortly after dark, the children drifted home and Nan, Betty, and Kim sat to catch their breath. In the silence, Nan noticed that baby chimp Abigail was chattering, but there was no sound at all coming from Big Boy's cage. She thought that perhaps he had escaped again and she ran back to his cage calling his name. What she saw was a sight she would never forget.

There was her beloved Big Boy, hanging limply from the top of his cage, a rope noose wrapped tightly around his neck. Apparently, what had happened was that the rope had caught, somehow, on the cage grating, and when Big Boy was dancing, he had slipped, fallen off the cage, and hanged himself. Nan spoke of it only once, briefly, but still remembers it as one of the saddest times of her life.

CHAPTER 32

The Coming of the Rain

It felt marvelous to flop into our Peace Corps bed with its mass-produced, government-issue mattress. This was one of many times that I would give thanks for *not* having to "live like the natives." I closed my eyes at eight o'clock and didn't open them again until 6:00 a.m.

The next day was June 1. The first few months seemed to have gone by slowly, but now I realized we'd been in Liberia for six months. The air was heavy, and the sky was dark with clouds. It felt like rain. Living in Tacoma, Washington, where it rains probably 80 percent of the time, gave me plenty of experience to know what impending rain felt like. My clothes hung heavy. My hair spray lay on my hair like a layer of glue and was sticky to the touch. I remembered how free I felt when the bush children had mussed my hair until the stiffness was gone and it fluffed loosely around my face. I washed my hair, took my scissors, and trimmed it as short as I could without looking shaved. Then I let it air dry. I loved it. I didn't use hair spray again until I got back to the States and once again fell prey to fashion merchandising.

Walking to school was exhausting, and trying to teach lessons in the brick building with no electricity and inadequate materials was a harsh comedown. Mrs. Carter was in Monrovia, so half the teachers and students didn't bother to show up. I took my class back to the house and I read them two stories. Then they began to make up their own stories, so I taped them and played them back to whoops and hollers so loud you could hardly hear the recording.

After a short math lesson the sky began to darken, and everyone agreed that the rain was coming, so I shooed them home. I figured it would be hard enough for them to keep dry under their leaky thatched roofs, and I didn't want them to come home drenched to begin with. They reminded me it was the start of malaria season.

Dale came home as they were leaving and announced that school had been dismissed early due to the impending rain. During rainy season in June–July and again in October–November, it rained every day, at least in the afternoon. I wondered if school would always be a half-day during the season. That turned out to be pretty much true.

I felt like we were preparing to watch a performance. I made some fresh Turkish coffee and got out the saltines and Danish butter. Mac Cat stalked an enormous flying cockroach that had managed to surface briefly in the kitchen and then scurry back to safety behind the counters. I didn't try to spray it. I knew Mac could outwait it. Under Mac's watchful and patient eye, that cockroach would meet its maker, and Mac would have himself a crunchy, tasty treat.

A gentle breeze blew the curtains through the open window slats. I waved at Robert Isaac just down the road. At that moment, he sprinted toward our front door, the skies opened up, and sheets of rain poured from above, thundering onto the tin roof with deafening thumps. The parched earth sucked up the rain almost before it touched the ground. The curtains blew wildly as the huge drops found their way through the window and landed with loud splats on the tile floor. Mac meowed loudly and ran for cover under the wicker couch, and Dale and I dashed from room to room, closing windows. We left the front and back doors open to the screen, for a cross breeze. It didn't let up for three hours. The three of us sat and played Scrabble, Robert wearing Dale's dry clothes, which were too tight and much too long.

We palavered endlessly over words Robert tried to tell us were part of the English language, and when the palaver reached the point of no return, out would come our Peace Corps-issue Webster's Collegiate Dictionary to settle the dispute. Every time Robert was proven wrong, he would howl loudly, slap his knee, and shout, "How you know! How you know!" More than a few times we let him win the palaver without proving him wrong, and he would look at us incredulously, slap his knee and boast, "You see! You muh try to learn more English from Robert!"

Being the efficient and exacting teacher he was, Dale wrote down the "questionable" words, saying he planned to look them up later with Robert. He claimed he didn't want Robert to learn improper English. I convinced him that Robert knew perfectly well he had won under false pretenses, and we should let it go in the spirit of fun.

In our future games of Scrabble, Dale and I used Robert's made-up words to great protests by Robert. We reminded him of his use of those very words in the previous game, but that didn't faze him. He forced us to look up the words in the dictionary, and when they couldn't be found, we argued that the dictionary was abridged and couldn't possibly contain all the complex words in the English language. We even made up definitions for the fake words and began using them in our everyday speech. It became an unspoken understanding that the only made-up words we could use were the ones contained in that first game of Scrabble played during our first rainfall.

Whenever anyone else joined our games, our poker faces, detailed definitions, and adamant refusal to back down finally convinced them that our made-up words were, indeed, part of the English language. We had countless laughs over our practical joke and looked forward to any newcomers joining our game. Our circle of conspirators became larger and larger, and often we had two games going at once.

In all the times we played Scrabble, not once did anyone "in the know" spill the beans—before, during, or after our games. By the time Steve joined our little circle, the joke was so entrenched that he didn't have a chance. To his credit, he palavered long and hard, but no one budged, and he eventually gave in. I wonder if he ever figured out the joke; to this day, he may be trying to convince someone else of those same words.

The rain cooled things off so much that I had to wear a sweatshirt. I looked at the thermometer, convinced I would be able to disprove the "temperature never varies either way of eighty-five degrees" proclamation. It read eighty on the nose, but I would have sworn it was lower. In any event, I was relieved to feel cool and glad for whatever was making me feel that way. After scarfing up all the saltines and polishing off nearly an entire tin of butter, we weren't hungry for dinner.

Robert stayed long past sunset playing Scrabble; then, after I went to bed, he and Dale played whist (similar to the game of "spit") far into the night. I could hear them laughing and slapping the cards down through the heavy whirring of the bedroom fan. Most days the rain would come around three o'clock. When you felt it coming, school would let out, and everyone would scurry home for cover.

Some days the rain would come in midmorning and catch us by surprise, holding us up in school while we waited for the occasional breaks between downpours. Other days it would already be raining, so I knew school was cancelled. But the most fun was when we'd be at the market and hear the rain coming. In the distance the rainstorm was visibly moving—a solid sheet of water—pressing its way closer. There was nowhere to hide. You either ran ahead of its path, or you stayed your ground and got drenched. The first time we saw the wall of rain approaching, we were struck dumb, riveted to the spot. Excited shrieks from the vendors woke us up to our two choices. There wasn't much time. Half the vendors put large cloths over their wares and themselves and hunkered down to wait out the first violent downpour. The other half scooped up their things and ran for the nearest inadequate cover.

The marketers, without exception, took off running in front of the rain in a race to beat it to their houses. We joined the exodus, moving so fast our legs nearly buckled under us. We darted into our house just as the first splashes hit the roof. A few others, whose huts were farther away, followed us inside. We collapsed and laughed until our sides ached. We didn't know any of the people who'd followed us inside, but by the time we drank a few beers and shared dinner together, we were old friends.

CHAPTER 33

The Electrical Storm

A few weeks into rainy season, we decided we needed an R & R in Monrovia. We were used to the rain patterns by then and knew we could fly out on an early morning plane and spend most of the day outside in Monrovia before the rains came. We called Jack and invited ourselves. We'd have to sleep on the floor because there were six others also staying over, but if we wanted to do that we were welcome. We almost declined, thinking that, even though we'd be separated in the Peace Corps hostel, we'd be on beds, but when he mentioned that John and Virginia were at the house, we jumped at the chance to see our buddies.

We took Mac Cat to the Carpenters, and they drove us to the airport. Even though Steve had had a glimpse of how possessive he was being with the car, he couldn't bring himself to let go for more than an instant. I knew I could righteously insist in the event of an emergency, but it was enough for me that he had reflected, however briefly, on his behavior that morning long ago at our house when we thought I might be in danger of getting rabies. Oddly enough, nothing else he did or didn't do after that day had much effect on me one way or the other. We coexisted, we socialized, we even played bridge, but we were never destined to become good friends.

The four of us—John, Virginia, Dale, and I—talked nonstop the entire first day in Monrovia. During the afternoon downpours we'd duck into a restaurant for a lukewarm Club beer. We shared all our stories— our first Club beer, the tropical sunburn, Mac Cat's disappearance, and our first cup of Turkish coffee. We howled over the account of catching my first chicken and Robert Isaac teaching me how to husk rice. We sympathized with each other over the lack of privacy. We cringed over red-eyed rats and the close encounters with cassava snakes, and were amused by the presidential chamber pot and my dramatic proof that

I was white all over. We were shocked anew by the retelling of Sarah's rape and deeply saddened by the hanging of Big Boy.

After dinner we took a money bus back to Jack and Evelyn's, shared a brandy with the rest of the PCVs, and listened to their stories. Jack and Evelyn had recently returned from a month's safari in the East African countries of Kenya, Uganda, and Tanzania. One corner of the living room was piled high with beautiful artifacts, and their slide show made my mouth water.

After a year in Liberia, we would be getting a month's vacation, and Dale and I didn't need to do more than look briefly at each other to know where we'd be going in that month. We couldn't afford a luxurious safari, but we could afford to fly over, rent a Volkswagen, and pay a small fee to bunk at people's houses or the occasional cheap hotel. The climate was dry due to the higher altitudes, and East Africa was attractive to tourists because of its vastly appealing big-game reserves and unspoiled tribes of Maasai and Kikuyu. Jomo Kenyatta was still president of Kenya, African genocide hadn't surfaced, and the brief local uprisings weren't considered a threat to our safety. It would be a nice blend of elegant and rustic. As my dad advised, always have something to look forward to. This was the carrot that would get me through some of the difficult times in the months ahead.

We finally fell into our place on the floor around 1:00 a.m. We had snatched a spot close to the wall and were smug that we wouldn't have people breathing in our faces. The grass mat gave us a little padding, but the floor was the main contributor to our stiffness the next morning. There were two light sockets in the wall next to us, and Dale managed to confiscate a small lamp and plug it in. As he lay reading, I could hear the deep breathing and soft snoring of the others as I, too, drifted off to sleep.

Some time later, I was jolted awake by a cracking explosion that felt like a slap in the face. Sitting bolt upright I waited, frozen, to see what would happen next. I didn't have to wait long. Another bolt of lightning streaked the sky, and a clap of thunder rocked the house, followed instantaneously by a torrent of rain that would have rivaled Noah's flood. My heart jumped out of my chest.

A steady stream of lightning bolts darted and crackled outside, and thunder rattled the house like an earthquake. Visceral memories of the

Alaskan quake made me more afraid that I should have been. I looked around at everyone else sleeping peacefully on the floor. I told myself I was being overly dramatic and there was nothing to be afraid of, but my heart would not be stilled.

Finally, I woke up Dale. He said I was being foolish and to go back to sleep. Those words were very familiar, but not the least bit comforting. Ever since I could remember, I had heard the words, "Don't be so dramatic. You're too sensitive. You make too much of things. You're being silly. Don't be such a baby," and every variation of the same theme. I always believed what others said—blaming myself, invalidating myself, as they did, for the very qualities that make me who I am—the gifts that allow me to be a creative, perceptive, and compassionate person.

I hunkered down and tried to quiet myself, but fear kept me paralyzed. I woke Dale again. He sat up, leaned against the wall, and didn't know what to say to me. "There's nothing to be afraid of," he sighed impatiently. Seconds later Evelyn appeared in the doorway with some urgency. She told us that we should move away from the wall and out of the path of the light sockets because lightning could come shooting through and fry us both. Dale jumped like he'd been touched by a cattle prod. The only consolation was in knowing that my feelings of fear weren't so stupid after all. This was only one incident in a lifelong journey to learn to trust my feelings, even though others may invalidate them.

Huddled under a blanket, I spent the rest of the lightning storm wide awake, while everyone, including Dale, snored around me. I think Dale may have felt some remorse for being so impatient with me, but he never said so.

I woke up raccoon-eyed from my vigilant night watch, though I didn't feel the least bit tired. The dawn was its usual majestic beauty, and I felt like getting up and outside before the sun got hot. I did my best to walk quietly over the sleeping bodies on the floor. I turned on the bathroom light, expecting to see cockroaches dancing on toothbrushes, but they had already gone back into hiding. Things looked a lot better in the light of day.

When I came back into the living room, John and Dale were talking. When I suggested that we move to the Peace Corps hostel for the rest of our stay, Dale said, "Hey, wanna stay at the Dukor one night?" I knew what kind of courage it took for him to suggest that. Dale was one of the most frugal persons, aside from my mother, that I'd ever known, and I could feel the magnetic pull of his hand on his wallet.

"Sure!" I said, before he had a chance to think about it. I could see him biting the inside of his cheek.

I found out that it was John who had suggested it. He was complaining about the uncomfortable accommodations on the floor and how the thunder and lightning had kept him awake half the night. Dale told John what Evelyn had said about lightning shooting through light sockets, and that was when John suggested we all treat ourselves to the elegance of the Dukor. Before Dale could offer resistance, I had already come back into the room.

We were about ready to go to town for breakfast when we heard a car in the driveway. We saw Jack getting out of his car with armloads of fresh bread. His generosity overwhelmed us. We had warm bread smothered in Danish butter and jam, crisp Danish bacon, and strong coffee as everyone talked of things to do in Monrovia. John and Virginia wanted to do one thing, Dale and I another, so we decided to split up and meet at the Dukor later in the day. Check-in time was eleven o'clock, so one couple would register some time after that and leave a message for the other.

We all showed up at 11 sharp and laughed heartily at our predictability. John and Virginia chuckled and spoke freely of looking forward to making love in an air-conditioned room on a soft bed. Dale looked at me sweetly, and I knew we would be doing the same thing that night, however briefly.

CHAPTER 34

CARE Food

Jack had asked us to drop by the next day for dinner because he wanted to introduce us to the man who ran the CARE food program in-country. I had heard about CARE Food only through TV ads that showed pictures of starving children in Ethiopia with skeletal limbs and distended bellies and pleaded for your money. I was always stricken by those pictures and thought what a noble thing to be able to contribute. But my parents warned that the money sent would never be used to bring food to the people—you could never be sure that the food actually got there. They figured that some middlemen along the way pocketed the money. I had no way to disprove their suspicions, but the wish to contribute never left me. Now, here I was with the perfect opportunity to talk with the distributor of CARE food in Liberia and find out firsthand how things really were.

Marianne and Donald arrived at the Reeders' each carrying a heavy casserole of food. They breezed past us through the door. "There's more in the car ... Hi, I'm Marianne, and this is Don," she motioned. While the four of us—John, Virginia, Dale, and I—brought in the rest of the food, Marianne popped the casseroles snugly into the already preheated oven and set the timer for one hour. It was enough to feed twenty people.

Evelyn smiled at our incredulous looks and said, "When Marianne and Don come to dinner, I vacate the kitchen. Marianne's a genius in the kitchen." I couldn't take my eyes off Marianne, who was smiling, humming, and moving efficiently around the kitchen like she was born to it. "I know," said Evelyn, "The first time she offered to bring dinner, I was just as surprised as you look—but now I simply sit back and revel in the show. You'll see. You're in for a real treat."

I said, "I'm already having the time of my life just watching her." Marianne laughed lyrically in response.

Later, at the table, I knew I'd never in my life tasted anything so good. I marveled at her humble acceptance of praise—like the meal was nothing too special, really. Don confirmed that she cooked like this all the time and whispered that he thought she got just as good an orgasm cooking as she did making love. Marianne blushed and laughed out loud, but I could see that underneath the humor was a grain of truth. Her whole being seemed to glow from an inner light. I thought how incredible it was that someone could be so fulfilled. I wondered if I would ever feel that way for more than a few moments at a time.

For the first time, I had a fleeting thought that tasks which I experienced as mundane—cooking, cleaning—could possibly be elevated to an art form by right intentions. It was a thought I would entertain from time to time but not experience myself until much later in life when I began to explore Eastern philosophies.

Don explained the CARE food program in-country and answered all my questions. Then he said, "So, do you want to start a CARE food program in Greenville?"

I startled briefly, then said, "Yeah, sure, but how do I start?"

"Well," he said, "You have a meeting with the principal and staff in your school and see what they think about a school lunch program. Then, if you think it'll fly, we'll load up a plane with food. Do you have a place you could store the food?" He said it would have to be a place that we could lock up, or it would disappear in a surprisingly short time. I thought of the Demonstration School's storeroom to which everybody and their cousins once removed had a key.

"What about the outside spare bedroom of our house?" I asked.

Dale looked at me. "Are you sure you want to do that?" he said. "When we have guests, they'll have to stay inside. Less privacy for everyone."

"That's okay" I said, too embarrassed to retract. I didn't want Jack to think I couldn't put up with a little inconvenience. After all, we did live in the most elegant Peace Corps house in metropolitan Greenville, and I was no softie. Plus, the excitement of a new project overshadowed any thought of a minor inconvenience. In retrospect, I realize I've always had a tendency to let my enthusiasm rule my actions. While others are weighing the pros and cons of an issue, I'm already halfway up the mountain. Then I suddenly find myself knee-deep in snow with my sandals on, while others have taken the time to fill their backpacks and don snowshoes. Nevertheless, because of my exuberance, I have had countless adventures others have only dreamt about. However, as the years have progressed, I've learned that there is nothing wrong with a little caution and evaluating all sides of an issue, as long as it doesn't replace enthusiasm with fear.

My proposal to the principal and teachers was approved, so I called Don and told him it was a go. He arrived the next week in a plane loaded with sacks of rice, flour, beans, sugar, and powdered milk, along with tins of lard, tomato sauce, Vienna sausage, and Spam. During the unloading process at our house, the yard filled with my neighbors lending a helping hand. It reminded me of the Old West barn raisings I'd seen on TV and filled me with awe at the speed and efficiency of the operation. I felt positively joyful. The little room was piled to the ceiling. Dale and I agreed that we should hire the only taxi in Greenville to take food supplies to school each day so people wouldn't steal it.

The next few days proved to me that I didn't have the first clue how to manage the cooking and distribution of food at the school, but it didn't matter. Without being asked, everyone brought bowls, utensils, pans, and plates from their homes, and someone actually got the gigantic industrial stove in the school kitchen to work. There was no running water, and I knew that any water used to prepare the food would not be boiled.

The first day with school lunch was an exciting day for everyone. I still have no idea how it was accomplished because, for the most part, I didn't have to do a thing. I sat back and watched, with admiration, as a people who had lived cooperatively for centuries simply took care of business. I couldn't understand why they would need anyone to supervise anything—CARE Food might as well just provide the supplies and leave them to it, because the people seemed perfectly capable of organizing distribution on their own.

On the days that I taught school out of my home, we walked back to school at lunchtime and stayed there the rest of the school day which, in rainy season, lasted only till about 1:00. As the CARE food program got rolling and everyone came to expect a good lunch, another problem surfaced. Word got around the town that the supplies were stored at our house, and soon villagers started showing up at my door at all hours requesting "a bowl of flour" or "just one bag of rice, M'Nancy." It was difficult to explain that the supplies were for the children's lunch at the Demonstration School. It was incomprehensible to them why the food couldn't be shared among all people who needed it.

Frankly, I agreed with them. Everyone who needed it should have access. I simply couldn't refuse a fair request. No one asked for more than they needed, and no one hoarded it "for a rainy day." When I called Don to ask for more supplies, he was surprised that they had gone so fast. I said the children at the school were big eaters. CARE Food kept supplying, and I kept handing it out. Our neighbors gifted us, in return, with fresh fish, corn bread, casseroles of collard greens, and anything else we could have needed. What we couldn't eat, we'd pass on to someone else.

A few months into the CARE food program, Don paid us a visit. He seemed pleased that it was going so well. He must have noticed that I handed out food to people who showed up at my door, but he never said a word. (In fact, after he returned to Monrovia, he began to send food more frequently.)

I apologized for my humble cuisine, even though he ate with gusto and complimented me as if I cooked gourmet-style like his wife. We spent the evening browsing through our book locker. He was an avid reader and enjoyed a good book discussion. He asked if he could borrow one of our books. I said, "Sure," before I realized it was my favorite *Liberian Folklore* book, but I figured I could do without it for a while.

When we visited in Monrovia some months later, I was browsing through his library and noticed the green-backed book on the shelf. I pulled it down and opened the front cover. My name had been crossed out and his had been written boldly in black ink beneath it. I was shocked. I asked him if this was the book I loaned him and he said, "Oh, yeah, sure, take it." I wondered how many of his other books were somebody else's.

However, through the years I've come to realize that a book is one of those things that, if you lend it, you may never see again. Some treasured books I don't lend, but most of the time I look at a book as not really belonging to me—it's just passing through—and I'm happy if it becomes a part of somebody else's life.

CHAPTER 35

VD

Saturday was laundry day. Robert showed up before dawn to begin the arduous task of pumping water into large kettles and putting them on the stove to heat. Then he plugged the bathtub and poured in enough hot and cold water to make it the right temperature for washing. Robert preferred the large blue cakes of local lard-based soap he was used to, so I had long ago stopped buying the European powdered detergent.

The few times I had to wash the clothes, I cursed the wretched cakes because they wouldn't lather, no matter what I did, and they made my hands feel like sandpaper. If that weren't enough, they smelled like a cheap imitation of Fels Naphtha. Needless to say, I was more than happy to leave the laundry to Robert.

Robert took pleasure in everything he did. Singing hymns in his full, beautiful African voice, he beat the dickens out of those sheets and scrubbed them on the huge washboard until there wasn't a speck of dirt left in them, and they were as white as if they'd been soaking in Clorox. His strong hands were used to hard labor, and he wrung those heavy sheets dry without any effort at all. Before we hired Robert, Dale and I worked as a team, holding the sheets with our four hands and twisting with our whole bodies—and still we couldn't seem to wring all the water out. Washing clothes was practically a full day's work for the two of us, and our hands were sore for days. Robert did it effortlessly in a single morning.

While he waited for the water to heat, he mixed enough batter for two loaves of banana bread and kneaded enough dough for four loaves of white bread. While the bread was rising, he finished the laundry and laid it flat on the grassiest part of the ground to dry. While the laundry was drying in the sun, he baked the bread.

By the time all the bread was done and we'd devoured our usual entire loaf of white bread slathered in Danish butter, the laundry was dry. Robert deftly shook out the dry laundry to get rid of any stray particles of dirt or crawlies and brought the folded articles inside. The entire process of laundry and baking bread was accomplished before ten o'clock. Then he set about cleaning the house, which took him less than an hour. I never saw anyone take so much joy in his work (with the exception of Marianne and her cooking), and I loved being in his sphere when he worked. Every so often he erupted into rich laughter at some remembered experience, and even though I hadn't a clue what had sparked his laughter, it was so contagious I laughed right along with him.

The only time I remember seeing Robert upset was when he showed up to work one day and asked to speak to "Mistah Dell" privately. It seems that Robert was having trouble urinating because his "penis was on fire." He was almost in tears as he spoke. Dale asked him if he'd had sexual intercourse recently. Robert blushed, lowered his head, and said nothing. In Liberia, relations between a man and a woman were an intensely private matter. I never saw a display of any kind of affection between a man and a woman in public. It was common to see two men or two women walking along holding pinkies, or with their arms around each other, but never opposite sexes.

At some urging, Robert admitted he'd been having sex with a young woman. It was his first sexual relationship, and she was the only one. He said that when he tried to have sex last night, it hurt a little, and by this morning he was really in pain. He was terrified that he might have a disease that would make his penis fall off.

Dale thumbed through the Peace Corps Medical Manual to find the most obvious diagnosis, gonorrhea, and read to Robert what it said. Then he told Robert he would go with him to the hospital. Dale's diagnosis was confirmed, and Robert was given penicillin. Robert looked vastly relieved when he came back from the hospital. Then Dale told Robert that it was his responsibility to tell the girl she had to go for treatment. Robert became agitated and indignant, saying that, since she gave him the disease, she deserved to suffer, and why should he tell her—it was her fault. Dale explained that this disease, as with all venereal diseases, doesn't stop with two people.

He asked Robert how he supposed the young woman had gotten the disease. Robert was thoughtful as he realized she had gotten it from sexual intercourse with someone else. He became angry and determined that she should suffer for her indiscretion. All sorts of conventions surfaced about men's and women's sexual habits—it was okay for men to have multiple partners, but not women. Wading through Robert's rising emotions, Dale calmly explained the chain reaction of passing on a disease like gonorrhea—that every person she had slept with could be passing it on to every person they might be having sex with, and did Robert see how this thing was a much bigger issue than hurt feelings and wounded pride? It took some time before Robert had worked through his anger to concede that Dale might be right.

The next step was getting to the girl and following the chain to the end. That's when I entered the picture. I offered to go with Robert to talk to the girl, and he accepted. I spoke while Robert translated. She was mortified. She never once looked me in the eye. She said that there was only one other person she had been with, but she wasn't seeing him any more. I told her that it didn't matter that she wasn't seeing him—he would have to be told, and he would have to tell everyone he had been with. She said she couldn't reveal his name. Robert pleaded with her to tell us.

Finally, she told us that he was an important official with a wife. I made her promise to speak to him, then come and tell me what happened. Then I took her to the doctor. A few days later, she showed up at my door, and we sat down to coffee. In her broken Pidgin English, I understood her to say she had spoken to the man. I thanked her for following through and asked her if she stressed the importance of his telling his other partners. She said she had. He had queried her about who else knew they had been together, and she truthfully answered, "No one." Then, without prodding, she told me his name.

She was right. He was an important official with a wife and family. Later, Dale and I talked about what we should do. We decided to do nothing and, for that choice, I've always felt a twinge of guilt. Today, as I read about the increasing AIDS epidemic in the world, I remember when it all started and how it has reached epidemic proportions, in part, because of a dangerous chain of ignorance, irresponsibility, and fear.

CHAPTER 36

U.S. Army Privates

One Saturday afternoon there was a knock at the door. We opened it to find two United States Army privates standing there. Looking past them, I saw two stuffed duffels and a stack of some kind of equipment. They said they had been assigned to Greenville to survey the road. Steve had directed them to our place as somewhere they could stay while they did their job. They were big and brawny with light brown hair and Southern accents. They were handsome and could have passed for brothers, and they were both from Texas. We asked how long they'd be staying, and they said a few days at the most. We could hardly refuse. They were government employees just like us; they'd be working all day, so we probably wouldn't see much of them; they offered to pay us for what they ate; and we had the largest Peace Corps house. And so it was that Pete and Joe moved into the spare room inside the house.

The next day was Sunday, their day off. I cooked the usual breakfast of Danish bacon, powdered eggs, fresh bread, and fruit. Then we sat around the whole morning talking of everything and nothing. Pete said they'd be receiving a large shipment of frozen T-bone steaks and some boxes of C-rations on tomorrow's plane and asked me if I had anyplace to store frozen food. I told them that all I had was a small freezer compartment above the refrigerator. It didn't occur to me to ask why they'd need so much food if they'd only be staying a few days, but I was soon to find out.

They stayed for a month. They had a hundred and one reasons why they "couldn't survey the road today": They had to work as a team, and Pete had a headache, or Joe had a headache, or Pete had diarrhea, or Joe had diarrhea, or they both had diarrhea. Or their alarm hadn't gone off so, by the time they got up, it was too late to begin. Or the sun was particularly hot that day, and Joe had already suffered once from heatstroke and wasn't about to go through that again. Or they had so much equipment to set up that day that, by the time it was all set up, the rains would be there, so why bother? Every other day it was something else.

They "worked" only enough days to keep us on the hook. The rest of the time, they lounged around reading from our book locker and smoking cigarettes until noon—then they dug into their store of American whiskey and drank until it was time for dinner. Then they'd cook their juicy T-bones with some of our rice and gobble it down, while we ate our varieties of Spam, canned roast beef, and the occasional fish or tough chicken. Conveniently, every time the plane came in, they'd receive a fresh shipment of T-bones and other frozen foods.

For all our naiveté, we were beginning to get the picture.

They left their dirty clothes for Robert to wash, for which they promised to pay him; we found out later that they never did. They left their dirty dishes lying around the kitchen, to the delight of the cockroaches, and their ashtrays full. I was welcomed into my living room at six each morning by the odor of stale cigarette butts and whiskey.

I was becoming increasingly angry. I wanted to be magnanimous but there was a limit. I couldn't school out of my home while they were there. They were spreading out and leaving less and less room for us, and I was too timid to say anything to their faces. Dale was also too timid, so we put up with it, resenting them the entire time. Finally, after a month, with no end in sight, we took courage and told them they'd have to leave. They protested that they weren't finished with the road, and where would they stay? We said, "Why don't you stay at Steve's?"

They moved in with Steve and his roommates that afternoon. They left the C-rations but took the T-bones. Within two days they had finished their survey and were gone from Greenville. Steve said they slept on the floor, shared their steaks, and were delightful company; he couldn't understand what all the fuss was about.

The next morning I woke up with a headache. I thought that maybe my headache was a result of the cigarette smoking of the two army guys and set about cleaning every inch of the house to rid it of the smoke residue.

I was familiar with headaches because, as a child, I had had headaches often, mostly on Sundays when my dad was home all day. My dad smoked cigarettes until I was nearly sixteen. At that time, you didn't know they were bad for you, and no one made the connection between allergies and cigarette smoke. I suffered many a Sunday in bed with a splitting headache, which often made me sick to my stomach. My mom would always cook roast beef on Sundays, and to this day I can't stomach roast beef.

In any event, it did seem that I was having a lot more headaches since coming to Liberia, and it concerned me how quickly I was going through bottles of Excedrin. One of the single PCVs in Greenville clued me in to Excedrin, because she had migraines and popped six at a time. Two Excedrin made me a little light-headed, and I knew six couldn't be good for you, especially as often as she took them. She seemed to take her ailment in stride; she'd just go into a dark room, put a cloth over her eyes, and sleep it off in front of a fan. Usually my headaches were short-lived—no more than a couple of hours—while hers sometimes went on for a few days. Watching her suffer, I prayed I would never have a migraine.

I was glad to see rainy season end in late July because I could go back to teaching out of my home, except for lunchtime. The days in rainy season, when I stayed in school, it was difficult to listen to the frequent sounds of switches smacking the backs of the hands of the children in other rooms. The children were stoic and didn't let out a peep, but I cringed every time I heard that whipping sound on young human flesh.

My memory of the San Francisco ghetto children was still fresh in my mind. The only difference I could see between their switching and the switching in Liberia was the intention behind it. In San Francisco, the intention was to humiliate, to belittle; in Liberia, switching was a natural consequence for not learning your rote memorization. No anger or harsh words accompanied the swats. The children simply held out their hands, and strokes were administered. I was criticized for not switching, but I couldn't, and even the sound became so intolerable that I eventually taught out of my home full time. I made it clear that any of the other teachers and their classes could come to my home at any time to join in the lessons, but there was one ground rule: no switching. I had a lot of visiting classes. The teachers would leave their switches on the porch on the way in and pick them up on the way out. After a time, they didn't bring them at all, and I like to think that I had something to do with making them think more consciously about the custom of switching.

CHAPTER 37

Tropical Itch

The first time I ever heard of a vaginal yeast infection was when I got one. During intercourse one evening, I was tender and felt a little swollen. I thought it was from the activity. I washed up and rinsed thoroughly, thinking I might be allergic to possible soap residue from my earlier bath. After we bug sprayed the bedroom and waited the usual twenty minutes, we went to sleep.

But sleep didn't come for me. I had begun to itch. Rubbing or scratching made it burn, after which the itch would return worse than ever. The itching escalated so rapidly that, by morning, I was climbing the walls. There was no flight out for two days, but I was alternately crying and moaning so badly that Dale ran to the Carpenters' to see if there might be a private missionary flight coming in or out. By the time we got a flight out that afternoon I was ready to be put out of my misery. I didn't care about anything—all I wanted was relief.

The waiting room at the doctor's office was full, and I moaned and cried for another hour. After a quick, painful examination, the diagnosis was simple: a severe case of vaginal candidiasis. He administered a cream in and around the entire area and gave us both a prescription. As he put it, "You both have to take the prescription because if you don't, you could pass this thing back and forth endlessly." He told me these things were pretty common in the tropics. Being hot and sweaty for long periods of time can upset the natural balance of bacteria and yeast in the body. Natural yeast cultures in the vagina become exacerbated by heat and humidity, and the balance quickly becomes disturbed, causing swelling, itching, burning, and a white curdish discharge.

He asked me if I was taking the birth control pill. I said yes, and he said, "That could be a contributing factor too." None of this was good news because I didn't see any way around the pill and the tropics. By the time he finished explaining the causes to me, the cream had already begun to alleviate the itching, and I could breathe easier.

The nurse took my blood pressure and weighed me. I thought surely the scale must be off because it registered twenty pounds more than the last time I was weighed before entering the Peace Corps. I had noticed, however, that even my loose tent dresses were getting a little snug on top but I blamed it on water weight and the humidity. Dale asked to be weighed. He had lost ten pounds. He never could keep any weight on. It was infuriating. I would have to cut back on saltines and Danish butter. Morning sickness was the reason I had started the habit, and that had long since passed.

After a trip to the pharmacy, we drove to the Peace Corps hostel. I went straight to bed and slept soundly till morning. Flying back to Greenville, I told Dale how relieved I was that it was all over. However, as it turned out, I was to be plagued by frequent yeast infections for the next eighteen years. Then, mysteriously, the vaginal itch stopped and hasn't been a concern since.

CHAPTER 38

Staff Meeting

One evening a month, the administrator at Dale's school held a secondary-school staff meeting. They took place after dinner, and he always came back from them full of energy and laughter, but he wouldn't tell me anything about them—he wanted me to experience a meeting firsthand.

We arrived at 7:00 p.m. Only one other person was there. As soon as Dale walked in, he was greeted with the elaborate Liberian handshake, after which he reached into his pocket and brought out a pack of Salem menthol cigarettes and gave one to his colleague. This surprised me because neither Dale nor I smoked.

Each person who arrived promptly greeted Dale the same way and was given a cigarette. If Dale didn't offer the cigarette immediately, the colleague lingered and looked longingly in the direction of his shirt pocket, while Dale pretended not to notice. Then, in mock remembrance, Dale dramatically pulled out the pack. In mock surprise, his colleague smiled broadly and said, "Ah, yes, Mistah Dell, you mu' please give me one Slahlem." The "Slahlem" ritual continued until the last two cigarettes were left in the pack. Dale took one for himself and offered me one, which I took.

When all the cigarettes had been smoked, it was the signal for the meeting to begin. Whoever felt the strongest about his complaint spoke first. The problem was put before the group, and the heated discussion was off and running. Everyone talked at once, furiously, emotions flying. The anger escalated so rapidly that I was afraid it would erupt into fisticuffs. Then, as in a perfectly choreographed performance, the whole group erupted into peals of laughter, whacking their knees and slapping each other's hands, and the palaver was over.

That was the signal for the stories to commence. One person got up and acted out an elaborate tale complete with gestures and broad movements, which ended in grand applause and slaps all around.

Then a second person got up and told a tale. Often, others would spontaneously jump in and act out what the storyteller said. This went on until everyone who wished to "perform" a tale had done so.

I was enthralled and completely entertained. After the "meeting" we walked home as a group, each person peeling off as they reached their hut, pleased with the evening's bonding experience. All future meetings I attended had the exact same format. I could never figure out what they were so emotional about, but I suspect all that palavering was just a way of warming up for the storytelling.

CHAPTER 39

Christmas

Santa Claus

The Carpenters had been in Monrovia for two weeks having a baby, and we missed them. One afternoon Dale and I decided to go to the beach to watch the sun set and to check on their house. We didn't go to the beach to swim too often, and when we did, we didn't stay long. We had learned our lesson well. We had a newfound respect for the tropical sun, and we never got sunburned in Liberia again. We checked their house, talked to the caretaker, and moseyed on over to the beach. We took off our shoes and strolled along, found a sitting spot, and watched the sun do its disappearing act, producing a panorama of color that rivaled the most exquisite Cézanne painting.

The only thing we ever had to endure from our little beach walks was the occasional chigger infestation. Chiggers are little bugs that bore their way through the skin on the bottoms of your feet and lay their eggs. You don't notice anything for a few days, until the eggs start to grow, and you begin to feel a sore spot when you walk. The remedy is to take a sharp pin and carefully widen the tiny opening, allowing the sac of eggs to ooze out.

We didn't arrive home till after dark. Both of us had a sort of an empty feeling that we couldn't attribute to anything but homesickness. A few weeks more and it would be Christmas—our first Christmas away from home and away from America. Usually, by this time, in the States, we'd be counting the days until Christmas, but somehow, in the tropics, it didn't feel like anything resembling Christmas.

The Carpenters returned with a healthy baby boy they named Christopher. The girls acted like they'd gotten a new doll for Christmas. John Mark beamed, and young Mark took it in stride. Betty looked like she'd never been pregnant. She moved through the event effortlessly, without the slightest drama. I loved being around her. It looked so easy that I felt, not for the first time, the urge to have children. I thought Dale would make a good father, and I loved children so much, how could I be anything but a wonderful mother. My better judgment intervened. I was simply not ready—not mature enough to take it on—and there were those occasional lingering thoughts about the marriage. Oh well, in the meantime, I could revel in the Carpenter children and young Christopher.

Our visits to the Carpenters grew more frequent, because I felt lonely and needed some reminders of home. One evening after dinner at their house, we were chatting, and I heard little Christopher start to cry. I jumped up to go to him, but John Mark and Betty said to let him be for a while. His usual pattern was to cry a little when he was put down to sleep.

Another few minutes of his crying and I asked if I could go see if something was wrong. Betty was busy in the kitchen, and John Mark assured me Christopher was fine. The crying stopped, and the reverend said, "See, he fell asleep." Almost immediately the crying resumed, but this time, softer. John Mark looked at me and saw I would not be reassured.

A few minutes later he came back holding Christopher. He said he had found Christopher face down, wedged between the crib and the mattress. He could have suffocated. Then he said tearfully, "You saved his life, Nancy," and handed me the precious bundle. I rocked him till he fell asleep. The reverend was to tell the story and express his gratitude many times in Liberia and even when I returned to the States and visited them in Georgia. I honestly didn't feel like I did anything unusual—I was just being me. Maybe that's all life is ever about—just being yourself.

Christmas was one of my favorite times of year—snow, hot chocolate and ice-skating, Jack-Frost-nipping-at-your-nose kinds of things—but I felt odd celebrating Christmas in the tropics. Coconut trees, grass-roofed huts, and red laterite dirt simply didn't fit the picture. The thought of Santa Claus all bundled up in a red velvet suit and patent leather boots was ludicrous in Liberia. (Funny, it never occurred to me, in Alaska, to question the familiar image of Jesus preaching in sandals and riding desert donkeys.)

The Carpenter girls went into the season with unbridled enthusiasm. Their church in Georgia sent Christmas decorations—sparkling tree garlands and icicles, nativity scenes, all manner of ornaments, and, of course, an enormous artificial tree, complete with cans of spray snow. They also sent boxes of gifts, all wrapped and ready to be put under the tree. We were invited to join their tree decorating ceremony, complete with mulled cider. We stayed over Christmas Eve and enjoyed a special time of quiet prayer and storytelling, reminding ourselves that our purpose was to share with the less fortunate and to live our lives every day in gratitude and simplicity.

My memories of Christmas mornings past consisted of getting up before the sunrise, racing to the tree, and shaking all the presents, then waking my parents so we could get on with the unwrapping. That was Dad's cue to get up slowly and linger over his orange juice, teasing us that we should really have a nice leisurely breakfast before we opened the gifts. Mom always intervened: "Howie, stop teasing the girls." We loved it. Dad continued to linger and tease until the coffee was brewed, at which time he and Mom would pour themselves large cups, and we'd all sit down. Ceremoniously, Dad would play Santa and dole out one present at a time. All the attention would be on the one person opening a present. Our unwrapping would go far into the morning, as each gift received its place in the spotlight.

The Carpenters did things a little bit differently. The girls woke up at 5:00 a.m. and then woke everybody else. Immediately, wrapping paper was ripped off and tossed helter-skelter as gifts were opened with abandon. By 5:30 all the gifts were opened, and coffee was on the way. We spent the rest of the morning lounging around and playing with their toys, until it was time to get ready for church.

The reverend gave an inspirational sermon about the life of Jesus and following his example of tolerance and love. In all the time I've known the Carpenters, they have been beacons of tolerance and love. In the 1970s, when I was an actress living in New York, I had the occasion to perform my one-woman show in Georgia. I had left my husband, and I was living the part of a gypsy actress in a time of free love. I showed up with a boyfriend in tow, and we were welcomed with open arms. We stayed with the Carpenters, albeit in separate rooms, but nary a reference was made about my "wayward" lifestyle—not even a sideways glance.

Over the years, we've kept in touch at Christmas and have followed each other's lives at a distance. Their entire family was deeply saddened to have to evacuate their Liberian home during the many years of civil war. John Mark and Betty have fostered many children since their return (as have their children), and they still have dreams about returning to Liberia one day.

That first Liberian Christmas we were visited by no fewer than four Santa Claus bands. A Santa Claus band consists of four or five kids with pots and sticks. One child is the Santa. He is dressed in a poncho, rope-tied at the waist, and wears a head mask. The beating of the pots alerts you to their presence in your yard. When you open the door, a wild dance accompanied by singing and beating of pots lasts for a good ten minutes. After the applause, the Santa comes forward, takes off his mask, and holds it in his hands, prayerfully. Then he lowers his head and begins his elaborate tale of woe.

He tells of how he and his friends had to travel around the world on a leaky boat, sleep without cover, and have nothing to eat and drink for weeks on end. Stranded finally in Greenville, they are now forced to go door-to-door performing and begging for the next meal. Real tears glisten in his eyes as he continues to embellish the tale. He ends with a dramatic flourish, accepting our appreciative applause with deep, Shakespearean bows.

Then, in the silence, it's our turn to speak. "How much money do you need?"

To which the Santa Claus replies, "Oh, M'Nancy, we could not possibly take less than $25,000, for true!"

With great fake deliberation, Dale and I whisper loudly to each other, debating for all to hear, the pros and cons of such a large contribution. It seems like an exorbitant request, and it would surely break us, and we'd have to leave our home and resort to begging on the street, but how can we refuse someone in such need? We are, after all, part of the same human race and must help each other.

Finally, sighing heavily, Dale reaches deeply into his pocket, pulls out a quarter, and hands it to me. I look at it longingly, as if to say my final good-byes, and then slowly I hand it to the Santa Claus. He looks at it, wide-eyed.

"Oh, oh, this is a magnificent contribution, Mistah Dell; thank you from God!"

Then, bowing graciously, beating their pots, they turn to go to the next house. At the end of Christmas day, Dale and I agree that our first Christmas in the tropics is a huge success, complete with visits from several Santa Clauses.

CHAPTER 40

East Africa and Amos Midamba

Amos Midamba and me

School had been out since the week before Christmas, and we were getting excited about our trip to East Africa. Dale controlled the bank account, and he had been socking money away. We still had a little we'd brought with us from home. He figured if we were careful, we could spend an entire month in East Africa. When we had visited Jack Reeder last, we'd met a Peace Corps couple who wanted to vacation in East Africa as well, so we decided to share the expenses of renting a Volkswagen for a couple of weeks. The rest of the time we'd be on our own.

We didn't know the couple very well, but they were stationed in Monrovia, had recently married, and were good friends of the Reeders. It wasn't an immediately familial feeling, like it had been with John and Virginia, but we figured it would be okay for a couple of weeks. We could certainly find something fun to do the other two weeks, and anyway, we wanted to look up Amos Midamba, who lived in Kenya.

Amos Midamba had been a Swahili foreign exchange student at our university in Alaska. He was a grand, good-natured fellow whom everybody loved. He was there to study business and, after graduation, would go back to Kenya to work for his uncle at a tea plantation. We magnanimously included him in all functions and parties. He laughed gustily as students teased him about his "natural tan" and asked him if he knew any cannibals.

We were all much too self-involved to really find out about him or his country, and I now think he must have been very lonely in America. We gave him a huge going-away party before his return to Kenya and bought him a magnificent set of bongo drums, which he played flawlessly at his party. We were shocked when we discovered he had donated them to them to the university before he left. Dale had gotten his address so that, in case we ever got to East Africa, we could look him up.

Dale wrote him when he found out we were going to Liberia, and Amos wrote back saying that as long as we were coming that far, why not come a little farther? He gave us his phone number. We wrote him from Liberia and told him that if we didn't hear back (since the mails were so slow) we'd call when we got to Kenya.

The temperature in Kenya was about the same as Liberia—or a little higher—but the humidity was low, which made it seem much cooler and, for me, altogether bearable. I didn't have a single headache the entire month in East Africa, which could have had something to do with the low humidity, or it could be that I was in a happier state of mind. A month seemed like an eternity, and I was going to take full advantage of having nothing to do but play. Robert Isaac was the gatekeeper of our house in Greenville, living there and taking care of Mac Cat, so I knew everything would be tip-top.

Phone service was readily available in Kenya, so I decided to call my parents. I'd wait till a Sunday evening when I was sure they'd be home. I was nervous and excited to hear their voices. Mom picked up the phone on the first ring. The phone reception was atrocious, and a loud echo forced us to wait eons between words in order to decipher what was said. We got through a few basic phrases about health and the weather, but any thought that we were going to share the real stuff of our lives was quickly shattered, and I ended the conversation holding in a lot of frustration. The frustration turned into tears when we hung up. I never tried calling home again, but we did manage to send a few audiotapes back and forth.

Nairobi was a tourist's dream come true: colorful shops and markets, artifact heaven, fancy English and Indian restaurants with waiters who served exotic foods in white gloves and attended to your every whim even before you asked.

Game reserves and guided tours were promoted on every street corner. We elected to hire a guide and open-topped Land Rover and take the brief tour of the Serengeti. It was everything we hoped it would be.

Adult lions lounging belly-up while their youngsters frolicked and practiced fighting for later life, Thompson's gazelles flowing in herds across the open plains, giraffes running slow-motion and stretching their majestic necks to nibble on the tallest trees. We saw a pack of hyenas and vultures feeding on the remains of a wildebeest the lions had left behind.

Our guide purposely got too close to a rhino and her baby, and she ended up chasing our Land Rover for a half mile, the ground positively shaking under her tonnage. At dusk, we sat in an English bar perched atop a tree, sipped Gordon's gin and watched an amazing assortment of animals drink from the watering hole below. I couldn't have asked for more, and I felt renewed even after just one day.

I hadn't realized the degree to which the daunting humidity in Liberia was affecting my mood and physical health (and probably contributed to the mild depression that eventually sent me home). In East Africa, I felt no such weight. The air was dry, and even though the heat was extreme, the sweat evaporated quickly, so my clothes never clung to my body.

The next week we decided to go on a guided tent safari to get a more in-depth experience of the animals of the plains. If we were really frugal with the rest of our money, we could do it. Those safaris cost a fortune, by our standards, and clearly catered to the wealthy. The Europeans showed up in fashionable safari khaki, and we showed up in our Peace Corps wardrobe, which didn't even approach khaki. In fact, we had chosen to pack only our homemade Liberian clothes so we'd fit right in.

Oddly enough, we were sought out for dinner conversation because of our curious West African garb. There were no other Americans in our particular group, so we had the opportunity to speak with many people from all over Europe and Australia. Being a Peace Corps Volunteer was still a novelty and carried with it a certain prestige that, even if we weren't wealthy, gave us passage to be accepted across "class" lines. (We all exchanged names and addresses, but after years of yellowing in the junk drawer, they were eventually tossed out.)

The following week we rented a Volkswagen with our Peace Corps friends and explored Olduvai Gorge, the excavation site of Dr. Louis Leakey and his discovery of the *Zinjanthropus* fossil. We drove across the African plains, pretending we were going where no person had ever gone before. We found the odd road or path and followed it wherever it led.

We were cautioned not to stay out after dark because that was when the big game did their hunting. And we were cautioned not to sleep in our car. Since there were four of us stuffed in a Volkswagen, there wasn't much danger of that.

Inching along slowly, we drove through a large herd of long-horned water buffalo that were blocking the road. We brushed by them in our tiny Volkswagen, their large, wild eyes peering intensely at us, their breath steaming our windows. We were thrilled at our adventure.

When we reached the next village, we stopped in a bar for a beer and to tell our story. The African bartender told us the water buffalo was one of the most unpredictable of all African animals, and we were lucky to be alive. He told us a story of a couple of tourists who had driven a Volkswagen, just like ours, through a similar herd of water buffalo. The animals attacked, and by the time they were through, the car was so damaged he said they had to remove what was left of the couple with a can opener. We ordered another ice cold beer and savored every sip.

Maasai women and children

We bought elephant hair bracelets and huge round beaded necklaces from the Maasai women and children who lingered around tourist hangouts. They refused to let us take their picture unless we paid them an outrageous two dollars each. The mystique of the untamed African native vanished but returned again when a group of seven Maasai warriors passed by, their tall, lean bodies glistening with animal fat and red ochre and their long dreadlocks slapping against their backs as they glided along, brandishing their decorative shields and long spears.

Everybody, including the Maasai women and children, stepped aside and let them pass. After that, I was glad to pay the two dollars for a picture of any Maasai, including the tourist groupies. Posing next to them, I noticed that many of them had open sores—some of them quite large, with maggots feasting on the dead flesh. Flies swarmed around them, landing in the corners of their eyes and around the sores. The Maasai were nomads and cow herders and used the cow for everything—leather for shields, tents, and clothing; meat, milk, and blood for food; intestines for rope, and stomachs for water bags. No part of the cow was wasted. There wasn't much to do about the flies—they just came with the territory.

We took a boat up the Victoria Nile to Murchison Falls and watched hippos bobbing up and down like giant water balloons with bulbous lips. The sight of dozens of crocodiles lounging on the shore or half out of the water chilled my blood, and I could believe that they were so perfectly adapted to survival that they hadn't needed to evolve since prehistoric times.

Amos's tea plantation, Kericho

We reserved the last week for visiting Amos Midamba. We said good-bye to our travel companions and rented our own Volkswagen. We had no idea what the accommodations would be like at Amos's house, but we figured if we had survived red-eyed rats in the bush, we could survive anything. He had a phone, so it couldn't be all that primitive.

The tea plantations were located in the highlands of Kericho, 7,000 feet above sea level, where the Lake Victoria rainfalls make it an ideal place to grow tea. The drive was breathtaking—a panoramic view of Nairobi and the surrounding plains and villages. We snapped a lot of pictures, but our little Instamatic camera couldn't do it justice—we weren't able to capture the vast magnificence of it all. It was cooler in the highlands, and road signs were conspicuously absent. We had followed Amos's directions to the letter, but it didn't look anything like we expected. We finally decided to stop at a huge mansion on the edge of a tea field and ask directions.

We were about ready to get out of the car when Amos bounded from the door, arms open wide in joyous welcome. *Nice hut,* I thought. He ushered us inside and introduced us to his wife. She was cooking and carrying a baby wrapped in a cloth around her waist. I asked how old the baby was. Amos translated the question in Swahili. Then he told us his wife had given birth yesterday. I shook my head in wonder as I watched her move smoothly around the enormous kitchen. The table was set for four with beautiful English bone china. The small, pink floral pattern reminded me of the presidential chamber pot, but I figured this was not the appropriate time for that story, however good it was.

So this was the little tea farm Amos was going to work for his uncle when he returned to Africa. I felt so foolish. In the year since his return from Alaska, he had taken over the entire plantation.

Amos's wife had prepared one of their favorite dishes, peanut soup: ground peanuts mixed with milk and herbs and served hot. I can only recall two foods I ever tried that I couldn't choke down if I had to: asparagus and peanut soup. Dale ate enough for two, I was humiliated that I couldn't take more than one bite, and our hosts were perfectly fine with both of us. When Amos noticed I wasn't eating the soup, he swiftly brought out a number of other foods, and lunch continued without another word about it.

Toward the end of the meal, we began reminiscing about our university days together. At one point I was overcome with the awareness of my youthful ignorance and American arrogance. My eyes started to water, and tears rolled down my cheeks. My reaction surprised me and baffled my hosts. Dale didn't know what to say, and Amos thought the food might be too hot.

I wanted to say how sorry I was for the way we all treated him while he was at the university and that we were just stupid and self-centered. I wanted to say how sorry I was that nobody cared enough to find out about who he really was—to ask him about his dreams and aspirations—to learn about his country and his way of life. I wanted to ask him how he put up with us—without once calling us on our assumptions or our cruel humor.

But I realized, in that moment, that he got through it by knowing who he was. He didn't need us to make him feel worthy. He lived among us and let us do whatever we did because he was sure of who he was. And he let us save face and learn our own lessons without feeling the need to teach us differently, not because he was a foreigner living among strangers, but because he already knew the secret of life—love and let live. That's what I wanted to say. But somehow I knew that he didn't need to hear it—that he already knew what I was thinking.

I blew my nose and said that once in a while I got a minor allergy attack, and it was over. He smiled at me, satisfied that all was right with the world. Dale looked baffled but, to his credit, said nothing.

Amos took us on a tour of his tea plantation. The fields were dotted with workers, placing their long sticks atop the bushes and picking only the tender young leaves above the sticks. Holding the leaves with great care, they deftly plucked each leaf and floated it over their heads to the baskets on their backs. The fields were divided like a checkerboard, and each picker had his square to pick. Amos told us that he shipped most of his tea in bulk to England. He said that, more than likely, any English tea we drink is really Orange Pekoe African tea. He laughed at our surprise. I recently discovered that in 1997 Kenya became the number-one tea exporter in the world.

We sat on manicured lawns underneath lush trees, sipped all kinds of tea, and talked of everything and nothing. I oohed and ahhed over the new baby and longed for one of my own. I hung around Amos's wife, and although neither of us understood the other's language, we communicated without words and thoroughly enjoyed each other's company.

In our private moments, Dale and I marveled at their life. We spoke about how little we seemed to really know others and how condescending we were to Amos in the United States. We assumed he was so lucky to have the opportunity to come study at our spanking new university in the supremely sovereign country of the United States. And maybe he was lucky, but because of our youthful hubris, we had missed a perfect opportunity to create a deep, lifelong friendship with a remarkable human being and now it was too late. There was a polite reserve, and that made me sad. However, I was intensely grateful to be able to see clearly the effect of my actions, and I vowed to live more consciously in the future.

The evening before we left to go back to Greenville, we treated ourselves to a magnificent feast at a white-glove restaurant, The Lion's Den (in Nairobi) where two waiters stood beside our table and attended to our slightest need. They practically fed us. We spent a fortune for the experience and decided we would have preferred a little less attention and a little more privacy. After dinner, I finished packing up the artifacts I had purchased. I had bought others and had them sent directly to my parents in Alaska. I had no doubt they would arrive safely. Nairobi was well westernized from years of British colonization.

CHAPTER 41

A Party

On the plane back to Greenville, I began to think about the past year in Liberia. I had trouble wrapping my mind around everything. So many of my perceptions and values had been challenged by the very experience of living in Liberia. I was a young bride in a marriage that wasn't satisfying, I had never been away from home, I was living in a climate that I found hard to adjust to, and very little of anything or anyone was familiar.

I also harbored the fear that I might never be able to go home—that I'd up and left, and now I couldn't ever go back. I wasn't enough of my own person yet to be comfortable with the discomfort that naturally comes from changing values. I didn't realize that one can never go back anyway—and that Liberia had nothing whatever to do with that. I was realizing that many of the values I grew up with were narrow and rigid, and even if I could go back, maybe I wouldn't want to.

I had the oddest feeling of being trapped. The feeling stayed with me throughout the flight. I tried to talk about it to Dale, but when he started chewing the inside of his cheek, I quit.

Even though I knew what to expect, Monrovia's humidity hit me again like a slap in the face. We stayed at the Peace Corps hostel overnight and grabbed a money bus to Monrovia Air Field the next morning to catch the local flight back to Greenville. John Mark picked us up. I felt better already. Mac Cat was happy to see us and, after a good petting session, hopped into his favorite drawer. Within minutes, the neighbors started showing up to welcome us home. The three dozen packs of Life Savers I'd bought in Kenya disappeared quickly into the hands of delighted children. All afternoon a steady stream of visitors came to the door asking for CARE packages. I didn't unpack until ten o'clock that night, after which I fell into bed and didn't see consciousness until the first "G'mahnin', M'Nancy!" at 6:00 a.m.

"Let's have a party," I said to Dale when we awoke. "We can ask everyone to bring a dish, and we'll show our slides from East Africa." The word spread quickly, and soon we had the RSVPs of at least a hundred people.

We wondered what we'd gotten ourselves into. I'd never given such a large party before, and I didn't know where to begin. But, as with the cooking and distribution of school lunch, it was handled quite well without my supervision. Six women came to the door at 10:00 a.m. to discuss the food. The meeting lasted a mere half-hour and all I remember saying was "Okay, sure, fine, good." I think my sole responsibility in the party was to provide the beverages and leave my door open. Over the next few days the requests for rice, corn flour, and sugar increased slightly, but CARE was happy to oblige. Excitement ran high. Mrs. Witherspoon across the street said she would bring fish and asked if I would like to accompany her to palaver at the shore the morning of the party.

I was thrilled. I'd never quite gotten the hang of the early morning fish palaver on my own. I'd always depended on her to bring me fish in exchange for other things. It was a long time since I'd gone to the fish palaver, but I knew it would be an interesting adventure with Mrs. Witherspoon. I told her I'd be happy to pay for the fish and gave her the money up front. At least I wouldn't have to argue with the Fante fishermen from Ghana. Their palavers never ended in laughter—they were in it for the money. There was never enough fish for the number of people who wanted them, so competition was fierce—arms flying and hands grabbing. It reminded me of rabid fans around a movie star.

Mrs. Witherspoon was fearless. She was not a large woman but she was clearly motivated and knew how to work it. I wish I had brought my camera, but stills wouldn't have done her justice. She parted the crowd like the Red Sea, insisting on this fish or that fish, flirting with the fishermen, then insulting them loudly and shaming them for asking such exorbitant prices. Before she was finished, they were begging her to take the biggest fish for whatever price she was willing to pay. She was the first to leave, carrying a large basket of gorgeous fresh fish, having paid a fraction of the asking price. I could almost see the fishermen scratching their heads as their eyes followed her away. I turned to her as we left and said, "You're my hero." She beamed. It didn't even occur to me to ask her for my change. The purchase—and the show—had been worth every penny, and she knew it.

Robert showed up promptly at 6:00 a.m., and by the time we'd gotten back from the fish palaver, the whole place was spotless. I asked him to go the market for pineapples, coconuts, oranges, and bananas for a fruit salad. He said he wanted to get the coconuts off the trees at the beach. Coconuts were easy pickings for Robert. I went with him. I loved watching him shinny effortlessly up the sharp, crusty trunk, using the soles of his shoes like suction cups, a machete strapped to his waist. Holding on with his feet and knees, he took the machete and with one quick stroke, cut the coconut from its umbilical cord and caught it. Using his free hand and his legs, he scaled back down the huge tree. The whole process took no more than a couple of minutes.

Once on the ground, he performed his own private milk-drinking ceremony. Taking his machete, he chopped away at the hard, outer husk and stripped off the coarse fibers to expose the nut. Rotating the nut in one hand, he used the butt of the machete to make a circular opening in the top, exposing the sweet milk inside. He looked inside, smiling and licking his lips. "Ahh," he said, as he put the coconut to his lips and swallowed the milk down in one gulp. "Ahh," he said again, and the ceremony was complete. He performed the entire ritual three more times. On the way home, he said his stomach was too happy.

At 5:00 p.m., the guests started arriving in their finest colorful party clothes. The women carried casseroles and armloads of food, and the men carried drums, cane liquor, or nothing at all. The jobs were clear: While the men drank, played drums, and danced, the women went to work in the kitchen laying out food and setting up service.

It was pretty much the same in my family back home with one exception. In the States, the men usually went to work, and women kept the house and took care of the kids. In the Liberian countryside, for the most part, the women kept the house and kids, carried water, marketed, and tended the small, subsistence farms; and the men, with few exceptions, ruled the roost by telling the women what to do, siring children, killing the occasional snake, palavering, and playing cards with each other.

The house throbbed with the beating of drums and clear, open vowel sounds of Liberian voices raised in song. The living room rocked as the men bounced up and down, their heads bobbing like ducks in a pond. The East African slide show was a highlight of the evening. The pictures of the Serengeti Plains animals brought gasps all around. Pictures of Dale and me elicited knee-slapping laughter. Liberians are not quiet people—they fully express all their emotions. A full-screen slide of me popped up. One of the men said, "Ah, M'Nancy, you getting fat—looking good!" Everyone agreed that I was looking mighty good and far healthier. It didn't sit well with me because all I heard was the word *fat*, and the worst thing you could be in my family was fat.

Party spirits were high, and we danced the traditional West-African Hi-Life far into the night. When it was time to clean up, the women converged in the kitchen and, with the efficiency and speed of a "Ginzu" chef, divided the leftovers so that each person got an equal share of every dish. Pots and dishes were washed, counters were wiped, and floors were swept. Even the beer and soda were divided up equally, including the empty bottles to be turned in for refunds. Then we said our good-byes, gave elaborate Liberian handshakes, and everybody left en masse. No one said thank you to anyone in particular because everyone had done everything. The entire cleanup took only twenty minutes. We looked around after everyone left. It didn't even look like we'd had a party.

---- CHAPTER **42** ----

Soldier Ants

The next day gigantic soldier ants visited us. I'd heard tales about the soldier ants, but I had yet to see one. There are pros and cons to everything. The plus side of a soldier ant is that it can be used like a stitch to close a wound. Grasping the large black ant directly behind its head, you hold it close to the wound. By centering it over the cut, the ant opens its pincer jaws and bites the flesh on either side of the wound, thereby closing it. Before the ant has a chance to let go, you snap its head off. Voilá. Instant stitch.

Another plus is that soldier ants usually travel in hordes that can be as much as three feet wide and at least as long. Their mission is to consume everything edible in their path. After they've been through an area, the place is free of cockroaches, bugs, and rats, clean as a whistle. The downside is that whatever you don't want consumed has to be evacuated, including yourself. Liberians love to tell horror stories of chickens, domestic pets, and even people being consumed by the voracious ants, leaving only bare bones behind.

So when Richelieu knocked excitedly at our door that morning and told us the soldier ants were coming, we moved fast. The only safe thing to do, if there was the threat of serious invasion, was to head for the river or the ocean. We asked Richelieu how far away the ants were and how big the horde was. He said the column was about a foot wide and very long.

Our thought was to keep a close watch on their path and simply stand aside or jump the column, but Richelieu explained that the ants didn't travel in a straight line or solely on the ground. They snaked along from side to side, up and down walls, in closets, and across screen doors. And once they were in the vicinity, it was too late. The neighbors weren't taking any chances—they were already heading for the ocean.

I scooped Mac Cat into my arms, and we headed for the Carpenters, who didn't seem the least bit concerned. The antidote for soldier ants

213

was to pour gasoline in their path. They had plenty of cans on hand if they needed to use them, and since they weren't worried, we sat down to a Southern breakfast of eggs, grits, and biscuits and talked of other things. It was always such fun to be with the Carpenters.

When Richelieu showed up a few hours later to tell us the ants had finished their business, we returned home. They had, indeed, made a path through our house, leaving it cockroach free. Mac Cat's food dish was picked clean. Miraculously, the bags of CARE food had managed to escape their appetite. The chickens in Mrs. Witherspoon's yard were spared—it appeared as if our house was the only house in our vicinity that was visited by the little creatures.

CHAPTER 43

The Decision to Relocate

Dry season was upon us again, with hot humid days and hot humid nights. In order to conserve water and thwart evaporation, I instructed Richelieu to pump water every other day, and just enough for our daily use. His look of surprise told me he was concerned for his wages. I told him his wages would remain the same, and he said, "Ah, if the wages remain the same, the arrangement is satisfactory." The thought crossed my mind that he might try to renegotiate for a raise when the daily pumping resumed, but that was all part of the game.

Time seemed to stand still and the days seemed to go on endlessly. We had a little over six months left on our tour of duty, and Dale kept talking about re-upping for another year. I think he was nervous about going back to the States and having to find a teaching job. Reminders of his one horrific year of teaching back in the States must have plagued him. Although I was sympathetic to his plight, I couldn't imagine spending another entire year in the heat and humidity of Liberia with its side effects of chronic yeast infections and frequent headaches.

Both of us had difficulty sharing our feelings with each other, probably because we suffered from the same fear of disapproval and the feeling of not holding up our end of the bargain. Neither of us had the slightest idea who we were, and neither of us had any experience in the art of self-discovery—we were learning as we went and saw ourselves as the fortunate or unfortunate recipients of whatever came our way. But we still had over six months to go, and that seemed like an eternity to me.

Dale continued to talk about re-upping, and I continued to be silent. I know I was expected to follow my husband, but wasn't he supposed to be my protector? Wasn't he supposed to know what I needed, and wasn't he supposed to make me happy? Needless to say, this way of thinking spoke volumes about our marriage and about me. No mate would have been up to the task. It was an impossible expectation, not least because I didn't even know what I needed to make me happy, so I couldn't have told him if he'd asked me, which he didn't.

The demon of depression was starting to creep in. In another two weeks, I was ready for another R & R in Monrovia. We stayed at Jack's house. After our arrival Saturday morning I came down with a serious headache that escalated so fast that the Peace Corps doctor paid a house call and gave me an injection of something that knocked me out cold. Aside from waking once in a fog and having to be escorted to the bathroom, I slept through till Sunday noon.

We were scheduled to fly back to Greenville Sunday afternoon but I was still so groggy I could hardly stand, and we stayed over another day. I have no idea what the doctor gave me, but from what I've learned since about strong pain medicines, I suspect it may have been morphine. Jack asked if I'd ever had a headache like that before and queried me about my medical history. He was surprised to learn of the increase in frequency of my headaches since arriving in the country and suggested we speak to the doctor again. Without the sophisticated CAT scan techniques of today, the doctor could only speculate on possible causes—humidity, heat, allergies, strange foods. I asked if the birth control pill could have anything to do with it, but he dismissed the notion out of hand.

Jack must have suspected some kind of depression, because he asked me if I was happy in Greenville. Other than feeling all alone at my job and isolated from the other PCVs in the area, I told him I was having a wonderful time. He was surprised to learn that I was teaching mostly out of my home and listened intently to my accounts of how the school was run—or not run. He allowed as how he knew the situation would be challenging, but he hadn't realized how isolated I felt. He also said, "Sometimes the singles leave the married couples alone because they assume you have each other." I felt ashamed that my marriage wasn't enough for me, but it wasn't Jack that made me feel that way—I was comparing my true feelings with what I thought they should have been, and I came up a failure.

Jack suggested that we might be happier if we moved closer to Monrovia. He thought the proximity to the big city might ease the isolation. There was a post available in the town of Buchanan, about ninety miles down the coast from Monrovia. The school was well run, and he was certain I'd find the job more satisfying. Buchanan would put us sixty miles closer to Monrovia, and there were plenty of taxis and money buses in the area, so we'd be able to ride to Monrovia as often as we liked. He asked Dale what he thought about it. To my surprise, Dale said he thought it was a good idea. Then he told Jack he'd been thinking about extending for another year, but he really hadn't realized how unhappy I was. A change of situation might just do the trick.

My father advised me to always have something to look forward to, and I was looking forward to being a member of a team of teachers in a school that worked. Dale would be teaching math at a Catholic high school and I would have fifth grade at the elementary school. We would move into the small, furnished house vacated by a departing Peace Corps couple, so our packing in Greenville would be minimal. Three new single volunteers would move into our house and take over the CARE food program. My heart felt considerably lighter as we sat on the plane back to Greenville.

We told the Carpenters first. They were used to the comings and goings of missionary and Peace Corps folk, but I knew they felt special about us, and we felt the same way about them. If not for their friendship, I'd have probably wanted to leave months earlier.

The headaches were not the only factor—they were merely the trigger. The brief interludes to Monrovia and East Africa alleviated the problem, but didn't solve it. I tried desperately to pin the problem on one thing or another (the humidity, the teaching situation), but that was too simple. I didn't think too deeply about my unfulfilling marriage—I wouldn't even admit that to myself for a number of years. I could tell that Dale really didn't want to move, but he tried to keep a brave face for my sake.

John Mark and Betty were sympathetic and said they understood how a person could feel isolated and lonely away from the familiar. They knew things hadn't been right for some time so thought the move might do some good. The girls were disappointed, and I confessed I would probably miss them most of all.

My principal, Mrs. Carter, couldn't grasp the idea that I would give up teaching at her school. She thought everything was perfect and was truly baffled. I didn't go into detail because I didn't want to offend her by telling her she was an ineffective administrator. After all, she had knitted two entire blankets in the time I was there. I assured her that the move was for personal reasons. I thought I was guarding her pride by sugarcoating the truth, but in reality, what I told her was closer to the truth than I was willing to admit.

Robert was deeply saddened by the news of our move. We had grown very fond of each other. I would miss his cheery disposition and easy humor. We put in a good word for him with the new tenants, and he was hired on the spot. He wanted Mac Cat to stay with the house, but we explained that pets go with the owners, not the house. I hadn't thought down the road to what we'd do with Mac Cat when we had to leave the country. Time moved slowly in the tropics, and six months still seemed like a long way off.

Each day after school, I began packing in earnest. In the past year and a half I had accumulated quite a store of artifacts, cloth, and school supplies. Dale's hopes of extending our tour of duty for another year were shattered when I told him I wanted to send most of the artifacts back to the States. Remembering the fate of our thirteen rolls of undeveloped film, we decided we would accompany our treasures to the airport and see them onto the plane. From there, we were confident they would reach their destination unharmed.

CHAPTER 44

The Baby

As far back as I can remember I have been the most deeply and emotionally affected by circumstances and events involving children. I will watch a TV movie about a child being taken from its mother, and though my heart breaks, I can't seem to turn it off. Those advertising people who put babies in the Michelin Tire ads really know what they're doing. So it's no surprise that one of my most poignant memories of my Liberian experience involved a child—a little girl.

I saw her for the first time on a Saturday morning, resting in her mother's arms. She had been born two days earlier in a hut near the edge of town. With all of the usual morning activity, I didn't notice the woman at first. I didn't notice her until I was sitting down to breakfast and happened to look onto the porch. She was sitting on the step cradling her newborn in her arms.

The entire time I'd lived in Greenville, I'd never seen this woman before. She was petite and pretty, with ornately plaited hair and beautiful purple-black skin. Her baby had the same fine features and rich skin color. It was difficult to tell the woman's age—but I guessed she was about twenty-three, my age. I said "Good morning," and went about my daily chores. She sat for about two hours. The next day she was back. And the next, and the next—every day for the next month.

During the time I'd been in Liberia, I'd gotten used to my neighbors showing up at my door any time of day or night—simply to sit or watch. It had become a common occurrence to turn and find a Liberian face peering through my window. The first time this happened, I was startled and felt violated. My mind quickly reviewed what I'd been doing for the last twenty minutes, but as soon as I noticed the man's face, he said "G'mahnin', M'Nancy!" He didn't seem at all chagrined or embarrassed that he'd been caught, and there was absolutely no indication of his having done anything out of the ordinary. Had I been older and more set in my ways, this might have unnerved me. But this custom of showing up and looking in the windows or coming into the house to sit for hours was a custom I would become used to, and even miss, when I returned home. So when the young mother and her newborn came to rest on my porch, it did not surprise me, nor did I think she wanted anything from me.

Two weeks before our move to Buchanan, I was packing trunks full of African artifacts while the woman sat watching me as I lovingly wrapped and padded my treasures for the twenty-two hour flight home.

I felt a strange sadness as she sat there holding her precious treasure, and we seemed to share this moment of melancholy. Was I nostalgic about leaving this town I had called home for a year and a half? Had I underestimated the impact I might have had on the people I had come to know as my neighbors? Or on this woman, who had come to sit on my porch two short weeks earlier, with whom I'd spoken no more than a few words and whose name I did not even know?

Admittedly, it had been difficult for me to adjust to the Liberian perception of duty, time, and responsibility. My Anglo-American Protestant work ethic was a strong fortress, and it would not be penetrated easily. I was there to help them; that was what President Kennedy said, that was what the trainers said, and that was what I had come to do. I wasn't programmed to include their needs. Had I underestimated the impact they might have had on me in the short time I'd lived in their country? I struggled with these thoughts as I tried to analyze why I was feeling the way I was.

During that final two weeks, there was a steady stream of visitors to our house. One person came with a gift of a Liberian gold ring in the traditional V shape, another brought earrings to match. Mrs. Witherspoon brought a basket and country comb she had made. Another neighbor asked why I must leave and gave me a piece of cloth for a lappa suit.

With only two more days left until our departure, the woman and child arrived as usual, at dawn. This time, however, she did not take a seat on the porch or come inside to watch me work. She walked boldly up to me, held out her baby and said, in her obviously just-learned Pidgin English, "M'Nancy, you muh' plea' ta' ma baby." Her look pierced my heart like a hot knife through butter.

Suddenly the last month made perfect sense. She wanted to give me her beloved child, and she had been observing me to see if I would be a fit mother. At that moment I felt nothing but the highest respect and deepest humility in the presence of this woman, who loved her child so much she was willing to give her up so the child could have what she must have perceived would be a better life. I told her I couldn't possibly take her baby—but we both knew I was lying. She said she would return with the baby tomorrow and left me standing stunned in the middle of my living room.

Dale and I had actually spoken about adopting a Liberian child, but it never seriously got past that romantic notion, and we'd certainly put no wheels in motion. Now here we were, presented with the perfect opportunity to test the depth of our dreaming.

It was a rough night for me. We talked far into the night, weighing and measuring each thought and feeling. The only feeling I couldn't admit to myself, and therefore couldn't possibly articulate, was the possibility that Dale and I weren't right for each other. We talked of everything else. We were both teachers, and there was a teacher shortage in Tacoma, so neither of us would have any trouble getting jobs; the adoption process and paperwork would be minimal trouble, the little girl was healthy and adorable, and we both loved children. We would keep in close contact with her birth mother and teach the child about her heritage, and she would have all the benefits of an American child in a middle-class environment.

But this was 1967, and it would be a difficult journey for a little black girl with two white parents. There would be the stares, the side-glances, and the whispered comments. There would be isolation and hurt feelings from cruel words that would not go away. I imagined myself sitting on the airplane, lovingly holding my baby in my arms. But the closer I got to America, her skin became the blacker and mine the whiter. The closer I got to America, the more clearly I realized that I would be taking this child from her native country of acceptance and love into a country where she would face stark prejudice for perhaps the rest of her life.

I tried to explain to the woman the next day why I couldn't take her child, but I'm not sure she understood, and I was left with a feeling of shame and embarrassment as I thought about how the Liberians had accepted me so completely as one of their own.

In the last forty years, Liberia has gone from a stable, peaceful country to one almost totally destroyed by civil war. Thousands of people have been killed, and thousands more have fled to neighboring countries to escape the ravages of war and starvation. I have lost touch with my Liberian friends. Risking sadness and regret, I often think of that beautiful little Liberian girl in a country wracked with war and wonder if I made the right decision. Had I taken her with me, she would be living in New York City—a city whose people have learned, at least partially, to accept people's differences. But I didn't take her with me, so I'm left to wonder where she is today and what has become of her.

CHAPTER 45

Buchanan

We left Greenville with heavy hearts, and for the first time I had serious doubts about the move. I loved Greenville. I loved my neighbors; I loved the children, the Carpenters, the house, the bridge playing with the Europeans, the board-game parties, and the kids coming to the house for school.

I began to think that I was expecting too much of myself. I'd somehow expected myself to transform the Demonstration School into a facsimile of a well-run stateside facility. I was focusing on the gap between the two, instead of the small good I was doing. I knew in my heart the headaches weren't caused by the job.

What made me think that a move at this time would be an improvement? It would be a change, that's all—different people, new jobs, different house, different town to get used to—and we'd only be there for six months, just enough time to get adjusted, and then we'd be going home. I had a sudden frightening feeling that no amount of hopping from town to town was going to do it for me. What in heaven's name had I been thinking? The move was Band-Aid therapy. The real work was within, and no amount of first-aid could substitute for the lifelong journey of self-discovery.

I created enough diversion to push these thoughts aside as we drove the loaded Peace Corps station wagon down the dusty red road toward the airstrip—Steve and Dale in the front seat and I in the back. I thought it ironic that the last person from Greenville that I would be saying good-bye to would be Steve Wilson.

Our transition to Buchanan was relatively uneventful. Our small house was clean and ready to be occupied. Our new houseboy, James Bondo, was efficient but shy and without Robert's appealing humor. Our house was situated in a private little nook off the main road and was flanked by two other small houses.

Our house in Buchanan

Drying clothes in our yard (notice the goat)

There was no water path beside our house, and I missed our water bearers' friendly "G'mahnin', M'Nancy" at six every morning.

We did have a substitute, though. A fine, big, red rooster found a home on our front porch railing one morning, and his loud "Cock-a-doodle-doo!" just before daybreak scared the bejesus out of us.

It took us more than a few mornings to get used to it. It wasn't long, however, before his wives accompanied him onto our porch, and I came to enjoy their soft clucking sounds. They'd all leave the premises after we'd fed them, but returned at dusk to roost for the night and wake us up in the morning.

I have no idea who those chickens belonged to, but we always had fresh eggs on our porch. One morning I counted one fewer chicken, which I assumed had found its way into somebody's chop pot.

I couldn't bring myself to look on them as anything but pets, so they were safe with me. I managed to catch one from time to time, just for the practice. I'd pet them, talk to them softly, and then let them go. I had names for all of them.

Years later, when I performed in children's theatre, I created a character called Mrs. Hen, modeled after one of my favorites. She had a skittish personality, jumping and clucking at the slightest thing, running in circles, then standing with one leg raised—beady little black eyes wide and staring at the imagined intruder. Then, suddenly, she'd stop in midstrut and start to waddle sensually, swaying from side to side, clucking and cooing deep down in her throat, like a pigeon's lullaby. Out of all the characters I portrayed in the eighty or so plays during my fourteen-year acting career (from dinner theatre to Broadway, from Henrik Ibsen to Jean Genet, Neil Simon to Lanford Wilson) audiences always loved Mrs. Hen the best. In truth, so did I. Nothing gives me greater pleasure than to see people laughing till tears roll down their cheeks.

The school in Buchanan was efficiently run with textbooks and plenty of supplies to go around. Most of the teachers actually had teaching degrees; and most of my days were occupied because there weren't nearly as many "vacation" days. The students were eager and disciplined learners, serious about their education, clear about their intentions.

It was a lot less work for me. I didn't have to create a curriculum and invent materials. The texts were dry, but the students loved them and learned them well, even though the subject matter, aside from math and science, was mostly unrelated to their experience. There seemed to be an abundance and variety of books sitting in a storage room, unused, so I suggested to the principal the idea of creating a lending library. He was thrilled, and the project was mine.

CHAPTER 46

Penelope

Penelope showed up at our doorstep one afternoon around three. A bone-thin mongrel of a dog, she had short, tan hair and wore a forlorn expression that would have melted even the iciest heart. I was wary at first because she wasn't wary enough. Stray dogs in Liberia are not friendly with people—they are much too street smart and are used to being whipped or kicked.

Was she someone's pet that had wandered off and couldn't find her way home? Or was she rabid and ready to attack at any moment? Mac Cat sidled right up to her, and I saw her tail wag ever so slightly, which convinced me she wasn't rabid. As I approached her, she lowered her head and her tail wagged in earnest. Her bony ribs were a stark contrast to her hard, distended belly.

James appeared at the door and told me he had tried to kick her away, but she kept coming back. I had already warned him not to abuse Mac Cat—now I extended the warning to include all animals.

The dog looked so pathetic I wasn't sure what to do. If I fed her, she'd never leave. She didn't look healthy, and I really didn't want to be responsible for a sick dog. My logical mind urged me to turn and walk away, but my instinct to help the poor creature won out. I went inside and filled a large bowl with leftover rice and canned roast beef. I knew she'd wolf the whole thing down in seconds (and then probably lose it) if I put the bowl down, so I slowly ladled out one spoonful at a time. She ate like a perfect lady, chewing each bite and looking lovingly at me when she finished.

By the time Dale got home, she was mine. He sighed heavily and reminded me we only had six months left in the country. I said it would be six months of steady meals she never would have had otherwise.

He said, "Now we have two animals we have to find homes for."

I couldn't answer that one.

After I bathed Penelope, she looked like an entirely different dog. I managed to scrape off the fleas that were matted around her ears and eyes. The ones on the rest of her body fell off and drowned in the bathwater. After she had dried in the sun, I let her come inside where she promptly lay down at my feet and fell asleep.

I stared down at her bloated belly. Probably worms. Worms were as common as malaria. We had worm medicine in our Peace Corps medical kit, but the dosage was for humans. I asked another Peace Corps Volunteer how she wormed her dog, and she said she ballparked the weight and proportioned accordingly. After a few days, Penelope was worm free. Since Mac Cat and Penelope had become inseparable, I gave Mac Cat a dose of medicine to be on the safe side.

I told James again that he was never to kick or hit our animals, under any circumstances. He asked, "Why not?"

I told him, "Because it's cruel, and we must be kind to animals."

Then he said, "Bu' M'Nancy, you whack the chicken, and you eat the chicken, is this not a cruel thing to do to the chicken?"

I countered that we didn't kill and eat our pet chickens—but I was caught. He followed the reasoning to the end.

"So it is all right to be cruel to animals if they are not yours." How was I going to get out of this one? I hadn't followed my own thinking to the end and was not sufficiently sophisticated to talk about the idea of animals giving their lives to the service of others, the kindness of treatment, and method of killing. I stood there thinking how we were going to get sufficient protein in a country with limited resources if we didn't eat meat.

I said, "No, it's not all right, but sometimes it is necessary to kill animals for food." I felt lame, but he seemed satisfied with my answer.

Another week went by, and I saw no improvement in the size of Penelope's stomach. She was gaining weight and seemed healthy in all other respects, so I began to suspect she was pregnant. My suspicions were confirmed when her teats became enlarged.

Dale was irritated and nervous. I had never had a pregnant animal, but I felt certain I was up to the task, even with Dale's doubts. I would begin immediately to seek homes among the Europeans and PCVs in Buchanan and Monrovia. Dale suggested that if I couldn't find homes for the pups, he'd have to drown them. He said it would be the kindest thing.

I had flashback memories of unwanted kittens being drowned on the farms in Puyallup, Washington, and of the poor little kittens in Greenville after the dog got them. I felt anxious and vaguely sick to my stomach. The anxiety scared me, and I tried to stuff it down by looking for something to distract myself. There was no community of bridge players like there had been in Greenville and no Carpenters to visit.

The other PCVs in the town had already formed friendships, and we weren't invited into their regular circle. They didn't actually exclude us, but neither did they seek us out. We invited them all over for an evening of board games, but their hearts weren't in it, so after a couple of tries at different games, we socialized for a little while, then called it a night.

James was a good houseboy but not very sociable, and I missed Robert's charismatic personality and humorous banter. And James never warmed up to Mac Cat, as Robert had, so I was never quite sure how he treated Mac Cat when we weren't there. I missed the children coming to the house for lessons and popping in to visit—especially Richelieu and Joseph. The grass began to look a whole lot greener on the previous side of the fence, as I realized that the move to Buchanan wasn't all I'd hoped it would be.

One night when I was feeling particularly low, Dale suggested we get a couple of other people and take in a movie. There was one movie house in Buchanan that showed American films. Great idea. When we got there, we discovered they were showing a Bette Davis double bill: *What Ever Happened to Baby Jane?* and *Hush ... Hush, Sweet Charlotte*, two movies least likely to snap me out of depression. I was still hiding my depression from the world and felt I couldn't very well say I didn't want to go to the movies after all, so I sat through them. Over the next few days, the horrific images in those films occupied my thoughts, plunging me deeper into depression.

I still had frequent headaches, and each time I got one, I'd get scared it would escalate, which caused it to escalate. I couldn't seem to the stop the cyclical effect. I didn't yet have the psychological and metaphysical tools to work it through. I looked to Dale to help me—an unfair and futile choice, because he didn't have the tools to help me, either.

Nobody did—which made me more anxious and contributed to the cycle of helplessness and fear. The triggers were deeply hidden beneath the surface, and I didn't know how to find my way out of the abyss. The waves of panic would come and go for no apparent reason. We finally called Jack, and he told us to get to Monrovia ASAP. When we got there, he sat us down on the couch and said the words I never expected to hear: "I think you should go home."

Dale sighed heavily, and I started to cry. I felt like such a failure. As if I wasn't already painfully aware of the fact, Jack said, "You realize, of course, that your readjustment salary will be used to pay your airfare home." Our eighteen-month readjustment pay was $2.00 a day, apiece. We would be left with nothing to tide us over until we could find jobs in the United States. Of course, he left the decision up to us, but it was clear there was no other choice.

There was no fanfare surrounding our departure from Buchanan—we hadn't been there long enough to bond with anybody. All our sad farewells had taken place in Greenville. I made the second of two phone calls to the United States, to tell my parents we were coming home. Naturally they were concerned for my welfare, but they were convinced that once I got back on American soil, everything would be fine. Dale called his folks, who expressed sadness that we couldn't finish out our tour of duty.

There was no way we could take Mac Cat back with us. We didn't have a place to live and no jobs. We found a good home for him, and though it was a tearful separation, I knew he'd be well loved.

Penelope was another story. Nobody wanted a pregnant dog. As our search for a home grew more futile, and I became increasingly upset at the prospect of her future, Dale told me to let him handle it. I had the vague notion he might kill her. I told him he had to find her a home, and he assured me he would.

A few days later I came home from work and noticed Penelope was gone. I asked Dale where she was, and he said he had found her a home, but I sensed he was lying. After some days, I did ask him to tell me truthfully what he had done with her. He confessed he had hired a taxi driver to take her far outside of town and leave her on the road. I was devastated, but we never spoke of it again. I know he thought he was doing the kindest thing, and I just wasn't able to pull myself together enough to fight it. What he neglected to tell me till only recently was that the taxi driver, in fact, had sold her for chop. Although I have struggled to forgive myself, the sadness and shame associated with that incident have never left me.

CHAPTER 47

Back Home

Our first stop in the United States was Washington, D.C., for what they called a debriefing interview. One of the people interviewing was a psychiatrist. The concept of therapy still carried with it the connotation of "crazy," and I was nervous I might be so diagnosed, but the interview was no more than cursory. He said that returning home was the wise choice and that I might want to talk to someone to help with the readjustment, but therapy was expensive, and we had no money.

The medical doctor suggested that I stop taking the pill for a time. The pill was strong medicine, and research showed that some women had difficulty getting pregnant and resuming normal periods when they stopped taking the pill. The pharmaceutical recommendation was to take the pill for a year, go off it for six months, and then begin again. I had been on the pill for one and a half years, and I knew how potent it was, based on how my body had reacted to it in the first place. I was relieved to stop the pill, and Dale and I went back to condoms.

The next stop was Tacoma, Washington, to see Dale's family. There was still a teacher shortage in Tacoma, so I interviewed with the superintendent of schools, who offered me a job for the fall, which I accepted. Dale found a job working for a tour company that was based in Alaska, so after a brief visit with his parents, we flew to Anchorage for the summer.

We mooched off my parents until Dale's first paycheck, and then we found a cheap, furnished sublet for the rest of summer. Though I hadn't gone into therapy, I was no longer depressed, and my severe headaches had ceased. I assumed it had to do with my leaving Liberia, but that explanation still didn't gel.

Years later, when medical research revealed that the birth control pill was responsible for depression and headaches in a large number of women, I felt the burden of uncertainty lifted. My symptoms seemed to fit the profile perfectly. I felt angry and betrayed and, once again, invalidated. But even those feelings quickly abated as I realized it was simply another small step in the process of learning to trust my own instincts. (Today, I'm aware that the pill was only one of several factors that contributed to the depression and headaches).

Back in the States, I discovered that people were only somewhat interested in my Peace Corps experience. I was naive and expected everyone to ply me with questions to satiate a boundless curiosity, but after a time I realized that others were pretty much involved in their own lives and lent only a passing interest in mine. The odd conversation that showed more than a casual interest was rare, and I now admit I craved it. I needed to talk about my experience, but even my parents expressed only a minor interest. Because of our shared experience, Dale and I found a strong bond together, which continues to this day.

At the end of the summer, we drove our new car to Tacoma. Dale confessed that he was nervous about teaching in the United States and thought he'd enroll in college to get a master's degree in business. Along with attending college classes, he substitute-taught (at the junior high school level!), drove school buses, and tutored high school students in math.

I taught elementary school for the next three years. I loved teaching, and I was good at it. I brought Liberia into the classroom, with all my artifacts, pictures, and stories, for a two-month-long instructional unit every year. My students made drums, tie-dyed and batiked everything in sight, and learned Liberian folk tales and some Pidgin English.

We created an environmental classroom and invited parents for a culminating evening of entertainment and Liberian chop. We prepared a dinner of chicken, rice, plantains, fresh pineapple, oranges, bananas, and coconut. The only thing we couldn't find was palm butter. The children wore Liberian dress and showed their parents around the room, performed their folk tales, played their homemade drums, and taught them the traditional West African dance, Hi-Life. Everyone left with armloads of mementos, from tie-dyed T-shirts to batik artwork.

CHAPTER 48

Through My Eyes

I tried to hold on to living the Liberian experience as long as possible, but naturally life moved on, and I eventually quit teaching and moved to New York City to pursue an acting career. When Dale and I divorced, Liberia seemed to take a backseat, surfacing only occasionally in a passing conversation.

Throughout much of my life, I have worn the filter of others' perceptions and evaluated my life through their eyes. Little did I know that the experience of living in my beloved Liberia would affect my every perception and influence the movement of my entire life—but that's another book. It has taken me a distance of over four decades to finally see my extraordinary Peace Corps experience for what it was— through *my* eyes.

Printed in the United States
137379LV00004B/2/P